Monster
in River Oaks

Monster
in River Oaks

Michael Phillips

SpindleTop

Monster in River Oaks

© 2010 Michael Phillips

Manufactured in the United States of America

Part of the proceeds of this book will be donated to charity.

For information about the publisher, please contact:

Spindle Top Publishing
Michael Phillips
3200 Southwest Freeway
Suite 3200
Houston, Texas 77027
(713) 552-9595

www.MonsterInRiverOaks.com

ISBN-13: 978-0-615-42197-1
10 9 8 7 6 5 4 3

This book is dedicated to trial dogs.

"Anything he said three times he believed.
Sometimes, twice was enough."

—John Le Carre, *The Night Manager*

Contents

Prologue xi

Acknowledgments xiii

  1. 77019. 1

  2. Joan and Luke 9

  3. The Blaffer Dynasty 19

  4. David Collie Comes Calling 29

  5. Dinny's First Conquest: Glennis Goodrich 37

  6. His Matters of the Heart: Michael Holstein,
      Michael Sambogna, and Clint Langford 47

  7. Life on the Home Front: 1996 59

  8. A Lock Down School for Wirt 73

  9. Hindsight 85

10. Taking It to the Bank 93

11. Beat Them Until They Surrender 103

12. The Gardener Sees It All 119

13. The Man Who Must Not Be Named 127

14. "Mommy, Don't!" 135

15. First Accusation of Sexual Abuse 145

16. Who Lies to Her Diary? 151

17. Moving Day 155

18. Heartbreak 161

19. Capitulation: She Buys Her Underwear at Walgreens 169

20. Surveillance 179

21. Death Threats 193

22. School Daze 201

23. Dinny's Grand European Trip 209

24. Seth's School Years. 217
25. Shyam, the Keeper's Brother 225
26. Final Days at 2933 Del Monte Drive, River Oaks 233
27. Joan Takes Back Her Life and Home 237
28. Dinny's Not Too Guilty Plea 247
29. Where Justice is Rendered 253
30. The Legal Battlefield. 257
31. The Jury Speaks 269
Epilogue 277
About the Author 279
Documents 281

Prologue

In certain Houston circles, love is eternal as long as it lasts. In some ways, this book is a love story as well as a monster story. A story of a predatory monster that set out to control and then dominate a famous Houston family, a family whose grandfather founded a company that would become Exxon. It is a story of child abuse, pedophilia, squandered fortunes, covered-up homosexual affairs, generous charitable donations, misguided parents, and desperate children. It is a story of love offered but not returned. Of love needed but not offered. The story is based on police files, private investigator reports and trial evidence, but that is not the significant point. What happened for six years at 2933 Del Monte Drive could not have happened just anywhere in America. It could happen only in River Oaks.

Acknowledgments

I would like to thank my family who supported me in this endeavor, the many editors who assisted with the work, and my secretary who provided proofreading and word processing contributions.

The Houston neighborhood of River Oaks is in one of the wealthiest zip codes in America. With property values that range up to $40 million, 77019 is home to professional athletes, self-made millionaires, old-school Texas oilmen, socialites, and career politicians. Pro basketball player Clyde Drexler owns a home in the neighborhood, as did infamous Enron players Andrew Fastow and Jeffrey Skilling. In River Oaks, old money—mainly Oil Royalty—mingles with first-generation wealth, and the River Oaks Country Club serves as the center of the area's sophisticated social fabric. The neighborhood is home to the rich, powerful, famous, and infamous. In addition to the likes of Andy Fastow, and Jeff Skilling, highly respected citizens live side by side. Joanne Herring and Lynne Wyatt call it home, as do Becca Cason Thrash, Dan Duncan, Carolyn Farb, and Fayez Sarofim. Elyse Lanier, wife of former Mayor Bob Lanier, once declared, "I am never moving out of 77019. I worked too hard to get here." When told that her plan to remove the back fence to the Laniers' huge property would open the stunning backyard to passing golfers on the River Oaks Golf Course, she replied, as any sensible River Oaks matron would, "Exactly. That's the point."

But behind the façade of opulence and power, there is a darker, sinister side to the neighborhood. Violence is a common theme. Socialite Joan Robinson Hill, heir to the Ash Robinson fortune, died mysteriously while under the care of her husband, Dr. John Hill. Slow poisoning was rumored. Thomas Thompson wrote a best-seller—*Blood and Money*—detailing the case; Farrah Fawcett would play Joan in the movie version. And River Oaks residents still snicker about the antics of Candace Mossler and her longtime boyfriend Melvin Lane Powers: Powers was once found naked and unconscious on the lawn of Mossler's mansion after having fallen from the roof early one morning. The reason for Mossler's being naked and on the roof remains unclear.

The center of society, of course, is River Oaks Country Club. For members, summer days there are ideal: long afternoons by the pool, pitchers of frozen margaritas while sprinkler heads click lazily in the background, dinners that begin at lunch. The waiting list for membership in River Oaks Country Club is so intimidating that it single-handedly spawned the formation of two other clubs. And if residents tire of the club, there will always be Tony's, the epitome of society dining. Tony Vallone first made a name for himself by turning away Frank Sinatra one famous night because The Voice would not put on a tie, as the restaurateur required of male guests. That night Ol' Blue Eyes had to sip his cocktails at Rudi's over on Post Oak Boulevard where Mike, the doorman and reputed made man, would not be so picky about attire. Tony's, Brennan's, and Maxim's would be jammed with the likes of Oscar Wyatt, Michael Halbouty, and Glen McCarthy, a rough-cut wildcatter who was played by James Dean in the movie *Giant*. Upon seeing the movie, McCarthy growled, "That's not me. He's a sissy." Multimillionaire Howard Marshall would be seen at Maxim's for long lunches with a not-yet-famous buxom blonde, Anna Nicole Smith, taking a break from lap dancing at The Men's Club.

———————

Set in the middle of the country's third-largest city, the quiet streets in River Oaks are a striking contrast to the concrete, traffic, and noise that surround it. It is now, as it has always been, *the* address in Houston. No other neighborhood comes close. Tanglewood, Memorial, Rice Medical, West University, the Villages are distant— sometimes jealous—cousins. This is the neighborhood that Joan Blaffer Johnson called home then and even today. It is where the story begins.

During the Christmas season, River Oaks' sprawling mansions create a memorable impression, with lights of every color draped over the Tudor- and colonial-style mansions; at twilight, residents from all over the city cruise the neighborhood's tree-lined streets to marvel at the decadent displays. December 2002 was no exception: Even Police Officer P. D. Nguyen—who regularly patrolled River Oaks on his beat—was warmed by the holiday lights wrapped around the neighborhood's signature live oaks and strung like diamonds from rooftops.

But amid the festive decorations, one house stood in bleak contrast: Surrounded by neighbors' cheerful, twinkling Christmas lights and elaborate nativities, the house at 2933 Del Monte Drive was devoid of seasonal decor; in fact, not even a porch light cut through the chilly moonlight that night.

To neighbors, the darkness that surrounded Joan Johnson's home was just one more sign that something had gone terribly, irrevocably wrong.

To Officer Nguyen, the darkness just made the house harder to see. After the 911 call came in, he had to circle the block twice before he'd identified the Johnson residence.

Early on the evening of December 14, 2002, Joan Johnson left her home to see a movie with her fourteen-year-old daughter, Kaleta, and her longtime friend and live-in financial advisor, Dinesh Shah (affectionately known to the Johnson family as "Dinny"). Dinny's brother, Shyam Shah—who sometimes lived at the Johnson home—dropped off the three in front of the area's Cineplex. At Kaleta's request, they saw Jennifer Lopez's new romantic comedy, *Maid in Manhattan*.

A few hours later, at approximately 7:45, a frantic 911 call came from the Johnson home.

Shyam Shah had placed the call, saying that his brother, Dinny, was in a rage and he feared for the safety of Joan and her daughter. Five minutes later, Officer Nguyen arrived at the home and began knocking on the front door, but there was no response.

After Nguyen knocked and waited for several minutes, a muffled woman's voice inquired as to who was at the door. But the door remained closed. Officer Nguyen explained that he was responding to a disturbance call. The woman replied, through the closed door, that everything was OK. No problems, she said. No disturbance. Go away.

Nguyen persisted; something just seemed off. Finally, the door cracked open and Nguyen came face to face with Mrs. Joan Blaffer Johnson. She peeked out, shielding the right side of her face, and insisted that she was alone in the house with her daughter, Kaleta. No one else was there, she insisted. Go away.

It was obvious to Nguyen that something didn't add up. Especially since Nguyen could see a man lurking in the darkness behind the door after Joan reiterated that she was alone in the house.

That's when Shyam Shah stepped out from behind the door and related the details of the evening that prompted him to call 911. Little did Nguyen know that he was witnessing the beginning of a chain of events that would culminate in two lengthy court battles and reveal to the entire River Oaks community a family warped by secrets.

As Shyam started talking, he seemed paranoid—repeatedly asking Officer Nguyen to keep his voice down and running to look up the stairway to make sure that Dinny hadn't heard them speaking. Shyam reported that his brother, Dinny, was upstairs and that Dinny had been beating Joan and Kaleta. He told Nguyen that there were guns in the house.

Mrs. Johnson said nothing, looking down at the floor.

Officer Nguyen immediately called for backup, and Houston Police Department Officers Kenneth Bounds, Escobedo, Read, and Paiz responded. Later, Nguyen and the other officers who arrived on the scene would comment on how unusually dark and gloomy the Johnson home was—someone had even tacked up heavy blankets and towels over all of the windows, blocking the sunlight and obscuring the views to discourage curious looks inside.

According to their later testimony, Joan and Kaleta claimed that after the movie, Dinny wanted to walk to a nearby Mercedes-Benz dealership and check out a few models he'd had his eye on. But what started out as a pleasant evening soon turned violent.

As Dinny walked the lot, Joan and Kaleta began to complain that they had to go to the bathroom. Dinny—who was known by the Johnson family to have a short temper—snapped at them to hold it. During their walk, Shyam Shah had come to meet the three at the car dealership. Shyam offered to take Kaleta to the bathroom in a nearby building, but Dinny crushed that idea. According to Joan, Dinny said that Kaleta was being a "rude little girl" and that she could pee in her pants if she needed to.

As Kaleta's pleas grew more urgent, Dinny's anger became uncontrollable; he whisked the two into Shyam's car and, in the ten-minute ride back to Del Monte Drive, had worked himself into such a rage that he began beating Joan savagely. Joan Johnson would later testify that, once they'd pulled into the driveway, she'd been "slugged" in the chest, had the wind knocked out of her, and was hit repeatedly over the head with her $5,000 alligator purse.

Now, one might argue that a reasonable person would not stand for such abuse. A reasonable person would protect her children at all costs. And a reasonable person would not willingly follow after her abuser but would run to get help. Yet what Joan did after being beaten by Dinesh Shah in the driveway of her own home seems to defy reason: After picking up the contents of her spilled purse, she followed him into the house.

As she climbed the stairs to her bedroom to use the bathroom, Joan Johnson testified that she could hear Kaleta screaming from her room. Dinny was later accused of beating Kaleta and pinching her in the crotch as she became more and more distraught, saying to her that he could "f—k you if I want." But, according to testimony, Joan didn't rush to her daughter's aid.

In fact, Joan waited in her room for Dinny to enter and continue his assault, allegedly pinching her in the crotch, too. The abuse continued, and at some point Joan recalled hearing Shyam pleading with his brother to stop; he feared that if Dinny killed Joan and Kaleta, they would both be in trouble.

Katela's own words in a 2008 civil trial would provide powerful insight into what happened that night. As she put it, after the family had arrived at the Del Monte house, Kaleta went upstairs and shut herself in her room. But she wasn't safe.

Kaleta: "I heard Dinny coming up the stairs and when he came to the room I had backed up over near my bed and he started hitting me and I fell onto the bed. He was standing over me and hitting me while I was on the bed. I put my arms up but he was yelling. He said, you know, 'Shut the f—k up' and yelling all these things. . . . In the midst of that, at one point he put his hand over my mouth and he grabbed me between the legs and he said, 'I've lived in the room next to you for years; I could have f—ed you whenever I wanted to.' And he left the room shortly after that and he went to my mother's room and I could hear him hitting her in her room . . ."

Attorney: "What happened next?"

Kaleta: "Dinny came running into my room, and he looked very frantic, panicked. He said get in the shower, take a shower and then, you know, if the police come, don't tell them anything. And I went into my bathroom . . . and I locked myself in the bathroom and I turned the water on but I was too frazzled to do anything . . ."

When the police finally arrived, they found Kaleta cowering in her bathroom, too afraid to open the door. In a later deposition, Kaleta's own simple words underscore the horror the young girl had endured: "On the night Dinny went to jail, he was mad because I asked to go to the bathroom while he wanted to look around the Mercedes dealership. He claimed Mom was teaching me to be disrespectful; he beat Mom in the driveway and in her room and beat me in my room, bruises on my back and shoulder."

While other police officers were coaxing Kaleta out of her bathroom, Officer Nguyen found Dinesh Shah upstairs, sitting behind a desk in the study. Officer Nguyen asked him to raise his hands in the air. Dinny complied and came downstairs without incident.

But he had a very different story from Joan, Shyam, and Kaleta.

Dinesh Shah would testify that, after seeing the movie on this Saturday night, it was *Joan* who suggested going to look at cars in the Mercedes-Benz lot. Shyam picked them all up outside the movie theater and drove them to the dealership. Dinny reported that he waited in the car for them to finish looking at the cars.

Upon arriving home, Dinny said that he took the Johnsons' dachshund, Vicki, for a walk. When he came back, ten or fifteen minutes later, the house was dark and quiet. He went up to his study to do some work when he heard a pounding at the door. That pounding was Officer Nguyen.

A calm Dinesh Shah explained to a court later that he had been with Joan Johnson when she opened the door, but Officer Nguyen didn't confirm that fact. According to Dinny, when Nguyen came to the house, Dinny suggested that perhaps Officer Nguyen was looking for Andrew Fastow, the former CFO of Enron. In the fall of 2002, the Enron bubble had just burst and investigations were under way. According to Dinny, HPD had mistaken the Johnson house for Fastow's many times over the past few months. But Andrew Fastow had already been indicted by a grand jury on October 31, and Officer Nguyen explained that he was, indeed, at the correct residence.

Dinny claims that he and Mrs. Johnson then invited the officer inside. He also alleges that he was pulled aside and arrested without being allowed to tell his side of the story. According to Dinny, Joan Johnson pointed an accusatory finger at him, and the Houston Police Department officers believed her without any evidence. He described the police officers that night as acting out of jealousy over Mrs. Johnson's expensive home, with a hunger to make an arrest for Kaleta's abuse; over the past several years, Child Protective Services had been called out to the Johnson home to investigate claims of child abuse.

Yet as different as Dinny's and Joan's stories are, there is one fact that all parties agree on: Dinny was booked into the Harris County central jail on Reisner Street that night, charged with injury to a child. By all accounts, he came quietly (though he loudly expressed concern and confusion over his arrest). And a terrified Joan Johnson repeatedly insisted that she did not want to press charges against her friend and financial advisor.

Later, as this warped story of longtime abuse unfolded, Joan's two other children, Wirt (who was living in Dallas at the time of the December 14 beating) and sixteen-year-old Seth (attending boarding school in Connecticut), would add their own sordid tales—helping to paint a picture of a family held hostage.

But on the night of December 14, Officer Nguyen had no idea that he had just uncovered the tip of the iceberg in this dark tale.

As the patrol cars pulled away from the Johnson home that December evening, many believe that Dinesh Shah's control over the Johnson family effectively came to an end. But the twisted story of a wealthy household in shambles; a prominent family with a history of abuse, suicide, and financial squabbles that usually ended in court; and a woman scorned by an ex-lover was just about to unfold.

Joan and Luke

In 1974, Joan Blaffer was in the prime of her life: beautiful, young, and privileged. The daughter of John Blaffer and Camilla Davis, Blaffer and her siblings were heirs to Humble Oil Company, one of the largest fortunes in America. Joan's trust fund alone was worth an estimated $70 million without taking into account the millions she shared with her sisters via other trusts created by their parents. After graduating from the University of Texas, Joan Blaffer found a job at Tiffany & Co., in the upscale Houston Galleria. That's where she met Luke Johnson, Jr.

Handsome and charismatic, Luke Johnson, Jr., was well-to-do in his own right. Though he didn't have access to millions like the Blaffers, his father, Luke Johnson, Sr., had started a very successful car dealership in 1955. One of the oldest dealerships in Houston, Luke Johnson Ford was well known throughout the city. Luke, Jr., set to take the wheel of the dealership when his father retired, had a promising future.

Joan and Luke married in October 1979. Joan Blaffer was twenty-seven years old; Luke was thirty-one. Joan took her husband's name, becoming Joan Blaffer Johnson. Their first child, Wirt, was born just ten months later, in August 1980. Seth, born in 1986, and Kaleta (who was given Joan's middle name), born in 1988, would complete the Johnson family.

By all estimates, the early years of Joan and Luke's marriage went smoothly. The two made a good match, young and handsome; playful and passionate.

But all was not well: Joan's family, particularly her mother, did not entirely approve of Luke Johnson, Jr. They especially frowned upon Joan sinking her money into Luke Johnson Ford. Since taking the dealership over after the death of his father, Luke Johnson, Sr., the younger Johnson had effectively run the thirty-year-old business into the ground. Luke, who was more interested in carousing, lacked his father's solid business sense, and frequently sought financial assistance from his new wife.

Going against her mother's advice, Joan invested heavily in her husband's dealership. She put up a substantial percentage of assets in the family trusts as collateral to keep the dealership afloat. The two borrowed large amounts of money to fund the dealership, but Luke Johnson Ford went broke anyway. It would take Joan until April 1994 to dig Luke Johnson Ford out of bankruptcy.

Even before Luke Johnson's business started having financial difficulties, Luke had been a drinker. A handwritten note from Joan on stationery from the Royal Sonesta Hotel in New Orleans shows the extent of Luke's alcoholism:

> *Luke's drinking makes him very angry and obnoxious. This intensified after Uncle Jack died. The party started about an hour ago. I'm dressed and he's asleep. He thinks he's in Houston.*

After using her own wealth to salvage Luke's business, as well as financing the child support and taxes he owed to his son and first wife, Joan had become a very angry and resentful woman. Cracks in their marriage were beginning to show, and the secrets hidden beneath this crumbling façade would tear the family apart.

In 1994, Luke found out that he was HIV-positive, and he confided in Dr. Alan B. Cooper, a prominent Houston psychiatrist who had been treating Luke on and off since 1977. But Luke's illness and infidelities weren't his only secrets.

Rumors began to circulate that Luke was carrying on affairs in the family bay house in Morgan's Point. It was said that in addition to his longtime alcoholism, Luke had become reckless in his extramarital affairs—and that his tastes ran to men.

Sometime in 1995, Joan and Luke separated as a result of mutual distrust and, of course, his HIV diagnosis. Wirt was around fourteen years old, witness to his own parents' separation. Seth was barely nine and Kaleta seven—not quite old enough to understand the import and all of the consequences of their parents' actions.

Luke had no place to go and ultimately moved into the family's bay house at 311 Bay Ridge in Morgan's Point, Texas, a small community (population 336) east of Houston. Soon after, Luke's life began to spiral out of control.

In March 1995, Luke Johnson was arrested and charged with abandoning Kaleta in his Morgan's Point home, a felony. As he and Joan had agreed earlier in the week, Kaleta was to stay with her father at the Morgan's Point home the night of March 3 while Joan attended a hockey game with her sister. Joan planned to come to Morgan's Point later in the evening to spend Friday night with Luke and Kaleta. Luke's secretary, Bernice, drove Kaleta out to the bay house and the three had dinner together. Shortly afterward, Bernice left and Kaleta went up to bed.

At 8:12 p.m., an officer was dispatched to the residence to respond to a home security alarm report. Officer Terence Cornell, a peace officer with the Morgan's Point Police Department, arrived at 311 Bayridge Road and walked the property. When he found no evidence of a disturbance, Cornell rang the doorbell. A child's voice told him to hold on a second—she was trying to open the door.

As Kaleta fumbled with the lock on the front door, Cornell was approached by Will Rea. Rea was a neighbor and worked as caretaker for the Johnsons' Morgan's Point home, and the alarm company had called to notify him of a possible disturbance. When the front door finally opened, Rea and Cornell found six-year-old Kaleta home alone and seemingly frightened, a fire burning in the fireplace. She told the officer that her mother was at a hockey game; she had no idea where her father was—he'd been in the home when she'd gone to bed that evening. Kaleta had simply woken up to find Luke gone. He'd set the home's motion detector alarms before he left the house, and Kaleta had set them off when she walked downstairs. Unbeknownst to Kaleta and Luke, Joan had decided not to join her family at the bay house; tired after the hockey game, Joan didn't feel like making the drive to Morgan's Point. Instead, she decided to return to her home in Houston.

Officer Cornell contacted Joan, who drove out to the house to pick up her daughter around 11 p.m. Later, in a sworn affidavit, Joan said that she was "shocked" by Luke's behavior, but she defended her soon-to-be ex-husband's actions, chalking up the whole incident to a case of miscommunication.

> *I am sure that the reason Luke left Kaleta that evening was based on several assumptions, some of them mistaken: 1) that I was on the way to the bay house from Houston; 2) that he would not be gone long; 3) that, as usual, Will Rea would be at the house quickly if needed; 4) that Kaleta would not wake up and come downstairs while he was gone (or before I arrived); and 5) that the alarm was on "stay" rather than "away" (thereby activating the movement alarm causing the sirens to sound when Kaleta came downstairs).*

Joan was also quick to point to Luke's alcohol abuse as a reason for his poor judgment on the evening of March 3. "Luke has wrestled with sobriety for years and has done well in general," she wrote. "I do not think he would have left the house had he not been drinking. . . . I know such a circumstance will never occur again."

Joan's affidavit ended with a request that her husband not be prosecuted for the incident. Luke was charged instead with a Class A misdemeanor, fined $1,000, and given one year of probation.

Adding to Luke's business troubles, alcohol abuse, legal issues, and his estrangement from his family was his failing health. In early 1995, Luke confided to Dr. Cooper that his immune system was compromised, making it necessary for him to start taking medication for HIV.

The Johnsons' divorce was finalized on April 3, 1995. Just one month later, on May 4, Luke Johnson turned forty-seven years old. He had a weekend celebration planned with his family.

But Luke Johnson never celebrated his birthday with his kids.

———

On May 5, 1995, Luke Johnson was found dead in the family's Morgan's Point home. The Harris County Medical Examiner's report stated that Johnson died "as a result of close range gunshot wound of the chest, through and through, suicide."

Morgan's Point Police Officer T. E. Hummel was summoned to the home at 311 Bay Ridge the day Luke Johnson died. The officer found Luke seated on a sofa in the living room, bleeding from the chest. A blue steel revolver rested on the sofa to Luke's right. Dressed in only a bathrobe and boating shoes, Luke's position seemed relaxed, his legs crossed at the knees, head resting on his hand. In his report, Officer Hummel noted that no disturbances were visible in the room; no sign of a struggle. Given Luke's domestic troubles, abuses, and his declining health, suicide seemed likely—on the surface.

But some things didn't add up: Caretaker Will Rea later showed investigators the blood splatters he'd found on the walls and floor in Luke Johnson's bedroom, and it was discovered that approximately $80,000 in jewelry was missing from the home. And most importantly, Luke had recently devoted much of his time to setting up a life insurance policy and estate plan that would ensure his children's financial security when he died—except in the event of suicide.

While the matter of Luke's death seemed to police like an open-and-shut case, those close to him didn't believe that he'd died by his own hand. Joan Johnson hired a private investigator and former FBI Special Agent Russ Brown to look into her ex-husband's death, desperate to prove that Luke hadn't killed himself. Taking over where police left off, Brown and his team uncovered the shocking truth about Luke Johnson's lifestyle—and in a series of highly detailed reports raised serious questions about the circumstances surrounding his death.

In the months leading up to his death, Luke's increasingly erratic behavior and his constant stream of overnight guests had been noticed by neighbors in the small community of Morgan's Point; in fact, the police had been alerted more than once regarding Luke's mysterious visitors. Arriving and departing by limousine, young men—flown in at Luke's expense from around the country—would show up at the home at all hours, staying a few hours, a few days, or sometimes longer.

An invoice from Action Limousines reveals that, between April 18 and May 4, 1995, Luke Johnson spent more than $2,800 on limousine and car services alone, transporting "friends" from Houston's two airports to his Bay Ridge residence. Luke's next-door neighbor, Mrs. Bean, recalled in an interview that she'd been visiting him in his home shortly before his death when a strange young man showed up at the front yard.

"Are you Scott?" Luke asked. The young man replied yes and entered the home. Another man showed up at the door; Scott introduced him as the limousine driver. Mrs. Bean, who had seen Mr. Johnson's guests come and go at a distance, was unnerved by the exchange. She told investigators that she felt "scared," and "feared that something bad was going to happen" to Luke. But Mrs. Bean wasn't the only one concerned about Luke's demeanor. Will Rea, one of the last people to speak with Luke before he died, recalled Luke's strange behavior on Wednesday, May 3.

Although he had little interaction with Luke's visitors, Rea was presumably well aware of his employer's sexual appetites. As caretaker of the home, Rea had seen his share of Luke's guests come and go. Early on the evening of May 3, Rea was getting ready to return to his own home for the evening when Luke asked him to stay until a guest arrived. Rea noted to investigators that it was unusual for Johnson to request that he stay for the arrival of a limousine, as Johnson had never requested this in the past. Surprised, Rea agreed and the two men watched a movie in the living room. Sometime between 6 and 7 p.m., a limousine arrived at the home, and Rea went out to open the driveway gates. The young man who stepped out of the car looked drastically different from Luke's other callboys; dressed in tall, lace-up combat boots and toting a large duffel bag, the man had black, shoulder-length hair and, in Rea's words, "a rough demeanor." He introduced himself as Brian. Rea informed Brian that Luke was waiting for him. As the visitor made his way toward the front door, Rea locked the driveway gate for the night and went home.

It was the last time he'd speak with Luke Johnson.

Rea said he'd stopped at the home briefly the next day, May 4, but he didn't speak with Luke or his guest. Using his key, Rea let himself in through the back door and picked up the "to-do" list that Johnson left for him. Rea didn't recall anything especially unusual, but he did notice Brian's combat boots in one of the guest bedrooms.

When Rea returned to Luke's home on the afternoon of Thursday, May 5, Brian was nowhere to be seen. Instead, Rea found Luke asleep on the couch with another male guest, who was awake. Rea motioned for him to come to the kitchen, and the young man introduced himself as Brandon. Rea told police that it was during his conversation with Brandon that he heard a "thud" from the living room where his employer slept on the couch. Concerned, Rea asked Brandon to look in on Luke; the young man complied and returned to the kitchen, assuring Rea that Luke was fine. Rea later told investigators that his employer was known to become "agitated" if someone tried to wake him up while he was intoxicated. Rea decided it was best to let Luke remain on the couch to sleep it off; a few minutes later, he left for his part-time job at the local hardware store.

Things, however, were anything but fine. A few minutes after he arrived to start his shift at LaPorte Hardware, Rea received a call from Brandon—something had happened to Luke, and he needed to return to 311 Bay Ridge, pronto.

When Rea arrived back at the home, police and EMS personnel were already on the scene. Luke Johnson was dead of a gunshot wound to the chest. Officers were in the process of interrogating Brandon, and they wanted to ask Rea a few questions too.

Both Rea and Brandon were quickly cleared of suspicion—the men's hands were tested for gunpowder residue; Brandon took and passed a polygraph test; and Rea, although he was willing, was never required to take one. During his interview with police, Brandon mentioned that he'd seen Brian leave in the same limousine that had dropped off Brandon at Luke's home. Police never questioned the limo driver to confirm the story; they were convinced that Luke's death was a suicide, plain and simple. Luke had most likely shot himself while Brandon and Will Rea were chatting in the kitchen: Sergeant Suggs of the Morgan's Point Police Department noted that the "thump" the men heard could be consistent with the sound of a .38 being fired in the next room—especially if the ammunition were old. When Brandon checked on Luke after the thud, perhaps, at quick glance, he saw Luke's body slumped in a sleeping position and failed to notice the gunshot wound.

But the private investigators Joan hired found that things were not as simple as they seemed. Blood was found in the upstairs bedroom and bathroom, and Luke had a swollen eye and several abrasions. And the blood wasn't the only unanswered question—who had the missing jewelry and why would Luke shoot himself in the chest rather than someplace presumably less painful, like the head?

On June 8, Investigator St. Circq—an investigator on the team Joan hired—tracked down Action Limousines driver Jean Pierre Montariol, who'd been driving for Luke since mid-April, picking up friends from the airport and sometimes transporting Luke to and from one of the gay clubs in Houston's Montrose area. Montariol remembered picking up Brian on May 3 and driving him to Luke's Morgan's Point home at around 6:30 p.m. Later that evening, around 10 p.m., Luke Johnson called Action Limousines again—he and his friend wanted to go out for the evening. Montariol told investigators that when he arrived at the home to pick up Luke and Brian, Brian ran out to the car in a panic. He told Montariol that Luke had fallen down in the bathroom and was bleeding profusely.

Montariol told investigators, "Brian wanted to leave . . . he didn't know if Mr. Johnson was on drugs or what, but he couldn't handle situations like this. Brian wanted to call his boss and tell him he [Brian] was leaving. Brian called and talked to his boss, who told him to stay and take care of Mr. Johnson."

Montariol waited outside while Brian went back in the house to check on Luke. After a few minutes, Brian came outside and told the driver that everything was fine; Luke was OK. Montariol offered to come in and check on Luke, but Brian refused—he insisted Luke was fine. Montariol left the residence.

The next day, Montariol returned to Luke's house to drop off Brandon. He recalled that Luke Johnson "had a cut above his left eye and his face looked puffy," probably from the fall the night before. He recalled giving Brian a ride to the airport, too. Unlike most of Luke's friends, Brian gave the driver a generous tip of $60.

That story explained the blood and the abrasions. However, the missing jewelry was still a mystery; Brandon's bags had even been searched before he left the residence. And there was the mysterious

Brian —the one whose appearance Will Rea had found so unsettling. For some reason, Luke's "rough-looking" visitor was never located or questioned by police after Luke's death, even though he'd been one of the last people to see Luke alive.

After several weeks of inquiries, however, investigators from Russ Brown & Associates finally came to the conclusion that Luke's death may have been an accident—Luke was intoxicated and he was hardly a gun expert. Considering the constant stream of strange men in the house, it was plausible that Luke kept the gun close for protection; it was equally plausible that the gun had accidentally discharged when the intoxicated Luke picked it up. But despite the mysteries and loose ends surrounding Luke Johnson's death, his cause of death is officially considered a suicide. Ultimately, the police never reopened their investigation of Luke's death, and the opinion of the Harris County Medical Examiner's Office remained:

> *In view of the history and findings, it is our opinion that the decedent, Luke Johnson, Jr., came to his death as a result of close range gunshot wound of the chest, through and through, suicide, and we so certify.*

Despite his struggles with sobriety and his out-of-control personal life, the death of Luke Johnson, no doubt, left a great void in the Johnson family, a schism between past and future. Joan, who had always depended on the men in her life, no longer had a husband or a father for her young children. At 43, Joan Johnson found herself alone—and vulnerable.

The Blaffer Dynasty

Looking back at the history of the Blaffer family, "vulnerable" is hardly the word that comes to mind. The Blaffer name, well known throughout Texas, is synonymous with power, society, and philanthropy. Joan Johnson's grandfather, Robert Lee Blaffer—the great patriarch of the Blaffer family—was cut from the same bolt of fabric as the epic "self-made man" that is rooted in American history, and particularly in Texas lore. A graduate of Tulane University, Robert Lee Blaffer moved to the Houston area early in the last century after working for Southern Pacific Railroad. He sensed the oil industry would create vast wealth and many multimillionaires. He made the right connections early in his career and with a group of close friends established the Humble Oil Company in 1911. Named for the early oil boomtown of Humble, Texas, the Humble Oil Company rose from modest beginnings to become a global power in the petrochemical industry. Blaffer's keen business sense and, when necessary, his ruthlessness led to staggering wealth and helped establish the Blaffer family's place among Houston's elite. Unbeknownst to Blaffer, his success also helped set the stage for a family drama that would last for generations.

Oil production grew steadily for Humble Oil (renamed Humble Oil and Refining Company a few years after its inception) after the construction of a refinery in 1917. With around 200 wells operating, daily crude production reached approximately 900,000 barrels. By the 1930s, Humble Oil had become the nation's largest domestic crude oil producer, especially during and after World War II, when affordable domestic oil was in high demand. By the 1950s, Humble Oil employed thousands of people and supported the local economies of many Houston-area refining towns. But that was just the beginning.

In the early days of Humble Oil, Robert Lee Blaffer and his partners, Ross Sterling, Walter Fondren, Sr., and William Stamps Farrish II—industry giants in their own right—sold half of the company's stock to Standard Oil Company of New Jersey to help finance the construction of a refinery. The relationship between Humble Oil and Standard Oil would prove to be longstanding: Decades later, Humble Oil was eventually consolidated with Standard Oil. In 1972, the company changed its name to Exxon; after a merger years later, it became Exxon Mobil.

Unfortunately, Robert Lee Blaffer wasn't around to see his start-up company's transformation. He died in 1942, leaving behind his wife, Sarah Campbell Blaffer, to raise their four children. Blaffer is buried in Houston's Glenwood Cemetery, final resting place of the rich and powerful: a plain rectangular stone that simply says, "Robert Lee Blaffer 1878–1942" marks his grave.

Sarah Campbell Blaffer, Robert Lee Blaffer's wife of 33 years, lived much longer than her husband—until 1975—and she never remarried. In the 1930s and '40s, Sarah Campbell Blaffer's home was considered one of the major centers of society in Texas. In a book titled *Bulldozed: "Kelo," Eminent Domain and the American Lust for Land* by Carla T. Main, the Blaffers make a brief appearance in the true-life story about a land grab for business property in Freeport, Texas.

Main, quoting from *Debrett's Texas Peerage* by Hugh Best, says that "Sarah Campbell Blaffer was the nearest equivalent of Texas royalty . . . the Blaffer-Campbell marriage combined two of the world's great oil fortunes. Texas Governor James Hogg later called the union 'the conglomerate of the century.'"

And, indeed, it was an ideal match of both power and money: Sarah and Robert Lee's 1909 wedding in the central Texas town of Lampasas was attended by the top figures of Texas society, including then-Governor Hogg. The governor's daughter, Ima, who would become a well-known Houston art patron, was Sarah's maid of honor.

Robert Lee and Sarah Blaffer had four children, three girls and a boy. Their first child and only son was John Hepburn Blaffer, born in 1913. He would be followed by Sarah Jane in 1915, Cecil Amelia in 1919, and Joyce Blaffer in 1926. They would make up the first generation of Houston-born Blaffers.

The Blaffer children were raised much as you would expect, given the Blaffer family's wealth and position in society: A French governess attended to the children, and they spent summers in France visiting the governess's farm in Charente. While abroad, the Blaffer children were expected to perfect their French, and this gave Sarah plenty of time to visit the museums in Paris. A notable art aficionado, Sarah Campbell Blaffer began collecting art in 1909, when she and her husband spent three months on their European honeymoon, touring the world's finest museums and art collections. Eventually, the Blaffers' Houston home became a literary salon, with Sarah Blaffer single-handedly attracting the finest in sophisticated art and culture that the period had to offer.

Even today, Sarah Campbell Blaffer's legacy of art and culture lives on in Houston. In 1947, Sarah Blaffer donated a large portion of her personal art collection to the Museum of Fine Arts, establishing the Robert Lee Blaffer Memorial Collection in honor of her late husband. Sarah later established the Sarah Campbell Blaffer Foundation to promote art education and to sponsor touring exhibitions at the University of Houston. Additionally, Sarah promised many of the major works in her personal art collection to the university, which opened the Blaffer Gallery in 1973, two years before her death. Among the donations were works by Paul Cezanne and Auguste Renoir. The collections would be rich with Old Master works as well as those of French Impressionists.

The Blaffer family's fortune is one of humble origins. Through the hard work of Robert Lee Blaffer, the Blaffer family established itself as Texas oil royalty. And there would be plenty of real royalty mixed into the family tree, as well: Cecil Blaffer became an Austrian princess when she married her third husband, Prince Tassilo von Furstenberg. Cecil was the stepmother of the late fashion designer Egon von Furstenberg, whose ex-wife, Diane von Furstenberg, is well known among international stylistas for her iconic dress designs of the 1970s. And the Blaffer's youngest daughter, Joyce, would marry the French Marquis Jacques de la Begassière.

But just two generations later, the Blaffer legacy would be badly tarnished. Sometimes ridiculed by family as well as the financial community as "one of America's most poorly managed family fortunes," the Blaffer fortune did not grow as it should have, causing bitter squabbles and legal disputes among Robert Lee Blaffer's grandchildren—Joan Johnson included.

Joan Blaffer Johnson is the daughter of John Hepburn Blaffer (the only son of Robert Lee and Sarah Campbell Blaffer) and Camilla Davis. In many ways, the marriage between Camilla Davis and John Hepburn Blaffer was a good match: Both were young, attractive, and from socially prominent backgrounds. But beneath the surface, the marriage may have been less than ideal, especially for Camilla. In 1940, Camilla Davis had a bright future: The daughter of Dallas real estate tycoon and multimillionaire Wirt Davis, Camilla came from one of the wealthiest families in north Texas. Camilla had just graduated from the prestigious women's university Wellesley College and had her sights set on a career; she'd always dreamed of going to law school after graduation. But that dream was cut short when her parents insisted she return home to Texas to find a suitable husband. It was the 1940s, after all. Shortly after receiving her degree, Camilla met her future husband, John Hepburn Blaffer, at her debut party, which was featured in the January 1940 issue of *Life* magazine. They were married several years later.

A year after Camilla's marriage, the first of the Blaffer children was born: Camilla, also known as "Coco." Joan, born in 1952, was the fourth of the Blaffer children, following sisters Catherine "Trinka" (born in 1943) and Sarah (born in 1946). The Blaffers' youngest child—and only son (who was sometimes the target of his sisters' ridicule and jealousy until his suicide in 1990)—was Robert Lee Blaffer II, born in 1959.

There is evidence to suggest that Camilla found life as a house-wife and mother unfulfilling at best, and it seems that her own children found her maternal instincts left something to be desired:

"My mother was, by some standards, an appalling mother," recalled Sarah, the third of the Blaffer children (now Sarah Blaffer Hrdy), who noted that Camilla was never one to comfort a crying child. "But I loved her tremendously."

In addition to raising their large family, John and Camilla Blaffer continued the Blaffer family patronage of the arts. They worked closely with the Museum of Fine Arts in Houston, organizing the first Beaux Arts Ball and fund-raiser in 1952. The Beaux Arts Ball is now a yearly event at the museum. Camilla and John Blaffer also donated an entire wing to The Kinkaid School, the oldest and arguably one of the most prestigious private coed schools in Houston that was founded in part by John's father, Robert Lee Blaffer. Camilla Blaffer was also a member of the Junior League and was active in developing the Child Guidance Center in Houston.

John Blaffer was an old-fashioned businessman, husband, and father. He took care of his family, always willing to listen to his children's woes and solving any problems that arose. He personally handled all of the family's financial dealings, so that

Joan and the other Blaffer children grew up without any financial worries. Although rumors circulated that John liked to carouse (a habit that his only son, R. L., would fall into himself once he reached adulthood), the Blaffer children had a comfortable, secure childhood. Joan and her siblings grew up surrounded by the finest things money could buy. Tragically, Joan's relationship with her father was cut short—he died in 1973, a year before Joan graduated from the University of Texas. Joan would never fully recover from the loss of her father. Over the course of her life, she would look for strong men to help fill the space he vacated, both emotionally and financially.

Joan's siblings grew up to discover their own triumphs and failures in life. After attending Bryn Mawr, Coco married a man by the name of John Royall and became an international jet-setter. She has owned homes in Houston, London, New York, Monaco, and Rhode Island, and has enjoyed the company of exclusive society worldwide.

Trinka married Nicholas Taylor, and the couple had two children. Today, Trinka carries on her family's support of the arts as a member of the committee that appoints the Texas poet laureate, state musician, and state artists, sponsored by the Texas Commission on the Arts.

Sarah Blaffer attended Wellesley College, her mother's alma mater. She may well have inherited Camilla's unfulfilled passion for education; she would later attend Radcliff, Stanford, and finally Harvard, where she received her doctorate in anthropology. She married fellow anthropologist Dr. Daniel Hrdy and today is a respected anthropologist and primatologist known primarily for her research on family structures in langur populations in India. Interestingly, Hrdy sparked a controversy after the 2000 publication of her book on motherhood. In *Mother Nature: Maternal Instincts and How They Shape the Human Species,* Hrdy theorizes that there is no true "maternal instinct." Inspired perhaps by her own mother's cold, distant approach to child rearing, Hrdy (who is herself a mother of three) claims that mothering is not innate to women. Instead, she theorizes that, for most women, motherhood is a constant balance of trade-offs and sacrifices. She goes on to say that women cannot raise their children alone but need the support of a network—a community of fathers, grandmothers, aunts, siblings, nannies, and teachers.

Though controversial, this particular aspect of Hrdy's research may well explain the Blaffer women's approach to motherhood. Camilla Blaffer could hardly be described as a "natural" mother, and at least one of her daughters—Joan Johnson, left without a husband and without the support of her extended family—seemed to struggle with the day-to-day trials of raising children. Hrdy has published three other books throughout her career and now operates a successful walnut farm with her husband in California—far away from her siblings and their financial squabbles.

Though the Blaffer siblings may have navigated their way successfully into adulthood, the journey was not entirely without conflict. And in some instances, the family's tangled web of finances and trust funds were the only threads that kept Joan and her siblings connected.

The first signs of trouble started after John Blaffer's death in 1973.

———————

Money was at the root of all evil in the Blaffer family. The way in which the wealthy preserve their wealth is to set up trusts for themselves, their children, and their grandchildren. Because of strict laws in Texas, trusts usually can exist only for a limited time after the death of the second generation. American law in general and Texas law in particular is set up this way to avoid some of the problems European nations have faced with trusts: Some family trusts in the Old World last for centuries, and they're often tax-free, since the governments can't touch them until they "expire."

In order to sidestep some of these laws, the Blaffers chose an interesting—and, by legal standards, unusual—system of cascading and interlocking trusts. The original John and Camilla Blaffer trust was extended to include each of their children. In addition, when each of their five were born, a portion of the John and Camilla trust was carved off in order to set up individual trusts for each child. Once each child reached adulthood, they had legal rights to two trusts: one in their own name and a portion of their parents' trusts that they shared with their siblings. The trusts were named by letter, such as "Trust A," "Trust B," and so forth. This system went on for years, extending all the way down to Joan's children and their cousins.

The most interesting choice with regard to the Blaffer family's financial matters was the apparent absence of professional control: Instead of appointing financiers as trustees, family members were chosen to manage the trusts. As is often the case when mixing business and family, this system of interlocking, family-managed trusts would be the impetus of much conflict and discord within the family. More than that, the trusts were not always properly managed; in fact, several were severely underperforming. By the mid-1990s, Joan's trust had been underperforming for decades.

These trusts formed the basis of contention and bad blood between Joan and her siblings; even Joan's own mother would resort to withholding funds from Joan. Article III in Camilla Blaffer Trammel's trust was designed specifically in regard to Joan. Camilla—who hated the fact that Joan had married the irresponsible, alcoholic Luke Johnson, Jr., and was sinking her money into his failing car dealership—added Article III to her will, stating that Joan could not access her portion of the trust as long as she was married to Luke:

> *Special Provision for Joan B. Johnson.*
> *Notwithstanding anything to the contrary in the Article III,*
> *during any period when my daughter Joan B. Johnson is married*

to or living on a full time basis with Luke Johnson, the following
provisions shall apply to the trust created for her benefit under
this Article III:
(2) The Trustee of such trust shall have no power to distribute
any principal of such trust to or for the benefit of Joan B.
Johnson, except to provide for her health needs.

To drive the point home, she wrote a letter to Luke, dated February 6, 1980, in which she says of Joan's investment in Luke Johnson Ford that ". . . [Joan] is very unsophisticated in business matters and emotionally involved with you . . . therefore I request that you cooperate with her retaining proper independent legal counsel in this investment. . . . I do not believe that my daughter's interest in this matter is adequately served by this arrangement."

The death of Camilla Trammel in 1991 after a bout with cancer—only a year after R. L.'s suicide—did little to stop the infighting among the family: All of the sisters' assets were tied together, with other relatives serving as executors of the trusts. The trusts included stocks, land, property, and businesses, with each of the sisters inheriting staggering fortunes. Litigation ensued as the sisters tried to divide assets and bolster profits in their floundering trusts. Joan remained close to Sarah, but Coco and Trinka seemed to start many of the problems concerning Joan's financial status. Each sister would need to employ a team of lawyers just to deal with the paperwork concerning all of their mutual court battles.

In an affidavit dated April 27, 1998, Joan describes the state of her family affairs in her own words:

For many years now, I have not had a good relationship
with either of my two older sisters named Coco Blaffer and
Trinka Taylor. My sister Trinka Taylor sued me and my other
two sisters for a property known as Midway Plantation in
Alabama. Prior to this lawsuit, my relationship with Coco and
Trinka had been strained and minimal. Today, my relationship

with these two sisters, Trinka and Coco, is nonexistent . . . My
relationships with my family are strained on all sides and I think
that it is due to jealousy and greed within us.

And so, after a tumultuous few years that included the suicide
of her brother, death of her mother, and suicide of her husband,
Luke Johnson, Jr., it would be safe to say that Joan Johnson was in a
delicate state of mind, emotionally stressed but trying to cope. The
financial and legal problems left strained relationships with those
she should have been able to turn to: her sisters. By 1995, distraught,
unstable, and with little support from her family, Joan Johnson was
in need of a friend, a confidante, an advisor. Her vulnerabilities
helped set the stage for exploitation, which is exactly when David
Collie and Dinny Shah entered the picture.

David Collie Comes Calling

Although Joan had lived in River Oaks all of her adult life, she had never entirely fit into the close-knit, country club community. While not an "outsider"—after all, Joan was heiress to one of the largest family fortunes in America—the later Johnson generations had not maintained the reputation achieved under their parents. In fact, Joan, despite her enormous wealth, was not even a member of the River Oaks Country Club although Dinny said she longed for membership. Perhaps Joan felt that membership to the exclusive club was her birthright: The Blaffers had belonged to the club until their membership ended sometime in the 1970s. For reasons that aren't entirely clear, Camilla Blaffer chose to let the membership lapse rather than renew it or pass it on to her children. Perhaps Camilla privately thought the family, including the despised Luke, did not deserve that perk. This may be true. However, another story goes that a Blaffer family member, after having a few too many drinks at the club, stood up on a table in the middle of the crowded dining room and urinated. According to this version of events, the Blaffers were asked not to return.

Despite her family's internal squabbles, Joan did have some close friends in River Oaks, one of them being Baron Enrico "Ricky" di Portanova and his wife, Sandra. Ricky di Portanova was the grandson of Hugh Roy Cullen (another prominent Texas oil king) on his mother's side. His father was the Italian actor Baron Paolo di Portanova. Ricky grew up mainly in Italy, but he maintained lavish homes all over the world, including a mansion in Houston. The di Portanovas were regular guests at fund-raisers thrown by fellow Houstonian Joanne Herring. Herring is a minor celebrity in her own right, thanks in part to the 2007 movie *Charlie Wilson's War*. The film chronicles Herring's efforts to influence Texas congressman Charlie Wilson to support American efforts to defeat the Soviet Union's invasion of Afghanistan in the 1980s. Herring was played by Julia Roberts; Tom Hanks was cast in the role of Charlie Wilson, who died in early 2010.

Joan Johnson had a very close relationship with the di Portanovas: They were even appointed guardians of Joan's two youngest children, Seth and Kaleta. And Joan was a regular attendee at the di Portanovas' weekly Bible studies.

The di Portanovas' home in Houston is situated on River Oaks Boulevard—the street itself a grand parade of some of the most expensive properties in Houston—and is a spectacle of baronial proportions. The French-style mansion calls attention to itself with its vast, bricked-over front yard featuring a cupid and fountain dead center. The backyard was one of the most impressive aspects of the home: di Portanova enclosed and air-conditioned the entire backyard, including the swimming pool.

It was among the opulent, aristocratic rooms of their mansion that the di Portanovas would host their weekly Bible study. Aside from the reverent preoccupation of the attendees, guests would also use the weekly opportunity to mingle, gossip, and drink wine; it was

as much of a social gathering as it was religious. And it was here, in the spring of 1996, that Joan met two men who would change her life forever: David Collie and Dinesh Shah.

Another regular attendee of the di Portanovas' Bible studies was a Mr. Henry Dyches. Well-advanced in age, Dyches was not a part of the River Oaks set, but he was a trusted and admired swimming coach and Spanish teacher to the wealthy families that lived in the neighborhood. Joan and Henry knew each other well: The two met at the di Portanovas' weekly gatherings and hit it off; as they grew closer, Dyches became privy to the intimate details of Joan's personal life, including her divorce and Luke's death. Dyches eventually became an honorary member of the Johnson family, and he appears in many of the family's personal photographs between 1996 and 2002.

Given their close bond, it makes sense that, in the spring of 1996, Henry Dyches tried to play matchmaker for Joan. Dyches, who did not drive because of his age and an early onset of Alzheimer's, lived in Houston's nearby Museum District, perhaps a ten- or fifteen-minute ride from River Oaks. And because he could not drive, he would often ask for rides to and from the di Portanovas' home. On one occasion, his drivers were two neighbors from his apartment complex on Portland Street: David Collie and Dinesh Shah.

Dyches introduced Joan to both Collie and Shah. Dyches, knowing that Collie was also single, was actually engineering a potential love affair between the two. But he couldn't have known the explosive consequences of the relationship between Joan, David, and Dinny.

Dinny's own testimony corroborates the story:

Attorney: "How did you meet Ms. Joan Johnson?"

Shah: "Well, I believe that we all had a common friend named Mr. Henry (Dyches), who was an older gentleman and he was very well loved by a lot of people in Ms. Johnson's community in River Oaks. He knew a lot of people. And he was attending a Bible study or a class at somebody's home in River Oaks and he didn't drive.

So he would ask me or some other friends to take him to the Bible study. And when I drove him one day, he said Dinny, would you like to come into Bible study. And I went in and he introduced me to some people and at that point I met Ms. Johnson."

Attorney: "Who met Ms. Johnson first, you or David Collie?"

Shah: "I did. I met Ms. Johnson first. That is for certain. And we didn't know who she was. David Collie did not know who she was, and I had no idea who she was."

Attorney: "Explain to the jury the relationship between your meeting of Ms. Johnson and David Collie's meeting of Ms. Johnson."

Shah: "Well, I think he also drove Mr. Dyches to the Bible study . . . and Ms. Johnson then met Dave at the Bible study because she was in attendance."

David Collie is tall, blond, and muscular, with a mischievous, boyish disposition—an attractive catch for many women. More than that, he comes from a wealthy and respected family in Houston, which is perhaps why Joan fell so hard for him. They looked good together, and in Houston, there are many couples who marry simply because they look good together.

David is the son of Marvin Collie, an admired Houstonian who served during World War II as an officer in the Office of Strategic Services (OSS), the predecessor of the CIA. After World War II, Marvin Collie returned to Houston and became a celebrated attorney, working his way up to managing partner of the Vinson & Elkins firm, one of the oldest and most respected corporate law firms in the United States. Among Collie's partners at the firm was former Texas Governor John Connally. After Marvin's death in 1989, David Collie inherited part of his father's fortune, making him an instant multimillionaire.

Sometime in the mid-'90s David Collie met Dinny Shah. The two were immediate friends, sharing the same interests and the same sense of inflated bravado. Although neither man had ever held a job in the financial sector, they liked to think of themselves as investors and analysts, as savvy financial pioneers. The two set out to form their own business venture: a video production company called Shah-Collie Productions, Inc. David Collie often presented himself as an "insider" in the Hollywood film industry, though there is little evidence that he had any actual connections. The production company, which was formed to produce commercials and movies, never actually did any business, but it did help the two fulfill their needs to feel powerful and important, to present an exotic image to the world, to impress. It also helped solidify the relationship between the two men.

By 1996, the two were roommates in the same complex on Portland Street in Houston's Montrose District where Henry Dyches lived. Collie and Shah shared common living areas but had separate bedrooms; they also housed the "offices" for their production company in their apartment.

After Dyches introduced Joan and David, their relationship escalated at light speed. In a 2008 deposition as part of the civil case Joan would file against them, Dinny Shah testified that Joan was dating several men when she met Collie. Her apparent willingness to start a new relationship so soon after her ex-husband's death may have had something to do with dependence on men, both emotionally and financially. And this may have been the very same reason why Joan soon was infatuated with David Collie. But during his video taped deposition, Collie was vague with the details of his early relationship with Joan:

Attorney: "When you met Joan, is it fair to say that you and Joan Johnson had a fairly intense romantic relationship for a handful of months?"

Collie: "Yes."

Attorney: "Three, four, five, six months maybe?"

Collie: "I don't remember, sir."

Attorney: "Did she tell you she loved you?"

Collie: "Yes."

Attorney: "Did you tell her you loved her?"

Collie: "Yes."

Attorney: "You discussed marriage?"

Collie: "We discussed it, yes."

The early details may have been fuzzy for Collie, but it's certain that his first date with Joan occurred not long after their meeting at Ricky di Portanova's house: Collie invited Joan and her daughter Kaleta to his shared apartment with Dinny for an afternoon cookout. Joan picked up some IMAX tickets and the group—Joan, Collie, Kaleta, Dinny Shah, and Henry Dyches—walked over to the Museum of Natural Science to see the show. David Collie, for Joan, was the perfect match: He was good with her children, he had enough money to support himself, and he was from a socially acceptable family—he even had a coveted membership to the River Oaks Country Club, something that Joan longed for. To top it all off, Collie was a younger man, some ten to fifteen years younger than Joan.

Collie quickly became a regular guest at Joan's house. He appears in many of the family photos from this period, and he took an active role as a substitute father in Seth and Kaleta's lives. In a matter of months, Joan and Collie began talking about marriage; Joan would testify that she and Collie even went engagement ring shopping.

At the same time, Joan became closer and closer to Shah. Shah often accompanied Collie on trips to the Johnson home; likewise, when Joan visited Collie at their Portland Street apartment, she ended up in conversation with Shah. Collie vouched for Shah, calling him a brilliant financier. This attracted Joan, who was experiencing legal problems associated with the trusts she shared with her sisters. Even though she was dating David Collie, Shah was the one Joan would often confide in, sometimes leveraging his friendship with Collie to influence her own relationship with him. On several occasions, Joan visited Shah at the "office" in his apartment. The two would have long talks about Joan's past, her financial problems, and her family problems. Shah, only twenty-nine years old at the time, was flattered to be considered the confidante of an older woman. He began offering her financial advice, something that flattered him and boosted his ego. Joan's innocent request for advice would set the stage for his later choke-hold on her finances.

But the three new friends didn't know that, less than a year later, in 1997, Joan's relationship with Collie would already be rocky. Joan testified that Collie did indeed ask her to marry him, and that she accepted, but most of the evidence indicates that Collie never made that commitment. And while her relationship with Collie cooled, Joan became closer to Shah, relying on his financial advice and his willingness to help her raise her children. Shah would outlast Collie in Joan's life, but only because Collie—who is not without blame in this family drama—was able to disentangle himself from the web of control and self-destruction that Joan and Dinny had woven.

Dinny's First Conquest: Glennis Goodrich

The real tragedy of this story lies with Seth and Kaleta: two innocent children—both very young, only ten and eight years old when Dinny Shah arrived on the scene—caught up in their mother's mistakes. And while no one—not Seth, not Kaleta, not Joan, not even Collie or Shah—could have predicted the outcome of their innocent meeting at the di Portanovas' home, the resulting events could have been stopped, or mitigated at the very least, before the December 2002 climax.

Had Joan been a little more mature in her friendships and romantic relationships, had she investigated David and Dinny beforehand, she may have been able to protect herself, her finances, and, above all, her children from Dinny Shah's physical and psychological stranglehold. Had she known that Shah was a habitual liar, a manipulator, and physically violent, she may not have been so quick to befriend him. Had she known that David Collie, a physically intimidating 6'3", occasionally served as Shah's muscle—often bullying people into complying with Shah's schemes—she may not have become intimate with him so quickly.

And had she known a woman by the name of Glennis McRary Goodrich, Joan might have distanced herself from these two con artists. It's here that Dinny Shah's story really begins, three years before he ever met Joan Johnson. The parallels between Goodrich and Joan—two women whose lives were upended by Shah, two women who never met—are uncanny and, on reflection, frightening.

―――――――――――

It was in May 1993 that Robert C. McKay first heard the name Dinny Shah. McKay, an attorney in Victoria, Texas, received an unexpected phone call from Jay Paxton, a Houston attorney who worked for the Stewart Title Company. A contract had recently come across Paxton's desk involving the sale of a home—a contract that Paxton described as "overreaching" and "nonstandard." The home belonged to a Mrs. Glennis McRary Goodrich, an aging, ailing widow, whose closest relation happened to be her nephew, Robert McKay.

Paxton had red-flagged the contract after reviewing what seemed like very suspicious terms. As Mrs. Goodrich's closest relation, McKay was contacted to review the contract himself. Paxton promptly faxed the contract to McKay.

A copy of the real estate contract listed the seller as Glennis McRary Goodrich; the buyer was a Mr. D. K. (Dinny) Shah. The property in question was Mrs. Goodrich's home at 615 Hunters Grove Lane, in West Houston's prominent Memorial neighborhood—a miniature version of River Oaks that was wealthy in its own right.

The home was to be sold to Dinny for nearly half a million dollars—$497,900, to be exact. And this was at a time when the median home sale in Houston was around $80,000. While Mrs. Goodrich's house was well above ordinary, what Paxton found disturbing was that Mrs. Goodrich was selling her property at its tax appraisal value, no more and no less—unusual in a time when property values were expected to rise. This was the first indication to Paxton that something was wrong. Why would a homeowner sell a home at the tax appraisal value instead of market value based on surrounding sales? What's more, it appeared that Shah was purchasing the home, literally, for nothing—no money down, no money in escrow, no loan agreement, and no written payment schedule for the duration of the thirty-year note. An unsecured thirty-year loan to an elderly woman with a limited life expectancy. The deal did not pass the smell test.

McKay was shocked at the grossly unfavorable terms of the contract and swiftly killed the deal: In a formal letter to Jay Paxton and Stuart Title Company, McKay stated that, as Mrs. Goodrich's closest relation and an attorney himself, he would further be representing his aunt's interests and that the closing on the house would not take place.

The next day McKay received a phone call from Dinny Shah. Furious that McKay had stopped the sale, Shah cursed and raged at McKay, even making veiled threats. During their conversation, Shah claimed to be a "very powerful man" and cautioned McKay that his brother was an IRS agent (he was not), implying major tax problems for McKay if he continued to interfere in the sale of the home. This pattern of tall tales, intimidation, and flat-out lies would continue three years later with Joan Johnson and her family. As for Robert McKay, it would take years of litigation before he would fully extract Dinny Shah from both his and his aunt's lives. In May 1993, McKay didn't quite know yet exactly the kind of damage Shah had exacted on Mrs. Goodrich's estate and mental well-being.

But he was about to find out.

————————————

It is believed that Dinny Shah and Mrs. Goodrich—two very unlikely friends—first met at the Houston Lincoln Continental Club, a club frequented by River Oaks residents and lovers of classic cars. Mrs. Goodrich was the owner of a 1963 pink Lincoln Continental with only nine thousand miles on it (the same year and model as the car in which JFK was assassinated) and a 1978 Lincoln Continental. Goodrich, well-advanced in age with no living relatives aside from her nephew in Victoria, was an easy target for Dinny: she a wealthy, vulnerable woman; he a conniving, manipulative opportunist. Dinny would have been in his mid-twenties at the time, a gulf of over half a century separating the two in age. One can imagine Dinny at work, ingratiating himself with a woman old enough to be his grandmother.

Dinny immediately befriended Mrs. Goodrich. And much like he would with Joan, he began to take over her life, little by little.

First, Dinny appropriated Goodrich's beloved Lincolns. There are no real records detailing how or why Goodrich gave the cars to Shah. It is noted, however, that being at a very advanced age, Goodrich was not always lucid in her daily interactions with others. It may not have been hard, in fact, for Dinny to convince the old woman that she didn't need the cars anymore.

Before Robert McKay ever received a phone call regarding Dinny Shah, Dinny had taken major steps to control Mrs. Goodrich's life and finances. Dinny would cause Goodrich's estate to take some major financial hits—like a substantial donation to her beloved alma mater, Baylor University in Waco, Texas, that her nephew McKay would not be able to reverse later. It seems that such a transaction was done for reasons that only Dinny would conjure. She did not need a charitable tax deduction at her age and there is no estate plan that would justify this contribution.

As with the sale of her home, it is probable that the entire idea was Dinny's concoction, taking advantage of Goodrich's weak mental state. Dinny made efforts to make the deal look legitimate, even going as far as hiring a lawyer to represent Mrs. Goodrich in the transaction, but really the lawyer was only acquiescing to Dinny's own desires—a faux semblance of a consensual contract. Dinny even had Goodrich document the transaction, allegedly dictating a note of sale to her that is written in childlike handwriting on the letterhead of her deceased husband, Baxter D. Goodrich:

I wish my house to be sold to Dinny Shah for just under half a million dollars. I do not wish to charge any interest. . . .

The letter trails off, the last sentence incomplete. Regardless, it is unlikely that the letter was written by a lucid, healthy woman; in reality, it is probably a coerced bill of sale dreamed up by Dinny himself.

In December 1993, Robert McKay filed a suit against Dinesh Shah on behalf of his elderly aunt, who had by then been declared an incapacitated adult. McKay's ten-page affidavit outlines a sordid and twisted tale of how Shah tried to ingratiate himself with Mrs. Goodrich, then take advantage of her by inflicting severe mental strain. The list of accusations included the unlawful acquisition of Goodrich's cars, the sale of her home on unfavorable terms, draining Goodrich's substantial estate, mental abuse, and harassment.

This lawsuit was prompted partly by McKay's visit to Houston the day after he received the phone call from Paxton about the bogus contract on Mrs. Goodrich's home—the day he learned exactly how far Shah had gone to control Mrs. Goodrich's life.

It was May 13, a Thursday, when McKay arrived at his aunt's home in Memorial. When he got there, he wasn't greeted by his aunt; instead, he found that the entire Shah clan was "camped out" in his aunt's home: Shah, Shah's brother, Shyam, Shyam's wife, and their parents. McKay could only guess why the entire family was there; perhaps they were all in on the scheme, or perhaps Dinny was lying to them too, telling them that he already owned the house. His aunt, he reported, was visibly "agitated, confused, and uncomfortable."

The Shah family remained at Goodrich's home until 10:30 that night when finally—and begrudgingly—they left. McKay, exhausted, rented a hotel room, hoping to return to his aunt's home in the morning to sort through her financial and living situations. But Dinny would beat him to it.

The next morning when McKay arrived at the home, he found his aunt curled up into a fetal position. He managed to learn through her tears and confusion that Dinny and "another man"—possibly David Collie or Dinny's brother, Shyam—had already been to the house and that Mrs. Goodrich had signed some papers at their request. When McKay asked his aunt what papers she had signed exactly, she could only parrot back to him, "What did I sign? What did I sign?" He would later learn that Shah had requested of the old woman a power of attorney over her estate, and that she had already signed the sales agreement for her home.

Goodrich was so mentally distressed that McKay decided to rush her to the emergency room at St. Luke's Episcopal Hospital. Doctors determined that Mrs. Goodrich was being given high doses of the over-the-counter diarrhea medicine Imodium, which made her dehydrated. It was at that point that McKay decided to move her far away from Shah's grasp, and he enlisted the help of Robert and Carolyn Feather, two Baylor University alumni and ambassadors. Goodrich, who was a Baylor alumna, had kept close ties with the university and was a major donor. Robert and Carolyn Feather were friends of Mrs. Goodrich through the alumni and donor associations at Baylor, and they were happy to help her in such a distressing time.

Goodrich had been planning to move to the Ridgecrest Retirement Center in Waco, close to Baylor University. McKay decided to speed up the arrangements, booking a flight for Mrs. Goodrich to Waco that very day. On their way to the airport, McKay stated that Mrs. Goodrich seemed more relaxed and lucid, saying that she never intended to sell her home and that that Shah guy "was crazy."

Carolyn Feather, who drove from Waco to Houston that day in order to escort Goodrich on the flight and who had a very close relationship with Goodrich, had never heard the name of Dinny

Shah before. While on the plane, Feather said that Goodrich became agitated again, fearful that someone was out to get her money.

————————————————

The Ridgecrest Retirement Center is an assisted living facility, complete with a hair salon, ice cream parlor, chapel, and movie theater. It was within the confines of this facility where Goodrich was placed in a private apartment—and where Feather and McKay thought she would be out of Shah's reach.

But even though Goodrich was now under the watchful eyes of McKay and Feather, Shah wasn't deterred. He told her he enrolled at Baylor University in the fall of that year. He would now be nearby.

According to eyewitnesses, Shah and other unauthorized guests were seen entering Goodrich's apartment on several occasions, starting in September 1993. Jack Tinsley, assistant administrator at the center, noted that Shah was observed four times attempting to gain unauthorized access to Goodrich. On one of those instances, September 15, Tinsley stopped into Goodrich's apartment to check on her. He reported her as being agitated, saying that "two friends" had come to visit her about "very important business."

Carolyn Feather would recall another instance when Shah allegedly visited Goodrich at the retirement center, a week before on September 7. Feather was supposed to take Goodrich to the beauty salon to have her hair done; when she called to remind Goodrich about the appointment, Goodrich refused to go. She sounded paranoid; she told Feather that someone was going to "do me in" and "take all my money." Around the same time, Feather also received a curious call from the phone company, reporting that someone had attempted to have phone company employees give out Goodrich's unlisted number. Feather's first suspicion was Shah.

Shah left tangible evidence of his visits with Goodrich in her Ridgecrest apartment. When McKay visited his aunt in Waco, he found Post-it notes strewn across the apartment. The notes, in

Goodrich's handwriting, said things like, "Robert McKay is evil, you must stay away from him," "Robert McKay wants my money," and "Robert McKay does not want me to give my money to Baylor University." There is no indication Goodrich felt that way about her nephew. More likely Dinny was at work again.

McKay, knowing that his aunt was fond of him, could only assume that these notes were the design of Shah himself. With little more to do, McKay filed suit and arranged for a restraining order against Shah. Fearful for his own life and his aunt's—and not knowing to what lengths the twenty-seven-year-old Shah would go to in order to sink his claws into Goodrich's money—McKay decided to simply buy off Shah.

In 1998, a settlement was reached between Shah and Robert McKay on behalf of his aunt. In the settlement, McKay and Goodrich agreed to not sue Shah or his family members. In return, Shah and his family members were to relinquish all claims to Goodrich's estate and power of attorney. But it seems that Shah ultimately got exactly what he wanted: Shah got to keep Goodrich's 1963 pink Continental and was awarded $30,000 from Goodrich's estate for cooperating with the terms of the agreement.

———————

In an interesting aside, Robert McKay had just one more thing to say about Shah. In 1996, McKay ended up selling Mrs. Goodrich's home in Memorial under much more favorable terms than those offered by Dinny. One day, McKay received a phone call from the new owners of 615 Hunters Grove Lane.

The new owners, who had recently renovated the house and put it back on the market for sale, said that they were visited by a Mr. Dinesh Shah. Shah claimed to be the adopted son of Mrs. Goodrich; he showed up at the home one day asking if he could visit the inside of his childhood home just once more. The owners let him in, and Shah proceeded to ramble through the house, reminiscing aloud about his fake childhood, even pointing out the bedroom that he claimed to have grown up in.

Shah's accounts of his childhood and formative years would grow more outlandish as time passed: He was becoming a better scam artist and by the time Dinny got to the Johnson family, he was making outrageous claims about having been a CIA agent, a paratrooper, and friend of presidents. And though such tall tales might seem unbelievable, his unshakeable belief in his own lies and his dominating personality somehow made them seem more palatable, though not probable. Anything he said three times, he believed. Sometimes, twice was enough.

Goodrich is just one example of how forceful Shah could be when it came to matters of scheming with other people's money. But as Michael Holstein, Michael Sambogna, and Clint Langford would later testify in 2008, Shah could be just as manipulative—even violently so—when it came to matters of the heart.

His Matters of the Heart: Michael Holstein, Michael Sambogna, and Clint Langford

Michael Holstein was missing. Or perhaps he wasn't really missing; he had simply skipped town one day in 1996, moving from Houston to Dallas without notice and taking a series of modest jobs to make ends meet. Holstein worked as a groundskeeper at a historical Dallas farmhouse, and he occasionally found work as a housekeeper. His family knew where he was, but they were the only ones who did—friends and casual acquaintances were kept in the dark. After all, Holstein didn't want word to get back to the person he was running from—his then-boyfriend Dinny Shah.

———————

"Missing Person: Please contact if you see him." On the surface, it was an innocent-looking ad: It appeared in the Dallas edition of *This Week in Texas*, sometimes known just as TWT, and listed Dinny's contact information; it even included a picture of Holstein. But behind the clear, bold-faced type and seemingly concerned message lurked something much more sinister.

TWT was a popular magazine in the Dallas gay community—
a community that Dinny knew his ex-lover had ties to.

As luck would have it, Dinny's search tactics were quite effective. It was only a short time after the ad appeared that a Dallas
local, Michael Sambogna, noticed the ad with Holstein's picture.
Sambogna was working with Holstein at the Henderson County
and Cedar Creek Lake, a historic house and farm an hour outside of
Dallas. Sambogna and his partner had also recently hired Holstein
as a part-time housekeeper for their condominium in Dallas' Oak
Lawn neighborhood. Although Sambogna didn't know Holstein
well—they had worked together for just a few weeks—he was concerned Holstein was in trouble.

Sambogna made the call.

He left his name, some brief personal details, and a promise to
call back later with more info. But he never got around to it. Only
later would Sambogna realize that the well-intended message that
he left on Dinny's answering machine would turn into the most
terrifying event of his life.

———

A few weeks later, Michael Sambogna had forgotten all about
the phone call he had placed in response to the missing persons ad.
It was a beautiful spring day, and he was outside his condo, doing
some gardening. As Sambogna pulled weeds, he noticed that he was
suddenly eclipsed by a shadow. He looked up to find a tall, blond
stranger standing next to him on the lawn.

The blond man told Sambogna that he had just moved to the
area, and the two men stood in the yard, making small talk:

"I'm from Austin," said the stranger.

Sambogna misunderstood him. "Boston?" he asked.

"No, Austin," said the stranger. "I'm new here; I'm just looking
around for any good restaurants, seeing what goes on in the neighborhood."

To Sambogna, there was nothing unusual about the man's approach. After all, Oak Lawn was a friendly, upscale urban community where residents often opted to walk instead of drive, and it wasn't out of the ordinary for strangers to greet each other. The two spoke for a few minutes, and the blond stranger from Austin said goodbye and wandered away. Sambogna went back to his gardening, unaware that his next meeting with his new "neighbor" wouldn't be a social call.

Just before sunset that evening, Sambogna's doorbell rang. The tall stranger was standing on his front porch.

And this time, he wasn't alone.

Dinny Shah lurked in the shadows next to the Austin man, holding a briefcase and looking angry. Only later, after the Dallas Police Department responded to a frantic call from one of Sambogna's neighbors, would Sambogna learn that the blond man from Austin was actually David Collie, who often acted as Dinny's "muscle." Sambogna opened his door to the two strangers.

That's when things took a turn for the worse.

Shah stormed into the condo. He pulled a picture of Holstein from his briefcase and began firing questions at Sambogna: Where is Michael Holstein? Is he here? Where could they find him? Collie stood by silently, his earlier friendly demeanor replaced by cold indifference.

Years later, in courtroom testimony in the civil case, Sambogna would describe Shah and Collie as "white-collar thugs." When he appeared before the jury in the 295th Judicial District Court he was nervous, apprehensive, frightened, and on edge. Dressed casually but wearing an effete cowboy hat, he would not look Dinny in the eye even though he was on the witness stand for forty-five minutes. His testimony unfolded as follows:

Worried that his former coworker might be in real danger, Sambogna tried to cover for Holstein. He didn't know where he was; Holstein didn't live with Sambogna; Holstein hadn't been to work for weeks. This was not what Dinny wanted to hear. Dinny's eyes bulged. He raised his voice and hissed his questions: *Where is Holstein? When did you see him last? Do you have his phone number?*

Then Dinny changed tactics. He patted his briefcase and told Sambogna that he'd make any information about Holstein worth Sambogna's while, intimating a bribe. But Sambogna stuck to his story.

Finally, abruptly, Dinny stopped asking questions and yanked open the briefcase—but he didn't pull out cash. Instead, a 9mm appeared and it was pointed straight at Sambogna's head.

Terrified, Sambogna shoved past Shah and Collie, vaulted over the rail of his front porch, and ran across the street into another condominium complex. Dinny ran after him, screaming and waving the gun in the air.

Sambogna, by this time a world-class hurdler, managed to jump another fence. But his pursuer hurdled over the fence behind him, and Sambogna suddenly felt Shah's weight barrel him to the ground.

Sambogna was screaming. The two men were wrestling, and then Dinny broke it off and bolted, yelling, "He's got the gun!"

Sambogna, driven by adrenalin, had wrenched the gun out of Dinny's hand during the fight.

Panicked, Sambogna tossed the gun into some nearby bushes. Sirens approached from somewhere in the distance. But Collie and Shah were long gone.

When the police arrived on the scene—a neighbor had heard the commotion and called 911—they were unable to locate the gun that Sambogna claimed to have thrown into the bushes. Perhaps Collie and Shah had doubled back to retrieve the evidence. Sambogna gave his statement and showed the officers the cuts and bruises he'd received in the altercation, along with a description of his attackers. A few days later, a Dallas Police detective came to visit Sambogna. He showed Sambogna photographs of possible suspects, and

Sambogna easily identified the two men whose faces were forever etched in his memory: Dinny Shah and David Collie.

Shah and Collie were arrested in Houston on charges of assault with a deadly weapon. They hired a crack team of high-powered Dallas lawyers—not the last time Dinny would resort to highly respected criminal attorneys—to represent them in pretrial hearings against their accuser.

But the case never went to trial.

Sambogna was still shaken by the events and frightened for his life. Since the attack, he'd lived in a constant state of fear and paranoia, unsure if Shah or Collie would show up at his door again to exact their revenge. He ultimately agreed to drop the charges, after some hardball tactics employed by Dinny's lawyers. In return, Collie and Shah were ordered by the court to stay far away from the Dallas city limits and Michael Sambogna.

Attorney: "Did you subsequently meet with the prosecuting attorney in Dallas regarding the aggravated assault with a deadly weapon charge?"

Sambogna: "Yes, sir, we met several times."

Attorney: "Was there any meeting in which Mr. Shah showed up with his lawyers?"

Sambogna: "He sent a legal team to meet with us at a pretrial conference or hearing or meeting. And, yes [Dinny showed up with lawyers]."

Attorney: "How did you feel about that?"

Sambogna: "Very intimidated . . . I was very scared because I really felt that the person [Dinny] would, you know, come get me."

Attorney: "Did you ultimately acquiesce in the dismissal of those charges?"

Sambogna: "I did."

Attorney: "Why?"

Sambogna: "Fear."

Attorney: "How did you feel as a result of that confrontation [with Collie and Shah], Mr. Sambogna?"

Sambogna: "Terrified and paranoid for a while, nervous about living on a busy corner with no fence or wall in between that person and me."

Attorney: "Why are you here then?"

Sambogna: "I think because I let my fear stop me the last time and I think we may not be here if I had stood up and I want to correct—try to correct—a wrong."

Perhaps that's why Sambogna agreed to testify on behalf of the Johnson family in the 2008 civil trial concerning Dinny's assault and battery on Kaleta and Seth. A decade earlier, Sambogna had let fear stop him from pressing charges against Shah and Collie. Even though he was never romantically involved with Dinny, testifying in Shah's civil suit was a way for Sambogna to correct a past wrong. Perhaps he felt a sort of kinship with the Johnson children—or a responsibility toward them. After all, Sambogna had something in common with Seth and Kaleta: Shah had come into their lives and changed them forever.

Unfortunately, other than a few drug-related arrests in the late 1990s, there is almost no information to be found about Michael Holstein. No records exist to document the nature of his and Dinny's relationship; there are no depositions or sworn statements from Dinny's ex-lover. Holstein either could not be found or refused to testify against Dinny in the 2008 civil suit. He seemingly vanished from the face of the earth.

To this day, the exact reasons behind Michael Holstein's disappearing act remain a mystery, as do his reasons for keeping silent during the civil suit. But not all of Dinny's former boyfriends chose to fade away quietly: Clint Langford, who dated Dinny for six months in 1996, did testify in the civil trial, giving valuable insight into what it may have been like to be romantically involved with the temperamental, manipulative Dinny Shah.

If Michael Holstein's story is anything like Langford's, the reasons behind Holstein's abrupt departure become abundantly clear.

———————

Clint Langford is an easygoing young man. Of medium height, pale complexion, and slender build, Langford appeared in court dressed casually in a sport shirt and jeans. His manner was low key and mild; a giver, not a taker. Significantly, however, he had a pretty girl, his girlfriend, with him. She would sit on the front row during his uncomfortable time on the stand, smiling encouragingly as he poured out his story to the jury.

In the summer of 1996, Clint Langford was eighteen years old and about to be a senior at Houston's Westbury High School. It was Saturday night, and Langford was on his way to meet some friends at a club called Heaven, located in Houston's predominantly gay Montrose neighborhood. Langford was stopped at a red light when a car pulled up alongside him. The man inside asked him for directions to another club in the area and then asked Langford where he was headed.

So Langford wasn't surprised when twenty-seven-year old Dinny Shah approached him later that night at Heaven. Dinny had obviously been cruising the neighborhood, and the teenager had caught his eye. The two talked and flirted for a while, and Dinny turned on the charm. By the end of the evening, Langford had agreed to go out with Shah.

Despite Dinny being almost ten years older than Langford, Langford and Dinny would date for about six months in 1996. But it wasn't long before Langford knew that he had to get out.

Attorney: "Mr. Langford, have you been subpoenaed to appear here and testify?"

Langford: "I have."

Attorney: "Would you tell us, sir, whether you are an eager or a reluctant witness in this case."

Langford: "Reluctant."

Attorney: "Why?"

Langford: "Um, Dinny makes me nervous."

Now a far cry from the teenager he once was, Langford was apprehensive about facing Dinny during the 2008 trial—and perhaps with good reason. On the stand, Langford recalled Dinny as being manipulative and controlling, and described how Dinny had attempted to "brainwash" him. "I was very young at the time," Langford told the jury. "He told me that I was handsome, I could charm people, and that I could be successful. He groomed me by telling me, 'You can have anything you want'. . . . Shah controlled virtually every aspect of my life. He was extremely manipulative towards anyone that had anything he wanted."

Langford's testimony reveals a pattern that became all too familiar to Joan Johnson and her children: Dinny Shah ingratiated himself to Langford; he made him feel special, cared for. And then there was isolation and ultimately the takeover.

As the relationship progressed, Dinny's erratic behavior began to make Langford uncomfortable. Early on, Dinny told his new lover that under no circumstances could Langford call him by his real name; instead Langford was to introduce him to friends and family as "Robert Cullen"—the surname of a wealthy Houston family with a background in oil. Why Dinny picked the famous Cullen name as an alias is unknown but suggests an intense interest in oil royalty as well as a healthy amount of historical research.

"I was not allowed to tell my mother or anyone else what Shah's real name was," Langford stated in his 2008 affidavit. "To this day, my mother still refers to Shah as 'Robert.'"

Langford's testimony also raises questions about the nature of Shah's relationship with David Collie. Langford knew that Dinny shared his apartment on Portland Street with a roommate. Langford recalled that there were two bedrooms in the apartment: Dinny's room was the smaller of the two, and it had a twin bed. David Collie had the larger bedroom, furnished with a queen bed. But during the six months the two dated, Langford never met Collie.

Dinny told his new boyfriend that he was never to show up at the Portland Street apartment unannounced, and Langford wasn't allowed at the apartment when Collie was around.

And Dinny went to great (and sometimes bizarre) lengths to keep his relationship with Langford hidden from Collie. In his affidavit, Langford said he was visiting Dinny at the apartment one day when "someone" came home unexpectedly:

"I assume but do not know for a fact that it was David Collie. When this person showed up, Shah made me hide in the bathroom," Langford said, adding that Dinny made him stay in the bathroom until the person left the apartment.

Soon after that, the lies started.

Dinny attributed this extreme secrecy about his personal life to his history as a former CIA and Secret Service agent. Langford, still just a teenager and obviously impressionable, believed it. But as time went on and Dinny's tales became more and more outrageous, Langford realized that perhaps his boyfriend wasn't the person he seemed to be.

Interestingly, Langford mentions Michael Holstein in a 2008 affidavit, though not by name. He recalls that Dinny was concerned about an ex-boyfriend who had suddenly moved to Dallas; he'd even taken out an ad in one of the gay newspapers, TWT, to try to find his former lover and make sure he was OK.

Langford didn't think much about it at the time, and he couldn't know that Michael Holstein's story was soon to be his own.

Clint Langford was still living with his parents at the time he and Dinny dated, waiting to graduate high school in the spring of 1997. Dinny, however, had other plans. According to Langford,

Dinny tried to drive a wedge between Langford and his parents, concocting lies in the hopes of having Langford all to himself.

"He told me that my mother had called him and harassed him because he was much older than me," Langford recalled. "He told me that my mom had said hateful things to him."

When the lies didn't work, Dinny offered to rent an apartment for Langford on Portland Street. He also offered to let Langford drive a pink 1963 Lincoln Continental—a "gift," Dinny explained, "from some old lady." That lady, of course, was Glennis Goodrich.

Fortunately, Langford was too smart to fall for Dinny's bribes; he got scared and promptly broke off the relationship.

But, according to Langford, after the breakup, things just got worse.

Desperate to salvage the relationship, Dinny began showering Langford with gifts and expensive designer clothes. When Langford rejected the gifts, Dinny became enraged.

Then, Langford testified, came the threats:

Langford: "Ever since we broke up, he's been constantly on my mind. He always told me he was a powerful man, worked for the CIA. . . . He always told me to watch my back, that at any time he could be around."

Attorney: "Would you tell us, sir, at the end of your relationship with the defendant, what conduct or behavior he demonstrated initially with respect to you?"

Langford: "He told me that I was making the biggest mistake of my life and that I would never be able to find a job in the city of Houston, again that he's an influential man and that I should always watch my back."

What Langford didn't know was just how serious Dinny was.

At the time, Langford worked part-time for Federal Express, manning a one-person, drive-through kiosk in a parking lot in the Upper Kirby district of Houston—a short drive from Dinny's Portland Street apartment. A few days after their breakup, Langford got a call at work: It was Dinny.

Dinny said that he could see Langford right now, that he was watching him. These harassing phone calls continued—seven or eight of them over a short period of time. Langford grew scared and paranoid. Dinny could be anywhere at any time.

And, it seemed, he was. One evening, Langford was out club-hopping with friends when he spotted Dinny in his car, following him. Panicked, Langford hit the gas, winding his way through the streets of Houston at full speed, Dinny's headlights reflecting in his rearview mirror. Langford eventually got away, but the traumatic evening was constantly in the back of his mind. And as he'd learned from experience, Dinny could have quite a temper. While they were dating, Langford noticed that Dinny was "volatile. . . . He could change the tone of his voice, his mannerisms, and his facial expressions in an instant." Even the smallest thing—like a guest showing up unannounced—could set Dinny off, Langford recalled, adding that when Dinny got angry, he'd scream and throw things.

Fearing what Dinny might do to him, Langford established a safety routine: He would call his parents before he went to work, while he was at work, and shortly before leaving work to go home, just so they knew where he was. Langford continued this routine for almost a year after he broke up with Dinny, until the phone calls suddenly tapered off.

As his testimony finished, Langford left the witness stand, studiously avoiding looking at Shah. Langford walked out of the courtroom, tightly holding the hand of the pretty girl. He had just closed a dark chapter in his young life, and he was lucky to get out unscathed.

But Dinny would not long be distressed by the breakup with Langford. After all, by 1997, Dinny was deeply involved with a new pet project: Joan Johnson.

Life on the Home Front: 1996

By late summer of 1996, Joan Johnson's romance with David Collie was in full bloom—and so was her friendship with Dinny Shah. As David began spending more and more time at the Johnson home, Dinny, too, became a regular visitor, slipping easily into the role of confidante to Joan and ersatz father figure to Seth and Kaleta. After all, Dinny and David seemed to work as a team; you'd rarely find one without the other. The two men quickly became fixtures in the Johnson household, and family photographs from this time period often include David and Dinny. In one set of pictures—taken at Wirt Johnson's sixteenth birthday party in August—David and Dinny appear in almost every shot.

On the surface, these photos show what appears to be a happy, well-adjusted family, gathered around a birthday cake and a table piled high with gifts. Seth and Kaleta seem happy and healthy; Joan and David and Dinny look cheerful. Even Wirt appears to be having a good time; the photos show no evidence of the teen's troubled adolescence. To an outside observer, there is nothing especially alarming or unusual about any of the photographs.

But something sinister lies just beneath the festive decorations and the brightly wrapped presents: Perhaps it's in the smile that doesn't quite reach Kaleta's eyes or Seth's stiff, unnatural posture as Dinny drapes an affectionate arm around him and mugs for the camera. Kaleta would testify later that Dinny's hands were busy indeed, running up and down her backside while Dinny smiled smugly at the camera, totally in control. In hindsight, of course, it's easy to read into these pictures; to search for hints that Joan and her children knew what was in store for them in the years to come. But by all accounts, in August 1996, things were beginning to turn around for the Johnson family and their new friends. Joan would later testify that she was already in love with David Collie by that summer and, as far as she knew, he was in love with her. They were in the "honeymoon" phase of their relationship, and there was even some talk—though nothing serious—about marriage. Dinny had taken an interest in the children's well-being, and he had even offered to help Joan sort out her messy financial situation.

To Joan, Dinny and David's presence must have been a huge relief. Luke had been dead almost a year, and there is evidence that suggests Joan had a rough time adjusting to her new role as a single mother. She was vulnerable. She was overwhelmed by her family's money squabbles and struggling to stay on top of Seth's and Kaleta's school performance. Though she had friends in the neighborhood, Joan lacked a solid support network.

No matter whose version of events you choose to believe, it was obvious that Joan was drowning in the day-to-day responsibilities of raising her children and running her household. Joan was desperate—throwing herself headlong into her relationship with David Collie and leaning heavily on both David and Dinny for emotional support.

It was clear that Joan Johnson needed help, and Dinny Shah was quick to volunteer for the job.

After all, Dinny wasn't one to pass up an opportunity when he saw one.

While nobody can deny that the Johnson family was struggling, the exact reasons for their difficulties differ depending on who's telling the story: According to Dinny, in the summer of 1996, the Johnson household was in a state of total disaster, mostly brought about by Joan's negligence. Joan, Dinny said, was either incapable of taking care of herself, her children, and her house, or she just didn't care anymore. Perhaps the loss of her husband had left her too paralyzed with grief to properly run a household.

At the top of Dinny's list to help Joan: hire a cook.

Shah: "The kids were not eating and there was no cooking going on. And the only time that they were eating was if they were eating out of the refrigerator or if I took them out to eat at a restaurant."

Attorney: "Did Mrs. Johnson cook for her children?"

Shah: "I think sometimes she would make a grilled cheese sandwich or something like that. Peanut butter or a grilled cheese sandwich. If you are asking me if she was an accomplished cook, I wouldn't say that she was even interested in doing something like that."

Dinny's further testimony painted an increasingly bleak picture. The plumbing, according to his 2008 testimony, was in such disrepair that there were no working bathrooms in the house in 1996. The children, he said, were bathing in the backyard pool, and Joan was showering every morning at the Briar Club, the private club on Timmons Lane where she went swimming. The house itself was overwhelmed with excess furniture to the point that the family could barely navigate through the rooms. Joan, he claimed, was battling alcoholism, and the children suffered from neglect and physical abuse. According to Dinny, there wasn't even any food in the house for the children to eat—all of this happening in the wealthiest neighborhood in Houston.

The Johnson family, of course, would deny these assertions in the 2008 civil trial. Kaleta would claim that Dinny's testimony was absolutely ridiculous, and that she "had bathed in a lake once or twice on a hiking trip, but never in my own backyard."

Joan would later testify that the house was simply a little disorganized in the aftermath of Luke's death. Things had piled up but certainly not to the extent that Dinny claimed. She recalled that David Collie volunteered to help clean and organize the house that had been neglected for so long. And according to his testimony, Dinny came along to help because, he said, he pitied Joan. That summer, David, Dinny, and Joan spent weeks sorting through Joan's home office, organizing the years of financial documents that had been haphazardly thrown around. They cleaned out the attic and garage, hanging family photographs that had been uncovered, clearing the clutter, and cleaning the house from top to bottom. Dinny saw firsthand the many Blaffer treasures that had been squirreled away in the Johnson residence, collecting dust: priceless antique furniture, clothes, and art.

Later, when Joan would accuse Dinny of stealing several priceless antiques, Dinny would claim that the items had been gifts. According to Dinny's 2008 testimony, Joan gave him various luxury items—Tiffany silver from the 1930s, an antique wingback chair dating back to the eighteenth century, Faberge picture frames, early American art, and even family portraits. It was, he said, her way of thanking him for his help around the house and financial services. Joan would claim that these items, among many others, were forcibly taken from her or that she unwillingly gave these items to Dinny under duress, echoing the story of Glennis Goodrich.

Around the same time, Dinny began a project of greater proportions: Joan's finances.

Dinny would testify in the 2008 civil trial that sometime that summer, Joan began to visit him at his office-apartment on Portland Street, chatting about her life, her finances, and her children. Sometimes she'd pump Dinny for information about David Collie. Other times, Joan would bring documents for Dinny to look at— sensitive financial documents—that he would help her sort through.

Joan trusted Dinny. After all, David had vouched for his friend early on, claiming that Dinny was something of a financial whiz. Dinny often represented himself as an expert in the world of high finance; sometimes he even claimed to have worked for Goldman Sachs and Chase Bank as a Wall Street investment banker.

In reality, Dinny had never held any sort of job, financial or otherwise. His expertise was limited to a small amount of online investing. But Joan couldn't have known that. In the summer of 1996, Joan was probably too relieved to be suspicious. Dinny, unlike Joan, seemed unfazed by the Blaffer family's complicated web of trusts and holdings, and it's likely that she was just glad that someone was handling things.

Though Joan admitted that she needed help taking care of the children and picking up the house, things were not as bad in the Johnson home as Dinny described:

Attorney: "Mrs. Johnson, you have three children, correct?"

Joan: "That is right."

Attorney: "At times it is difficult raising your kids, correct?"

Joan: "It is a challenge."

Attorney: "And sometimes, I take it, you lose your cool being a parent?"

Opposing counsel: "Objection, relevance."

Attorney: "I'll rephrase. By the way, your husband died in 1995, correct?"

Joan: "That is right."

Attorney: "And you asked Mr. Shah to help you in your business affairs?"

Joan: "Yes."

Attorney: "And sometimes you lose your cool as a mom, right?"

Joan: "Yes."

Attorney: "And you've also had problems with substance abuse, correct?"

Joan: "Never. No, that is very incorrect."

But Dinny's help wouldn't end with Joan's bank statements. As Joan became closer to Dinny and David, the two men—especially Dinny—started to take an interest in Seth and Kaleta. Dinny and David were spending an increasing amount of time with Joan and often had dinner at her house; at some point, Dinny began helping the children with their homework after dinner. It seemed, according to Dinny's testimony, that the house wasn't the only thing that Joan had neglected: Seth, Kaleta, and even Wirt were starving for attention.

Some of Dinny's more outrageous claims about the Johnson children were easily discredited. During his 2008 civil trial, Dinny testified that Seth, who was nine years old in 1996, had never had a haircut in his life and didn't know how to eat with a fork. Dinny would later change his story when early photographs presented at the trial clearly showed Seth sporting a freshly cropped head of hair. While Seth's hair was perhaps a little unruly—in the fashion of many young boys—he had indeed gotten his hair cut often in his life. Seth would counter this claim in court by relating the details of trips with his father and older brother to Estevan's, a local barbershop in nearby Greenway Plaza that was a favorite among River Oaks families.

Dinny also claimed that the children were not involved in sports of any kind when he arrived on the scene, and he credited himself with getting the children interested in athletics. It was because of his encouragement, Dinny told the court, that Kaleta joined her school track team. And, he continued, Seth had absolutely no interest in sports until Dinny signed him up for baseball. Dinny said he often drove Seth to practice, and initially he nearly had to force Seth out of the car.

In truth, Seth had been involved in Little League baseball for years before Dinny arrived on the scene, and Joan had pictures to prove it. Photographs from 1994 show a smiling Seth dressed in his Post Oak Little League uniform, clutching a baseball bat.

In the picture, Seth's hair is neatly groomed.

What is probably true is that after Luke Johnson's death, the kids were in need of mental stimulation. In one of his more believable statements, Dinny said that he often noticed Seth and Kaleta "just sitting around," playing video games or on their computers. It's very likely that Dinny really did encourage the Johnson children to go play outside occasionally; it's even plausible that, in her grief, Joan had become less proactive about taking her kids to various practices and games. But Dinny's testimony that Seth and Kaleta were completely inactive prior to his arrival was an exaggeration, at best.

Dinny's claims about the kids' school performance, however, are not so easily dismissed. It seems that, early on, Dinny took a particular interest in Seth's education. Kaleta had always earned promising grades, bringing home report cards filled with straight A's and B's, but Seth was the complete opposite, Dinny said. While his little sister seemed to breeze effortlessly through school, Seth struggled with even the most basic tasks, like reading and writing. He barely squeaked by with C's and D's.

Seth's poor grades may have been related to his spotty, nomadic enrollment history: School records show that he bounced around from school to school every couple of years. He attended a preschool called Pooh Corner for three years, and then he enrolled at The Fay School for kindergarten through second grade. By the third grade, he had transferred again, to The Parish School. He would start his fourth-grade year at Memorial Hall School—his fourth school in six years. Although it is unclear exactly why Joan repeatedly transferred Seth, evidence suggests that she was much more concerned with Kaleta's schooling—doting on her, even— and that when Seth suffered in school, she would pull him out and place him in another school that could deal with his learning problems.

Joan was also known to have run-ins with school administration, such as at The Kinkaid School. Joan's grandfather was one of the school's founding trustees, so Kaleta was naturally accepted to the school's pre-K program in the fall of 1993. Joan, however, had a problem with the school's carpool: It seems that some of the other Kinkaid parents were unwilling to allow Kaleta in their carpools, and Kaleta was having trouble making friends. In a fit of anger, Joan pulled Kaleta out of Kinkaid. Glenn Ballard, Kinkaid's respected headmaster, wrote a letter of rebuke to Joan: "I am disappointed that you presented me with a fait accompli, Joan. Also, I'm disappointed by your expressed reasons for withdrawing Kaleta, namely, the unwillingness of parents to include Kaleta in a carpool and classmates who are sometimes unfriendly. All of this sounds rather childish."

Joan then enrolled Kaleta at the prestigious St. John's School, which she attended until graduating high school. Despite her troubled home life, Kaleta managed to excel at St. John's, maintaining high grades.

––––––––––––

Dinny was concerned about Seth's grades. He made an appointment for Seth to see Dr. Rae Battin, an educational psychologist, to help identify the source of Seth's troubles in school. According to Dinny, at the age of ten, Seth could barely read or write. Dinny's involvement in Seth's education continued for the next six years, until 2002. Dr. Battin would be one of the first professionals that Dinny would hire to evaluate and help Seth, along with a litany of tutors to supplement Seth's homework and the personal attention that he was allegedly (according to Dinny) lacking from Joan. And, it was Dinny—not Joan—who discovered that Seth was particularly lagging behind on his homework; he'd been lying to both Joan and Dinny, telling them that he didn't have any. But there's only so long that a little boy can lie about his homework. A quick phone call from Dinny to Seth's teacher revealed a stack of homework that had never been completed. Moreover, Seth had been written up for cheating on tests. Dinny took such an interest in Seth because, he said, Joan would not: All of Joan's attention, he claimed, was focused on Kaleta, which, he theorized, may have contributed to Seth's educational and behavioral problems:

Attorney: "In the dynamic between Ms. Johnson, Seth, and Kaleta, which child seemed to be getting more attention to you when you first arrived, Seth or Kaleta, from Mrs. Johnson?"

Shah: "Well, out of respect for Mrs. Johnson, but I have to say that she was totally ignoring Seth and she was all over Kaleta, all over her, talking all the time and just really involved with Kaleta. It was as though Kaleta was the great one, you know, and just totally ignored her other children. To her, Seth was a nuisance. He was just a nuisance. And she was like, you know, get him out of my way so I can concentrate on Kaleta, who is really the great one."

Despite, as Dinny claimed, having her mother's undivided attention, Kaleta also had her own unique set of problems. While she managed to keep her grades fairly steady, her frustration at home manifested itself in behavioral issues at school. Though she managed to excel academically, Kaleta didn't get along with many of the kids at school, and when David and Dinny first arrived on the scene, Kaleta had been cited and disciplined at school for hitting some of the other kids in her class.

Strangely, it was Dinny and, occasionally, David Collie—not Joan—who would take the kids to school and keep track of their homework. Joan, Dinny would testify, was better at adding to the problems and the drama that the family faced rather than fixing them. He looked on her as the "fourth child" in the family. It was during this time that Dinny and David made up nicknames for the family—tongue-in-cheek, derogatory pet names. They called Joan "Delta," which Dinny explained meant "chaos," for her erratic behavior. Seth and Kaleta became "Cajun Boy" and "Cajun Girl" because they were wild and, in Dinny's words, "stupid." Dinny and

David would also sarcastically refer to Kaleta as "Darling," because, they explained, that's how they wanted her to act, like a darling, well-behaved child.

If anything, Kaleta's angry, violent tendencies were exacerbated at home. According to Dinny, Joan and Kaleta often fought more like siblings than like mother and daughter. Dinny and David witnessed many spats between the two—screaming matches that usually ended in physical violence; he claimed to have seen Joan hit and kick the children "more than fifty times" over the years. In his 2008 testimony, Dinny described Kaleta as "very mean spirited at the time," which is, perhaps, an accurate description. After all, the eight-year-old girl had no father and a less than ideal relationship with her mother. Seth and Kaleta, naturally, would fight often, but not in the normal way that brothers and sisters do, said Dinny. These fights were "really physical," atypically violent fights that sometimes ended in bloodshed.

Years later, during the civil suit, Kaleta told the court about those fights with her brother, admitting that they did, on occasion, get out of hand. In her 2008 testimony, Kaleta recalled a particularly nasty fight with Seth that ended in a trip to the emergency room. The two were riding in the backseat of the car and, Kaleta recalled, Seth was teasing her. Unable to control her anger, Kaleta threw her small flashlight keychain at her brother, hitting him directly above the eye. Seth's forehead split open, gushing blood. Joan immediately turned the car around and took him to the emergency room, where Seth received eleven stitches. Dinny, who was in the car with them during that fight, tells a similar story, with one notable exception: According to his testimony, Seth did end up in the ER that night. But in Dinny's version, the damage was done by something larger than a keychain. It was a baseball bat, swung by Kaleta.

Regardless, it would take years before Kaleta's violent tantrums calmed down. If Joan noticed Kaleta's behavioral problems, she didn't do anything to stop them. Dinny and David often excluded her from family outings as a punishment for her outbursts, but this strategy did little to control Kaleta's rage. Kaleta's temper tantrums continued to escalate considerably until her early teens, until Dinny had effectively terrorized the little girl into submission.

In addition to supervising Seth's and Kaleta's education, Dinny claimed that he also tried to impress values on the children, to motivate them, and to introduce a little fun into their lives. On one occasion, Dinny taught the ten-year-old Seth how to drive. During the civil trial, Dinny recalled how happy and excited the little boy was, sitting in Dinny's lap and slowly guiding the car up and down the driveway.

It appears that Dinny took a particular interest in Seth, perhaps to make up for what he felt was Joan's perceived lack of interest in the boy. When Seth expressed an interest in history, Dinny bought Seth several history books in an effort to encourage his interests. He also took Seth on outings to the Lone Star Flight Museum in Galveston, and the Eisenhower, Truman, and Franklin D. Roosevelt presidential libraries. And, of course, David Collie was always just a step behind, ready to take the children to the movies or treat them to dinner at a restaurant. Dinny and David also lavished Seth and Kaleta with gifts ranging from the latest Harry Potter book to a brand-new computer. Whether the attention was genuine or merely a carefully constructed façade designed to ingratiate them with the Johnson family, it worked; Joan, Seth, and Kaleta were swept away by Dinny and David's generosity. For better or worse, the two men had ingratiated themselves to the Johnson family.

Even early on, however, Dinny and David sometimes found the Johnson children hard to handle, According to Dinny, Seth and Kaleta were spoiled; they made sure to let everyone know when they didn't get what they wanted.

Shah: "Well, when I first came to the house in '96, when I first met them [the kids], they were crying a lot."

Attorney: "What about?"

Shah: "They would cry a lot."

Attorney: "Over what?"

Shah: "They would cry at the drop of a hat. And if Kaleta didn't get her way with her mother, she would throw a tantrum. And this continued on for many years, both Seth and Kaleta, for many years."

Kaleta, Dinny recalled, once threw a fit in a local bookstore, Bookstop, after he told her that he wouldn't buy her all the books she wanted. She needed to pick one or two, he said. Kaleta had cried and kicked her feet, screaming, "Don't you love me? Don't you love me?" She was immediately ushered out of the bookstore.

According to Dinny, Kaleta's tantrum was proof that she was a spoiled brat, used to getting everything she wanted. And there may be some truth in that; after all, Kaleta had grown up surrounded by fabulous wealth. But as every parent—rich or poor—knows, all children throw fits from time to time when they don't get what they want, whether it's a new video game, a pair of shoes, or a stack of books.

But Dinny, who had limited experience with children, was horrified by Kaleta's behavior. He was, after all, only twenty-nine years old at the time, and not a father himself. Later, Kaleta would explain her behavior, saying that she resented Dinny since he often excluded her because of her behavioral problems. She wasn't allowed to go with Dinny when he took Seth to restaurants or baseball games—though she eventually learned, she says, that if she acted nicer, Dinny and David would allow her to join the rest of the family.

If you asked David and Dinny, they would claim to be the heroes of this story: They were two men who, with no real obligations to the Johnson family, helped to pull them out of the darkness that was quietly smothering them. They played husband and father to the Johnsons, all out of the goodness of their hearts. Indeed, Dinny and David did probably have a positive influence on the family, especially when it came to Seth's and Kaleta's schoolwork. As

Dinny and David became more involved with the Johnson family, there would later be violent consequences.

But in the summer of 1996, Joan, Kaleta, and Seth enjoyed the attention they received from both David and Dinny, especially since Luke Johnson's untimely death. Seth and Kaleta seemed to flourish under the men's guidance, and Joan was probably grateful for their help raising her children and overseeing her finances. She couldn't know that allowing David and Dinny such control would be something she would come to regret.

In fact, it seems that only one member of the Johnson family proved to be immune to David and Dinny's gestures of friendship: Wirt.

A full six years older than Seth and eight years older than Kaleta, it was probably to Wirt's disadvantage that he was so much older than his siblings. While Seth and Kaleta lived under the umbrella of their youth and innocence, Wirt was witness to and fully aware of the problems surrounding his parents' separation and subsequent divorce. In 1995, the year of Luke's mysterious death, Wirt Johnson was nearly fifteen years old and attending a prestigious boarding school out of state. Unlike Seth and Kaleta, there was nothing to protect Wirt from his painful memories.

Adolescence is hard enough for the average person, but Wirt's particular circumstances certainly added to the upheaval of his early teenage years. In 1996, Wirt left school and moved back into the Johnson home in River Oaks. He told his mother that he wanted to attend nearby Lamar High School.

That's when Wirt's problems became apparent, particularly to his family.

By the time Wirt celebrated his sixteenth birthday in August 1996, his behavior was spiraling out of control, causing added pain to the Johnsons' already confused family structure. At first, Dinny and David tried to win over the teenager with attention and gifts, much like they'd done with his younger brother and sister, but Wirt didn't take the bait. He was hostile and aggressive, often challenging

Dinny and David. It was clear that Wirt resented the two new men in his family's life, and he would often take out that resentment on his mother and younger siblings.

To Dinny and David, there was only one thing to do: They needed to convince Joan to get rid of Wirt.

A Lock Down School for Wirt

In May 1995, the year of Luke Johnson's death, fourteen-year-old Wirt was away from home, attending seventh grade at the Eaglebrook School in Deerfield, Massachusetts, an all-boys intermediate boarding school reserved for the sons of well-heeled families. The boys that attend Eaglebrook are groomed in academics and sports and propelled to some of the best private high schools—and by extension, universities—in the nation. All of this takes place on the rugged natural school grounds in eastern Massachusetts, over 1,800 miles from the Johnson family's Houston home.

There's nothing inherently unusual about a boy attending boarding school—especially a boy of Wirt's privileged, wealthy background. But Wirt wasn't at Eaglebrook because he needed to be challenged academically or because he was expected to attend a top-tier high school. He wasn't there to build leadership skills or to excel at sports. He was there, it seems, because Joan and Luke Johnson simply couldn't handle him any more: They wanted him out of the house.

Before he was shipped off to Massachusetts, Wirt had been enrolled at Kinkaid, the same prestigious private school where the

Blaffers had been longtime patrons and which was founded in part by R. L. Blaffer, the family patriarch. Students at Kinkaid come from Houston's wealthiest families and live in some of the city's most exclusive areas—like Memorial, West University Place, and, of course, River Oaks. Wirt didn't do very well at Kinkaid; his behavioral problems disrupted class constantly. These problems followed him home from school, manifesting in constant fights with Seth, who was much younger and smaller than Wirt. It was Luke who first suggested that Wirt attend Eaglebrook, feeling that Wirt needed a more structured environment than he was getting at home.

Little is known about Wirt's stay at Eaglebrook, but it can be assumed that, if Eaglebrook didn't necessarily agree with Wirt, it was at least more agreeable for the rest of the Johnson clan to have him out of the house. When Wirt graduated from Eaglebrook in June 1996, he had no interest in attending any of the prestigious, out-of-state high schools where many of his classmates would eventually matriculate. And he can't be blamed much for that, anyway. He was, after all, only a teenager, faced with the monumental burden of having to cope with his parents' divorce and his father's subsequent death.

So in 1996—right about the time that Dinny and David joined the family—Wirt came back to live at the Johnson house in Houston after attending Eaglebrook for two years. The plan was for him to reenroll in Kinkaid. It would have been a good plan, for an average family. But between Wirt's emotional and behavioral troubles, Joan's difficulty managing her own life—let alone her family—and the uncharted dynamic that Dinny and David would exert over the Johnsons, the results would be disastrous.

———

Although Joan's grandfather, Robert Lee Blaffer, was one of the founders of Kinkaid, by 1996 Joan and Wirt had built up quite a different reputation. Kinkaid turned down Wirt's application to reenroll; in a letter to Joan, the school's administration says, diplomatically, that Wirt would be "better served by continuing his education away from Houston." The boarding school experience, they felt, was the right direction for Wirt.

Despite this setback, Wirt insisted on coming back to Houston. With no real fallback, and with the new school year fast approaching, Joan enrolled him as a freshman in the nearby public school, Lamar High School, located at the corner of Westheimer Boulevard and River Oaks Boulevard. Over the years, many wealthy children from River Oaks attended this impressive and prestigious school so that at one time River Oaks Boulevard became known as "the only street in America with a country club at each end, River Oaks Country Club on one end and Lamar High School on the other." Joan had to bargain with Wirt in order to get him back in school. Wirt believed that, if he waited long enough, perhaps until the next year, Kinkaid would eventually let him back in. Joan begged him to enroll at Lamar in the meantime, just until Kinkaid had enough time to reconsider. Wirt finally agreed to attend public school but reluctantly and with a few strings attached. He had plans of his own.

First, Wirt asked Joan to buy him a car—and not just any car. According to Dinny, the sixteen-year-old asked for a Maserati. Joan refused Wirt's request, but she eventually consented to a less expensive ride. To make the half-mile trek from the family's River Oaks home to Lamar High School, located outside the entrance of the neighborhood on Westheimer, Joan bought her son a brand-new Chrysler Jeep Cherokee. The price tag on the new Jeep—Wirt's first car—was a hefty $42,000.

Wirt's second demand was probably a welcome relief to the entire Johnson family, especially Seth, who often bore the brunt of Wirt's violent rampages: Instead of living in his childhood bedroom, Wirt wanted to move into the empty apartment over the garage. In the few weeks he'd been home, Wirt had already had a few run-ins with his younger brother, and the fights were growing increasingly brutal. Later, in his 2008 testimony, Dinny claims to have witnessed an instance when Wirt stormed into Seth's bedroom, ranting that Seth had been playing in Wirt's room, messing up his clothes and papers. Wirt picked Seth up and threw him against a wall, Dinny recalled, pushing Seth down every time he tried to get up off the floor, all the while "beating the hell out of him." It was Dinny who finally intervened, pulling the six-foot teenager off of his ten-year-old brother.

Soon after this incident, Joan gave her older son permission to live in the garage apartment. To Joan, the arrangement was just one more way to avoid dealing with Wirt's behavioral problems. After all, if Wirt wasn't in the house, he wouldn't have the opportunity to pick fights with Seth. But as Joan would soon find out, giving the troubled sixteen-year-old his own apartment came with an entirely new set of problems.

And Wirt's demands kept coming. Like his $42,000 car, Wirt's move wouldn't come cheaply to Joan. The garage apartment, Wirt said, needed a few updates in order to make it livable. Joan agreed to let Wirt take care of the remodeling, thinking that the project would be a nice diversion and a nonviolent outlet for some of his energy.

A few weeks later, Wirt showed his mother the proposed remodeling budget. For a person who had never worked a day in his life, a person who had just recently acquired a driver's license—a teenager—Wirt Johnson had already developed a taste for the finer things in life.

Preliminary estimates for Wirt's upgrades ran between $40,000 and $50,000. According to the sixteen-year-old, making the apartment "livable" included essentials like marble and wood floors and limited-edition designer fixtures in the bathroom. Dinny would report that Wirt wanted a $35,000 sound system, too. Joan was flabbergasted. Once again, she turned to Dinny for advice.

Dinny later recalled that his advice to Joan was to simply be straight with Wirt. "Just because you have money doesn't mean your kids can get whatever they want," he told Joan. "Just tell them no. Just tell him that if he wants to fix the garage up, he has got to have a budget." Joan followed his advice, offering her son a firm decorating allowance of $15,000.

It would be an understatement to say that Wirt didn't like the initial budget that Joan gave him. After pleading unsuccessfully with his mother to raise his budget, Wirt took a different approach. In 2008, Dinny testified about Wirt's reaction to his mother's budgetary cuts: He "kicked the hell" out of Joan's Ford with a pair of outdoor work boots. Wirt had never liked that car anyway, Dinny said; Wirt thought that since his mother was wealthy she should drive a more expensive car, a Jaguar or Mercedes.

After assessing the damage to the car's windshield and bumper, the hood and the body, Joan—or perhaps more accurately, Joan and Dinny—decided to cut their losses with the Taurus and buy a new car. According to Dinny's testimony in 2008, Joan actually did want to buy a Mercedes, but Dinny talked her out of the purchase. Always the voice of reason, Dinny suggested that a Ford Crown Victoria would be a simple, inexpensive replacement for the Taurus.

"I said, 'We don't need a Mercedes. We can just get a basic car. That's all we need,'" Dinny told the court.

Listening to his testimony, it's interesting to note Dinny's use of the pronoun "we," which just goes to show that as early as 1997 and as late as 2008, Dinny still considered Joan, her family, her finances, even her car, partly his.

Dinny would eventually step in to play mediator between Wirt and Joan during the garage renovation affair, since Wirt would also include Dinny in his appeals for a larger budget. When all was said and done, the three managed to reach a compromise. Wirt's remodeling budget for the one-bedroom garage apartment was inflated to $35,000. But even though a car and a newly renovated garage apartment were a part of Wirt's agreement with Joan to attend Lamar High School, Wirt never held up his end of the deal. He was habitually tardy for his morning classes, and as he fell behind in his subjects, he eventually stopped attending altogether. At home alone all day, Wirt's attention turned to other things: television and booze, drugs and parties, and, of course, terrorizing his family. Hordes of teenagers would gather at Wirt's apartment, even on school nights. The parties and the complaints from neighbors prompted Joan to hire a patrol officer to keep an eye on Wirt's apartment and report any unusual activity. Inside, according to Dinny, beer cans and drug paraphernalia littered the polished wood floors of Wirt's newly renovated garage apartment, even after the parties stopped. Joan had no idea how to motivate her son to get out of bed and do something, anything. Dinny would try having a few heart-to-hearts with Wirt, attempting to convince the teenager to clean up his act and go to school but to no avail.

Despite his mother's pleading, Wirt made no effort to attend school, and he showed no interest in getting a job. Wirt was simply killing time at the Johnson home, biding his time until Kinkaid allowed him to reenroll. He continued to drink heavily toward the end of 1996 and on into the next year, and he continued to fight with his mother and younger siblings.

The breaking point came in late 1996. One night, Dinny and Joan arrived home from dinner with Seth and Kaleta. As they walked through the door, they noticed a recent addition: A picture of Joan hung on the wall near the garage door, but it wasn't in a frame. It was held up by a screwdriver, driven precisely through Joan's photogenic forehead and into the wall. Wirt, upset that he had been denied permission to go to a party, stabbed the picture with a screwdriver and left it there as a warning to the family.

Wirt's outbursts continued to escalate: Joan complained to Dinny that Wirt was constantly criticizing her appearance and how she spent her money. In Wirt's opinion, Joan should have been flashier with her money, showing off the family's wealth. Wirt was also spending less time in his garage apartment and spending more and more time in the Johnson home, where he inevitably got into fights with Seth and Kaleta. Dinny recalled that, on one occasion,

Wirt picked up Seth and threw him down, hard, onto the concrete that surrounded the family's pool. X-rays showed that the fall had bruised Seth's spine.

Relief would finally come one weekend when one of Joan's childhood friends, Mary Griffith Wallace of San Antonio, told Joan about a boarding school with a reputation for turning around troubled teens: Rocky Mountain Academy.

The seed was planted in Joan's head, and Dinny and David would cultivate that seed, tending to it carefully, until Joan was fully convinced to pack Wirt off to Rocky Mountain Academy.

Rocky Mountain Academy was owned by CEDU Educational Services, a company that operated several behavior modification boarding schools that specialized in rehabilitating and educating at-risk students, including those with emotional, behavioral, or drug- and alcohol-related problems. Some of the more famous Rocky Mountain Academy graduates include Paris Hilton and children of Barbara Walters and Roseanne Barr. Former students often refer to it as a "lock down school." No further explanation is necessary. Rocky Mountain Academy and other CEDU schools were eventually sold to another company, Brown Schools, in the 1990s, but the spot where Rocky Mountain Academy was once located—somewhere in northern Idaho—is vacant now, closed after Brown Schools declared bankruptcy in 2005.

As part of Rocky Mountain Academy's enrollment process, parents were asked to fill out an application and write a letter detailing the reasons the school was a good fit for their child. This process not only gave the school a better understanding of each student's background, but it also told administrators exactly what sorts of problems they were up against.

Joan's letter to Rocky Mountain Academy isn't short: It goes on for five pages, giving a rambling account of Wirt's violent outbursts and the family's fragile emotional state since his return. Dated July 30, 1997, the letter is a laundry list of Wirt's emotional and behavioral problems. Joan starts the letter by writing, "Wirt appears to thrive on the torment he is able to inflict on us. He has little or no consideration or respect for others and their feelings. As a total ingrate, he has no appreciation whatsoever for the exceptional and numerous advantages I am able to provide on his behalf." She also includes several grievances, like the "jealous" and abusive behavior Wirt exhibited toward Seth and Kaleta. On several occasions, Wirt would throw away Kaleta's homework or the ribbons and trophies Seth was awarded on his basketball team. And although Joan had given Wirt a credit card for gas and other expenses that might come up, he had somehow managed to get his own card in his own name, racking up a bill that Joan had to pay.

Joan goes on to describe Wirt's school attendance as "dismal." As the spring semester of 1997 rolled around, Joan pulled Wirt from Lamar High School after he failed to show up for his fall semester final exams and enrolled him in an alternative school, Alexander-Smith Academy. Wirt stopped attending after a few days. A second school was selected, this time the Houston Learning Academy, which he also refused to attend.

Joan concludes her letter with this sad fact: "I do not care to have Wirt live here in my home with me and my two younger children until he matures sufficiently to appreciate his family and the extraordinary opportunities afforded him." But the accompanying handwritten application that Joan submitted to Rocky Mountain Academy has a less polished, less diplomatic tone.

In that document, Joan calls Wirt a "spoiled brat" that rebels against her authority instead of accepting changes in his life. "He is on strike," she writes. "He does not attend school. He blames me." In one section of the application, Joan is asked to describe Wirt's goals and motivations.

Joan's reply is chilling: "Wirt's goals are to destroy me and his younger siblings and take control and waste our lives."

Later, in a space on the application marked "Additional Comments," Joan writes, "Wirt will kill me in the future if something is not done." This statement may seem inflated and overdramatic; it's easy to assume that Joan was simply overreacting to her son's out-of-control behavior. However, in the margin of the application is a small note, set off in parentheses, that may show the true reason why Joan believed that Wirt was capable of matricide: "(Wirt told Dinny that he would kill me.)"

Did Wirt ever threaten Joan's life—or was that just a clever concoction of Dinny's to finally rid the Johnson home of its nuisance of a son?

Much attention was paid at the 2008 trial over this issue: Who decided that Wirt should be sent to Rocky Mountain Academy? Joan or Dinny? Joan claims that Dinny pushed her to make that decision; after all, Wirt was an obstruction in Dinny's plan, draining Joan's pocketbook and eating up her attention. Dinny would deny Joan's allegations, claiming that "in truth, I actually liked the boy and wanted to help him, tried to help him." He testified that it was Joan who wanted Wirt gone. Wirt, however, would forever blame Dinny for engineering his stay at Rocky Mountain Academy.

———————

Joan: "Wirt was not going to school. He had stopped attending class at Lamar. And I was really afraid that he might not, that he might become a permanent high school dropout."

Attorney: "What was the defendant, Mr. Shah, telling you about Wirt during this time?"

Joan: "He was getting me pretty worried about Wirt—more worried than maybe I would have. . . . Dinny told me if I didn't get Wirt off to a school, you know, out of town or force him to go to school that he would, well, at a certain age children don't have to go to school anymore and I was afraid that Wirt would get so far behind that he would not finish high school. . . . And so, Dinny and

David and I went to the House of Pies and met with two men one night and we arranged for the two men to come the next day in late May—the 28th of May, I believe—and take Wirt off to Rocky Mountain Academy."

Attorney: "So Wirt was gone from the house as of May 28, 1997?"

Joan: "Yes. And he told me that morning, I remember it, he said, 'Mom, you're making a big mistake right now.' And I realize that he was absolutely right."

Though Joan would refer to Wirt as her "bully son," she probably would not have sent him away without encouragement from both Dinny and David. Wirt was shipped off to Idaho in May 1997. Joan wrote a check for the full amount of his tuition—about $17,000 for the three-month semester.

When Wirt left for Rocky Mountain Academy, he was effectively exiled from the family. And it appears that Joan didn't want him back home; during the two years Wirt attended Rocky Mountain Academy, there were only a few letters of correspondence between him and Joan, mostly concerning financial matters and his progress at school. Wirt's relationship with Joan would continue to deteriorate to the point where he would eventually apply for emancipation from Joan, dropping his last name and changing it to Blaffer. Seth would testify in 2008 that after Wirt left the house in 1997, he wouldn't see his brother for five years, until December 2002.

Wirt would hop straight from Rocky Mountain Academy to college: In 1999, Wirt enrolled at a private college in Santa Barbara, California, where he planned to major in engineering. He'd later transfer to Dallas' Southern Methodist University after a couple of semesters. But that wouldn't please Dinny Shah.

At the 2008 civil trial, Dinny would be accused of following Wirt, harassing Wirt with threatening phone calls, and even hiring a private investigator to pry into Wirt's personal life, an intimidation tactic meant to keep him away from his own mother and younger siblings. By the late 1990s, Dinny was fully in control of the Johnson family, and he didn't want Wirt—now a grown man living only a five-hour drive away, instead of five states away—meddling in his affairs.

Hindsight

Meanwhile, life in the Johnson home went on, with the additional, constant companionship of David and Dinny. Joan, of course, was admittedly in love with David Collie at the time, willing to do anything she could to please him—including apparently risking her own safety and that of her children.

Not until 2008, nearly twelve years after the fact, that Joan complained openly in court that Dinny and David slowly isolated her from her friends and neighbors. Joan, ever hopeful that David Collie would propose to her, didn't notice what David and Dinny were actually doing until it was too late. The isolation started gradually, she testified, in the late summer of 1996 when Dinny and David started "tying up her time" so that she lost touch with her friends and neighbors. David and Dinny became more than close friends of the Johnson family; they became chauffeurs, disciplinarians, and tutors to her children. At first, the men's gestures seemed innocent enough; it's likely that Joan, overwhelmed with her family responsibilities, appreciated the active role David and Dinny took in her family's life. But somewhere along the way, her friends' "helpful" gestures took a darker turn: Before long, Dinny, not satisfied with Joan's definition of nutrition, was supervising mealtimes at the Johnson home. David and Dinny became advisors concerning every detail of Joan's life: what kind of car she should buy, how she should handle Wirt's discipline problems, which gym she should go to. Later on, their opinions would dictate Joan's life down to the smallest detail, like the kinds of clothes she should wear and even how she should style her hair.

By the time Dinny Shah was arrested in 2002, Joan had all but given up her rights and responsibilities as an adult and a mother. When Shah effectively seized the role as head of household in 2000, the family's every move was carefully monitored and controlled. But ironically, as is the case of predators, in these early years, David and Dinny were helping to breathe life back into the Johnson family. The two men organized weekend family excursions to the movies, shopping trips, dinners at nice restaurants—all healthy, welcome distractions for a family that had faced so much adversity in the early 1990s. But these family adventures were exactly that: shiny distractions from a darker reality. In fact, Dinny and David had altogether given up their side businesses, including their video production venture, Shah-Collie Productions, for a new full-time hobby—supervising the Johnsons' lives.

And it worked: From 1996 to 1997, the Johnsons were sweetly and gently lulled into a new pattern of life, artfully dictated by David and Dinny. Joan, none the wiser to David and Dinny's grand scheme of exerting ever greater control, seemed impressed by their seemingly generous gestures. What she didn't realize was that, by 1997, she was quickly on her way to becoming completely cut off from the few friends and neighbors she had; to being wholly isolated behind the walls of the false world Dinny and David had built for her.

———————

Later, witnesses confirmed Joan's accusations of isolation, and at least one claimed that it was inherent from the start of Joan's relationship with David and Dinny: Sharon Bryan, Joan's River Oaks neighbor who lived directly across Del Monte Drive.

At the civil trial in 2008, Sharon Bryan was a strong witness, speaking with the authority of an embedded River Oaks matron. Her testimony was blunt and believable. She was not cowed by cross-examination. She welcomed it, ready to tell the jury of her recollections. According to Bryan, when the Johnson children were very young, Joan and the kids would often stop and visit with the Bryan family. Seth and Kaleta would play with Bryan's son Charley while she and Joan drank tea and chatted. Sharon Bryan and Joan were, as far as neighbors go, very close; they'd walk their dogs together with the other neighbors in the afternoon and compare notes about what their children were doing in school.

Bryan distinctly remembered meeting David and Dinny in 1996, when Joan first started dating David. She described David as friendly and nice. Sharon and her husband, Chip, even invited Joan and her new beau to dinner one evening. But according to Bryan's sworn testimony, David's friendly disposition wouldn't last long.

"I noticed that Collie and Shah began spending an increasing amount of time at the Johnson house," she said. David, she noticed, "would come and go at all hours of the day and night. He was at the Johnson house quite a bit." Bryan became increasingly suspicious when she "became aware that Joan Johnson and her children were being isolated from me and others. I had known Joan Johnson since 1994, when she moved to her Del Monte house. Before Shah and Collie, I'd seen the children playing outside and Joan Johnson running her daily activities. After Shah and Collie, the Johnsons were increasingly isolated and kept out of public view in the neighborhood. The children, who previously had played outside frequently, quit playing outside, and were always inside the house. Over a two-year period, I rarely saw Seth or Kaleta Johnson outside their house."

David and Dinny's influence in the Johnson home—and the increasing isolation of the Johnsons—did not go unnoticed, at least not by Sharon Bryan. Once the two men showed up on the scene, the Johnsons were slowly and inexplicably cut off from the outside world.

As Sharon Bryan illustrates, the isolation didn't stop with Joan; Wirt, of course, was exiled from the family, and Seth and Kaleta's personal relationships were also curbed. Kaleta, in particular, may have suffered the most from Dinny and David's strict regime. It was no secret that they both took more of an interest in Seth. By 1997, Dinny was already scouting out prestigious boarding schools for Seth's future education; the eleven-year-old had recently received satisfactory marks, a major improvement from his previous academic scores, from his fourth-grade teachers at Memorial Hall School (thanks, no doubt, to Dinny's tutoring sessions, another example of how a dominant personality can bring temporary good results). Tragically, Joan even voluntarily signed over guardianship of Seth to Dinny—not once, but twice: On April 10, 1997, a hand-scribbled note from Joan appoints Dinny as Seth's legal guardian. This occurred after the recent death of Seth's previous godfather, Ricky di Portanova. In a more formal legal document dated September 27, 1997, Joan lists Dinesh Shah as Seth's first legal guardian and Sarah B. Hrdy, Joan's sister, as Seth's secondary guardian. Joan's reasons for appointing Dinny as Seth's guardian are unknown; one can only guess that it was done at Dinny's own request. Inexplicably, Joan was handing over her son's welfare to a man she hardly knew.

Because of what Dinny would call "her mean-spirited behavior," Kaleta was frequently blacklisted and banned from family activities. And because she wasn't always allowed to participate in the fun activities that Seth did—the visits to the ice cream shop and early evenings at the movie theater—Kaleta began to harbor a deep resentment toward her mother's friends, especially Dinny. In a 2008 statement, Kaleta recalled one instance in 1997 when Dinny searched her room and found her diary. After reading the second-grader's most private thoughts, Dinny became enraged by an offhand remark "about how mean he [Dinny] was." Dinny angrily confronted the eight-year-old with the same fervor as a recently scandalized public official, frightening her to the point where she stopped keeping a diary altogether. According to her 2008 testimony, Dinny's reaction to her diary entry affected her to the point that "to this day, [she doesn't] like to write things down." This is how Dinny put his brand on Kaleta.

After the discovery of Kaleta's insulting diary entry, Dinny became even more iron-fisted with the little girl, denying her any pleasure he could. For instance, every summer beginning in 1994, both Seth and Kaleta had attended a four-week camp near Hunt, in the Texas Hill Country. Seth went to Camp Stewart, an all-boys camp, while Kaleta attended Waldemar, the nearby camp for girls— both extremely prestigious summer camps where parents fight for admission.

But in 1997, Seth went off to camp alone; Dinny wouldn't allow Kaleta to go to camp that summer, or any summer after that. It was only after the disastrous events of December 2002 when Dinny was finally excised from the family, cut off like a cancerous growth, that Kaleta would finally be able to attend her last year at camp in the summer of 2003. Incidentally, as Dinny's chokehold tightened around the family, Seth wouldn't be allowed to attend summer camp either, making 1997 his last camp excursion.

While she sat at home alone that summer, not even allowed to play outside, Kaleta found a creative way to express her contempt, her frustration, for her situation: Before Seth arrived home from camp, Kaleta allegedly stabbed his pet rat, Nimh, with a pencil. But at the 2008 trial, Kaleta denied Dinny's claim that she purposefully killed Nimh:

Kaleta: "The rat bit me."

Attorney: "And you dropped the rat and the rat's back got hurt when you dropped the rat?"

Kaleta: "Yes. And I kind of threw my hands up and the rat fell to the floor."

At least, that was Kaleta's version of how she accidentally broke Nimh's neck. But the very idea that a rat—a rodent that can survive a fall of several stories—would suffer a broken neck begged credulity, but Kaleta stuck by her story. Either way, Seth's homecoming from summer camp was bittersweet when he learned that one of his pets had passed away; he had repeatedly asked about Nimh's well-being in his letters from camp, but no one in the Johnson family had had the heart to tell him about Nimh's demise. One must imagine the reaction that Seth had to the news, Kaleta looking on.

The summer of 1997 was only the beginning of the unjust and heavy-handed punishments that Kaleta would receive from Dinny. Had she known what was in store for her, perhaps the little girl might not have been so angry or surprised that she wasn't allowed to attend summer camp; in the coming years, she wouldn't be allowed to have any friends or to attend any adolescent social gatherings that weren't carefully monitored under Dinny's watchful eye. Though Seth and Joan would suffer through Dinny's controlling and abusive behavior, it is perhaps Kaleta who suffered the most dramatic isolation—a little girl kept tightly under lock and key, denied even the simplest pleasures of slumber parties, school field trips, and phone calls from friends as her delicate childhood years swiftly passed by.

What Joan didn't mention in her 2008 testimony is that despite the increasingly rigid rules that were being imposed by Dinny and David in the Johnson house, there were some people that Joan was actively trying to isolate herself from—namely, her family. In 1997, frustrated with the massive financial entanglements of her family trusts and the fights with her sisters, Joan confided in David Collie that she wanted to move away from her family, to break free from the archaic trust system that had plagued the Blaffer family wealth. She asked for David's recommendation for a financial lawyer that, she hoped, could end her financial relationship with her siblings—a relationship that had ruined any personal ties with her sisters years before.

This was, of course, the perfect opportunity for Dinny to make his next move. He and David had already taken over much of the family's business—from Joan's choice of salons to the children's education. But as they celebrated the dawn of a new year, Dinny was making his own plans.

In 1998, Dinny would finally get what he cared about most: control of Joan Johnson's finances.

Taking It to the Bank

At Dinny Shah's 2008 civil trial, Joan Johnson summarized her pre-Dinny financial situation simply: "I didn't understand my money," she told the jury. "There was just too much of it."

For the most part, this was probably true. Joan had always relied on either her father or her husband to take care of the family finances, and for the most part, she was ignorant of her own money matters. The only alternative she had was to rely on the good judgment of others to take care of her massive financial portfolio. And truth be told, in the beginning, Dinny Shah was actually a helpful presence for the family's money problems, although helping out as he did permitted him to obtain insider information about Joan's vast wealth.

Joan's financial situation up until 1998 was disorganized, at best. She was having particular trouble with one of her brothers-in-law, the executor of the Johnson family trust which had been underperforming for years. Additionally, the trusts that were set up for the benefit of Wirt, Seth, and Kaleta were also stagnant, mainly due to the archaic trust system that the original Blaffers had set up. Dinny Shah, acting as Joan's financial advisor, learned all of this: By the summer of 1996, just a few short months after his initial meeting with Joan at the di Portanovas' home, he was entrusted with helping Joan organize her home office where memos from legions of lawyers and accountants, tax documents, private investigator reports, police reports, and quarterly bank statements would float across his desk. Dinny, the designated custodian of those records, would later use them as part of his defense in the civil case Joan would file against him. Ultimately, thousands of such documents that he was given to review, monitor, personally manage, and organize would be exchanged between legal counsel as part of what lawyers call "discovery." Discovery consists of depositions, requests for production of documents, written interrogatories, and other pre-trial tools the Texas Rules of Civil Procedure authorize for use in civil litigation. Once documents are exchanged between counsel, they may become part of the public domain depending on how they are used, unless one of the litigants asks the court for a protective order. That apparently was not done in this case. Instead, Joan's trial team demanded—and received—all of the sensitive documents that Dinny had in his possession. Some of them were not flattering to the Johnson family, Joan especially. Many of them were marked as trial exhibits. Many of them were admitted into evidence.

Since the beginning of their friendship, Joan had often turned to Dinny—and to a lesser extent David Collie—for financial advice. David, whose father was managing partner at the prestigious Houston law firm Vinson & Elkins, was well-connected to a network of top attorneys, accountants, and financial planners. Dinny, on the other hand, was a self-proclaimed financial genius. And most importantly, Joan believed that the two men had her best interests in mind. They were her friends, after all; Joan trusted them.

When Joan mentioned to David and Dinny sometime late in 1997 that she was unhappy with her lawyers and wanted help extracting herself financially from her family, the two men seized the opportunity. They wasted no time in helping their prized possession—the fabulously wealthy Joan Johnson—with her multi-million dollar dilemma.

David began making calls in early January 1998 to his lawyer friends at Vinson & Elkins, but a conflict of interest prevented the firm from taking on Joan as a client. David then contacted a childhood friend, Michael Leary, who worked for Andrews Kurth, another renowned Houston law firm.

Sometime in early January, Joan met with Leary and another Andrews Kurth lawyer, Terri Lacy, to discuss her financial situation. There were two flies on the wall in that room—David Collie and Dinny Shah. In fact, a thank-you letter from Andrews Kurth to Joan Johnson—dated January 30, 1998—states that "as we have discussed with you and your colleagues, David Collie and Dinny Shah, our firm is pleased to represent you in connection with your general estate planning needs."

After the meeting with Andrews Kurth, Joan's two "colleagues" didn't waste any time securing the rest of Joan's assets, moving them around in order to get a tight grasp on Joan's finances. At David's recommendation, she transferred her entire stock portfolio into several Merrill Lynch accounts in March 1997 using David's own Merrill Lynch broker. A document dated March 17, 1998, lists Dinny Shah and David Collie as executors on Joan's Merrill Lynch accounts, essentially giving them the ability to direct her investments as they saw fit.

On the Merrill Lynch account documents, Collie is listed as "self-employed," which, he explained in the 2008 trial, meant that he was working for his own family partnership, developing tracts of real estate back when the real estate boom typified Houston. At about this same time, Dinny conveniently opened up his own Merrill Lynch brokerage account using the same broker, so that he and David could call up a single broker to direct any of their accounts, including Joan's. Dinny also listed himself on these documents as "self-employed": He made a meager living trading stock on his personal e-Trade account. At the civil trial in 2008, Dinny refused to describe any part of his private stock trading experience—not the amount, not the frequency of trades, not the stocks traded. He was forced to admit, however, that there were many years he felt it was not necessary to file a federal tax return: The "expert" had no reportable income. He paid no income taxes.

Shortly after, in the early summer of 1998, Dinny and David contacted Bessemer Trust Company of Florida to help Joan confront the massive problem of the interlocking, family-run Blaffer trust system. In a letter dated July 23, 1998, Jeffrey Pfleger, senior vice president at Bessemer, lauded Dinny and David for their deep concern over their friend's situation:

> *I would like to thank you for arranging my visit to Houston on Tuesday. . . . I realize that both of you have done a tremendous amount of work to help Joan with gathering her documents, dealing with all the trusts, and, most importantly, providing support to her and her children.*

The letter goes on to say that Pfleger would review the documents that David and Dinny had provided in order to make a recommendation about their next move concerning the Johnsons' trusts. These letters—from both Andrews Kurth and Bessemer Trust Company—reflect one continuous theme: David and Dinny had effectively presented themselves as sympathetic characters to the many financial professionals that were contracted to help Joan. They were the selfless saints; concerned friends who wanted to help the mega-wealthy Joan, an overwhelmed single mother, with her money problems. And they seemed to pull off the bleeding-heart act successfully. There is no reason to think that the lawyers, the CPAs, or the brokerage houses had any actual knowledge of the emerging relationship between Joan and her two new friends. But if questions were asked, it is clear that Dinny, David, or Joan had an answer that satisfied everyone.

Once they had gained full control of Joan's finances, Dinny and David needed just one more document to protect them legally:

power of attorney. They already had control over her Merrill Lynch accounts, but they were about to take everything just one step further.

In October 1998, a few short months after David and Dinny launched their campaign to free Joan's finances, Joan signed over complete power of attorney to her good friends and trusted advisors David W. Collie and Dinesh K. Shah. The most interesting part about the power of attorney documents is that they gave Dinny and David total control over almost all aspects of Joan's life—a role normally reserved for a spouse or the close relatives of incapacitated people. But David and Dinny, not related to the Johnsons by blood and relative newcomers to the family, had almost unlimited power over the Johnsons' lives: the authority to buy and sell any of Joan's property or personal effects; to make stock and bond transactions and handle tax and insurance matters; to control Joan's banking and financial transactions and manipulate her estate and trusts; they even had medical power of attorney. In a series of simple signatures, Joan had—quite literally—handed over her entire life to Dinny and David.

When asked about it years later, Joan would admit that she'd signed the power of attorney documents "at [Dinny and David's] strong suggestion." Just as in the case of Wirt's discipline problems, Seth's difficulties at school, or even the befuddling question of what car she should buy, Joan listened to the advice of her friends before making any decisions; their words had become her sole compass.

In his 2008 video deposition, David Collie backed away when asked exactly why he and Dinny held such power over Joan's personal affairs. Although David's name is listed first on the power of attorney documents, he claimed that he was only a backup power of attorney. The documents, he explained, were really structured for Dinny Shah.

To a certain extent, Collie's statement was true: Although David Collie's name appears first, Dinny Shah was listed as the primary power of attorney on these documents, and he was the one who called the shots for each and every Merrill Lynch account in Joan's name, including trusts that listed Seth and Kaleta as beneficiaries. Moreover, Collie denied ever suggesting or introducing Joan to any of the financial advisors and lawyers that were contacted to sort through Joan's financial mess: He didn't want to seem as if he had a vested interest in Joan's millions, at least not in front of a jury.

By the time all was said and done, Dinny and David had equipped Joan with a small army of lawyers, advisors, CPAs, and bankers to help her manage and make sense of her massive financial portfolio. And as they worked to extract her from her family's tangled trust system, she simultaneously handed over control of her finances to David Collie and Dinny Shah, naming them executors on her accounts. Moreover, David and Dinny literally held the power to make life-and-death decisions for both Joan and her youngest children. Such seemingly ill-advised legal moves concerning two men that weren't family—two men she'd known for just two years—makes even the most casual outside observer wonder: *What was Joan Johnson thinking?*

It is no big secret that Dinny Shah was a habitual liar. He was not, as he claimed to be, any type of seasoned financial advisor. He hadn't graduated from Baylor University or Rice University, and he didn't have a degree in economics or finance. One of the few verifiable claims he made was that his birthday, February 12, was the same as Lincoln's. He frequently pointed to this as if it were some badge of honor.

Over the years, Dinny's lies would become more and more outrageous: He was a CIA agent, a former Marine, and a paratrooper; he was a U.S. diplomat who had been stationed in India. He was descended from Indian royalty, and he and his brother owned blocks and blocks of property in his family's city in India; the people there would bow in awe when they returned for a visit.

As Glennis Goodrich and her nephew Robert McKay learned years before, Dinny's power stemmed from his uncanny ability to lie. It would take a rigorously trained psychologist or an abnormally perceptive person to challenge any of Dinny's tall tales; he told them with such earnest conviction, such belief, that a normal person could be easily convinced that the most outlandish lie was undoubtedly true.

Joan Johnson, unfortunately, did not possess above-average skills of perception, or at least not enough to penetrate Dinny's thick tangle of lies. Rather, she seemed to accept at face value each and every one of Dinny's outlandish exaggerations without question. Joan trusted him blindly, and her willingness to go along with his plan would make Dinny Shah an overnight multimillionaire.

Ironically, the working relationship that grew between Dinny and Joan was mutually beneficial: If Dinny is to be believed, he actually helped Joan's trusts—and those of her children—grow in the years between 1998 and 2002. Dinny would testify that his efforts increased the asset value of the children's trusts as well as that of Joan by at least $40 million. This feat seems too good to be true, but when the family CPA, Reed Jordan, testified, he would not deny that the trusts had experienced substantial increase in value during the time Dinny was helping to direct them. Other financial witnesses from Houston trust companies or investment firms would also not deny that the value of the trusts dramatically increased during the time Dinny was in charge. In fact, during the entire civil trial in 2008, no witness was called by the Johnson trial team to refute the $40 million claim. Whether the asset value growth was due to Dinny's skill or to a phenomenal run-up in the stock market during this period is open for argument, but it is undeniable that, at a minimum, Dinny helped Joan become disentangled from some of the family trusts and other business deals. In the process, of course, he became intimately familiar with the operations of each trust. He had Joan exactly where he wanted her.

After working so hard to manage the Johnsons' extensive wealth—after all, Dinny had started giving financial advice and managing Joan's home office since 1996—Dinny made his next move. He had Joan, who understood little about money and was completely reliant on his so-called "expertise," trapped in an advantageous position. That's when he played his hole card: He threatened to leave Joan, claiming that he had been offered a job at Bechtel, a huge construction company in California, with a whopping salary of over $800,000 a year; a second job offer arrived shortly, this time from Goldman Sachs in New York. These job offers were, of course, two more of Dinny's carefully crafted lies. But Joan didn't know that.

Truth is, Dinny had no real qualifications to work in the financial sector other than what he learned trading his own stocks—though he did seem to have an eye for a good investment. In the 2008 civil trial, Dinny openly admitted that he had never received any type of degree in business administration or finance and that he wasn't a qualified or licensed CPA or investment banker.

In fact, it seems the only official license that Dinny held back in 1998 was a Texas driver's license. But either Joan didn't care or she never took the time to find out for herself. Feeling the pressure of losing Dinny so soon after her finances had started to bounce back, and not wanting to deal with her financial matters herself, Joan decided to give Dinny a monetary gift, in an amount suggested by Dinny himself. That's how Dinny became a full-fledged, bankrolled member of the family, and a multimillionaire to boot. April 27, 1998, was a red-letter day for. D. K. Shah, for that is the day the money began to move. A signed affidavit from Joan Johnson reads:

> *My name is Joan Blaffer Johnson and I am a resident of Houston, Texas. . . . I am desirous to give and to gift stocks to D. K. (Dinny) Shah that are located in my Merrill Lynch account in Houston, Texas. The amount of stock which I desire and wish to gift and to give to D. K. (Dinny) Shah is one*

million two hundred thousand ($1,200,000.00) dollars. I
understand that I can give and gift up to six hundred thirty-
five thousand ($635,000.00) dollars tax free and that the
additional five hundred sixty-five thousand ($565,000.00)
dollars is taxed. I understand that I, Joan Blaffer Johnson,
donor, bear the gift tax burden on the additional five hundred
sixty-five thousand ($565,000.00) dollars which will
amount to approximately two hundred twenty-five thousand
seven hundred fifty ($225,750.00) dollars. I wish to give to
D. K. (Dinny) Shah this stock for all of his helpfulness as a
family friend. I also understand that I could have gifted this to
any one of my three (3) children but I chose not to do so.

Though the transaction wasn't made in dollars but stock, the stock's value was worth $1.2 million. What's more, Dinny was cunning enough to have Joan pay the taxes on the gift, which is highly unusual for a donor, saving him almost a quarter of a million dollars in taxes. Gifting of amounts this huge with the provision that the donor prepaid the tax should have set off alarm bells in legal and accounting quarters. But there is no indication Joan was urged to change her mind or if she was urged that she acted on the warnings. At the civil trial, Joan's lawyers would offer evidence that the total amount of "gifts" over time was on the order of $2.5 million.

Once Dinny had made his small fortune, why didn't he leave, just pick up and find the next wealthy woman to exploit? If the stories of Glennis Goodrich, Michael Sambogna, Michael Holstein, or Clint Langford tell us anything about Dinesh Shah, it's his relentless personality that makes him so dangerous. He loves the game, loves the chase. He wasn't going to leave Joan right after he made his first million. He'd stick around until 2002, when he was forcibly removed from the home, but only after he'd made another easy million dollars in tax-free gifts for his "helpfulness as a family friend" in the span of six years. Joan, he knew, was a cash cow that had plenty more milk to give.

For Joan, heir to the Exxon Mobil legacy, the $2.5 million that she gifted Dinny was a drop in the bucket of her seemingly bottomless coffers. And the unchecked power of attorney that she granted Dinny and David was just a symbolic gesture compared to what was in store for the Johnsons in the coming years. The physical, mental, and sexual abuse ushered in at the end of 1998 would continue until that fateful December night in 2002, when Dinny was finally evicted from the family's lives—thanks in part to Dinny's own brother, Shyam, and an alert officer with the Houston Police Department. Those four years would prove to be much more costly to Joan, and above all to Seth and Kaleta, than all the money in the world.

Beat Them Until They Surrender

It had happened so often that by the 2008 trial, Joan Johnson couldn't remember the date that Dinny Shah and David Collie began to beat her. Neither could Seth.

But Kaleta, who had been watching Dinny and David closely, partly out of suspicion and partly out of her resentment for the way the two excluded her from family events, could recall—clearly—the first time it ever happened to her: in the spring of 1998, during a family vacation to Palm Beach, Florida.

It was spring break: Seth and Kaleta were out of school, and Joan was in the market for a new summer beach house. David, too, had expressed interest in buying a getaway condo in Palm Beach. So the entire family, with Dinny, David, and family friend Henry Dyches in tow, headed out to sunny Florida.

The vacationers checked into The Chesterfield, a luxurious four-star hotel located on scenic, palm-shaded boulevard just minutes from the Atlantic. In his 2008 deposition, David Collie stated that they rented a double suite at the Chesterfield—Dinny and Seth in one room, Joan and Kaleta in another—with Henry and David sleeping on the sofa beds in the living room. The sleeping arrangements were somewhat unusual, but Joan didn't seem too concerned. She would not question the idea of Dinny bunking with Seth. Kaleta later testified that the sleeping arrangements were standard for all of the Johnsons' vacations with Shah: Dinny and Seth always in one room, Joan and Kaleta in another.

While in Palm Beach, Joan and David met with Jeff Cloninger, a high-end realtor and acquaintance of Henry Dyches. The two looked at various beach houses and luxury condos but didn't put in any offers. Perhaps they were just browsing, passing the time between shopping, dining out, and relaxing on the beach. Everyone, it seemed, was having a great time—everyone, that is, but Kaleta.

For Kaleta, the thought of that particular trip would bring tears to her eyes and an uncomfortable lump in her throat. Far from being a fun family getaway, the trip to Florida was a living nightmare for her. It was during this vacation that Kaleta, only nine years old at the time, got her first glimpse at the darkest, most sinister sides of her mother's closest companions and the men Joan appointed as guardians for her children.

One evening, as the six were driving back to the hotel after dinner, Seth and Kaleta began fighting in the backseat. Seth was pestering Kaleta, calling her names and teasing her, and Kaleta was yelling at Seth to stop. It was nothing serious, nothing violent—just a typical brother-and-sister spat. When she was annoyed past her breaking point, Kaleta turned to Dinny and David for help, but they just ignored her, refusing to intervene.

When David and Dinny didn't leap to her defense, she began to complain. Kaleta's list of grievances would be instantly familiar to any parent who's ever been trapped in a car with warring siblings: It wasn't fair, Kaleta whined. If the situation were reversed—if *she* was the one bothering *Seth*—she was sure that Dinny and David would have punished her. Seth always got his way, she told the men. They always took his side.

Perhaps there was some truth to the little girl's complaints: When David and Dinny finally did intervene, it didn't work out to

Kaleta's advantage. Instead of parking the car when they reached the hotel, David and Dinny dropped off Joan, Seth, and Henry at the front door of The Chesterfield. Kaleta remained in the backseat of the car. David and Dinny needed to have a talk with Kaleta, they explained as they pulled away from the hotel. But there wouldn't be any talking.

Instead, Dinny and David drove Kaleta to an alley behind the hotel. There, they ordered Kaleta to get out of the car. David Collie was already standing outside with the door open, removing his leather belt as Kaleta shut the door.

Kaleta: "And David took off his belt and, you know, whipped me with his belt. He had me bend over the seat and he whipped me, and he counted it out slowly. And then, you know, they were laughing as they did it. And after that, they took me back to the hotel, and they told me not to speak out against them anymore."

After the beating, David was leaning on the car, breathing heavily. Dinny and David made their point clear with one last verbal threat: Kaleta was to never criticize them again. Ever. That would be a lesson that Kaleta took to heart, never daring to speak out openly against David or Dinny, as she wiped her swollen eyes and was ushered into the lobby of The Chesterfield between her two abusers.

The welts left from David's belt, which eventually gave way to large, discolored bruises, were placed carefully: All of them were conveniently hidden beneath Kaleta's clothes where no one—not Joan, not Kaleta's friends or teachers—could see what David had done. As time went on, Kaleta testified, David and Dinny got sloppier. The beatings increased over the years, and sometimes Kaleta had to cover up the marks they left:

Kaleta: "Several times he [Dinny] would take off his belt and whip me and I would have long welts on the back of my legs. And he would tell me to wear biking shorts under my [school] uniform and, you know, he said not to take them off when I changed for P. E. so no one would see the markings."

David and Dinny, for their part, denied beating Kaleta in that alley in Florida. They would, in fact, categorically deny every single accusation of physical abuse against any member of the Johnson family that was brought to light in court.

———————

No one called police the night that Dinny and David beat Kaleta in that Palm Beach alley. There's no evidence that anyone even found out about it—Kaleta, fearful of the two men, wasn't going to tell anyone. She was the perfect victim. But she wasn't the only one.

Though she was ignorant of the abuse that took place in Palm Beach, it would have been impossible for Joan Johnson to ignore the subsequent "punishments" that David and Dinny meted out regularly. After all, Joan herself soon became the recipient of their violent outbursts. And as things turned out, she was also the perfect, tight-lipped victim: She never said a word to anyone—not her neighbors, not her lawyers, not anyone.

Once the family returned from Palm Beach, things began to change in the Johnson home. David and Dinny had gotten away with beating Kaleta, and now they were getting cocky: They wanted more power, more control over the kids and Joan. Joan's money wasn't enough for them, not anymore.

In the summer of 1998, the isolation and physical punishments increased both in frequency and degree. Once, when Kaleta yelled at Seth for going into her room, Dinny burst into Kaleta's room to intervene; the noise had interrupted whatever he was doing. In a rage, Dinny collected all of Kaleta's stuffed animals and trinkets, including a few favorite mementos that her father had given her, and put them into three large, plastic garbage bags, which he set out on the sidewalk for the week's trash collection.

On another occasion, Dinny beat Seth for eating a banana. David and Dinny had sent Kaleta and Seth to their rooms for misbehaving—a preferable punishment, no doubt, to one of their brutal spankings. While the kids were upstairs, David found a banana peel in the trash can. That banana peel sent him through the roof—one of the children had dared to disobey his authority, leaving their rooms without his permission. When the kids were sat down and interrogated by David and Dinny, it was Seth who finally confessed: He had snuck downstairs because he was hungry.

That's when a grim Dinny took Seth by the arm and led him into his room and beat him for disobeying. Joan, this time fully aware of what was happening, did nothing. The outrageous was rapidly becoming the norm.

Eventually, Seth and Kaleta—like prisoners in a POW camp—learned to work around Dinny and David's demands, sometimes through compliance, sometimes defiance. They already knew that their own mother wouldn't be of any help and wouldn't or couldn't intervene once David or Dinny were bent on delivering a swift and brutal punishment for some type of misbehavior. Kaleta recalled how she and Seth "would only play very quietly. If we were too loud, David or Dinny would punish us"—and that punishment, in the years following 1998, was usually a spanking, or something much worse.

The abuse was sometimes too much to take. Trying to escape another unjust punishment, Seth found the courage to fight back:

Seth: "I've been hit by books, cane, his [Dinny's] fist, his [Dinny's] shoes."

Attorney: "Did you ever try to fight back?"

Seth: "Yes."

Attorney: "Can you describe that?"

Seth: "There is one incident where I jabbed a Lego—it was the closest thing I had—I grabbed it and I jammed it in his [Dinny's] ear."

Attorney: "What did he do?"

Seth: "He quickly got off me. As soon as I saw him go for my wooden blocks, I jumped behind my bed."

Attorney: "What happened next?"

Seth: "He threw wooden blocks at me, which at a good force he put some little dents in my wall."

Attorney: "Did he hit you with any of the wooden blocks?"

Seth: "No. As soon as he got close, I would duck."

Seth managed to avoid each of the projectiles, eventually tiring Dinny to the point of retreat. But the divots on the wall left from the flying blocks, Seth knew, had all been meant for his forehead.

As is often the case with dominants, Dinny would go through periods of remorse and subsequent "good behavior," so that things weren't always so bad in the Johnson home. Between the harsh punishments, Dinny would boast of making headway with Joan's finances. And the two friends kept the family entertained with movies and dinners out on the town, buying little gifts for the children when they were good. They could be, just like any family members, generous and loving, or purposefully overbearing and insufferable. But the point is, David and Dinny weren't family members. And they certainly didn't have the right—as does no one—to slap around two children and their widowed mother. Needless to say, the mixed messages and the erratic behavior from Dinny and David kept the children constantly on guard: They were never sure if Dinny or David would laugh and make a joke, or take their belts off and shut the door. As Joan described it, "Dinny could be very nice, and very mean. His mean behavior was always followed by being very, very nice." In this way, David and Dinny could artfully calm and appease Kaleta, Seth, and Joan after one of their battering sessions.

———————

Despite the fact that these strange events were going on inside the Johnson home, the family was able to keep up regular appearances. It's true that Joan had slowly been distanced from her neighbors and friends, but most everything else appeared to be normal: The kids went to and from school. They were getting good grades. Joan kept up her regular appointments, going out to the occasional charity fund-raiser or social function with David on her arm, hobnobbing with the wealthiest families in the city. To most everyone who had known Joan casually before she met David Collie and Dinny Shah, nothing appeared to be any different.

And then the gate broke.

It was August 1998, and Joan Johnson couldn't pull into her own garage anymore. The electric gate that would swing open and close at the touch of a button was frozen, the mechanisms worn from too much use. Not wasting any time, Joan and Dinny ordered a new wrought-iron gate from the Four Seasons Development Company, a local construction and design firm. It would eventually send ripples of hushed whispers down Del Monte Drive as the summer slowly melted into autumn.

A new gate would normally not cause a big stir among the neighbors, especially not the tasteful, expensive gate and fence that now guarded the Johnson residence. It was the large sheets of black plastic that were then draped across the length of the brand-new gate that caused the commotion.

At first, the neighbors assumed the tarps must have been put there as part of the construction, a temporary measure. But as Joan Johnson's neighbors Sharon Bryan and Olabelle Hall noted, the tarps didn't come down—even after the construction was obviously complete. Weeks, and then months, and eventually years passed, but the tarps remained in place, completely obscuring any view of the back of the home from the street.

Olabelle: "This beautiful iron gate that went across her [Joan's] driveway where you could visibly see up the driveway but the gate would stay closed, it was electric, that they hung black plastic all over the gate. Black plastic all over it."

Once it became clear that the tarp wasn't a temporary construction measure but a permanent feature of the Johnsons' gate, the neighbors started talking. Sharon Bryan had already noticed that Joan and the kids weren't stopping by for their afternoon chats. And Olabelle Hall, who would often walk her dog with Joan, had noticed just how quiet the Johnsons' home had become. The black tarp was a disturbing physical reminder of the friend they no longer saw and the two children who might as well have just disappeared.

It was Olabelle Hall, standing at her window one day not long after the new gate was installed, who noticed another strange detail about the Johnson home, something more disturbing than even the black tarp. In her appearance at the 2008 trial, Olabelle Hall described her chilling discovery:

"Well, first of all, I was paying attention to the house because Joan had disappeared and the children had basically disappeared," Mrs. Hall said. "My awareness was heightened because I couldn't figure out what was going on and why the situation had just basically changed."

Mrs. Hall, unlike Sharon Bryan, had not had the pleasure of meeting David and Dinny. But Olabelle Hall had already noticed that, ever since the new gate and tarp had been installed, all of the shutters to the Johnson home had been closed tight—even the shutters on the sides and back of the house. It was impossible, she said, to glimpse any sign of life inside. But the closed shutters weren't the reason why.

Olabelle Hall's upstairs window affords a perfect view into Kaleta's bedroom. And just by happenstance, Olabelle Hall's keen perception noticed something that the other neighbors had missed: There were sheets hanging over Kaleta's window in addition to the drawn shutters.

Olabelle: "I pointed out to my husband when I was standing at our window looking down and I said, 'Look, there [are] sheets hanging over the shutters.' I said why would anybody, if you have shutters and they're closed, why would you hang material or sheets up?"

Every time Olabelle Hall walked her Brittany spaniel down Del Monte Drive with her husband, she'd look at the Johnson home, searching for changes or signs of the Johnsons' well-being.

Olabelle: "I pointed out to my husband when we were walking the dog, I said Joan had beautiful drapes and beautiful things in her home . . . the drapes were covered with white lining, and I said,

'Look, there is something hanging over the top, hanging down . . . now they've covered up the drapes.'"

What Mrs. Hall saw through the windows was only half the story: Every single window in the Johnson home was covered. Blankets, quilts, and even towels were draped across Joan Johnson's windows, preventing any light from coming in. Joan had hundreds of thousands of dollars worth of drapes hanging around her house, but they were obscured by the random linens that had been thrown haphazardly over them.

What *was* going on in that house? According to Joan's testimony, David Collie allegedly covered the windows—hanging sheets and blankets and towels, whatever he could find—after Dinny had convinced them that they were "being watched." Joan, like she did with Dinny's financial and parenting advice, went along with it.

Joan: "Dinny was convinced that people were coming to peep in the windows and somehow they could look in the windows and see what was going on. I really held this belief that Dinesh had worked for the FBI, the CIA, Chase [Bank] . . . I believed him to be all these things. And I had a lot of respect [for him]. And so, I thought, this guy knows a lot. I better, I'm just, you know, a housewife here. I better listen to him because I'm not—I didn't know any of those things."

And so a false paranoia spread through the house, instigated by Dinny. Though he claimed that the Johnsons were being "watched" by some unknown threat, the tarp and the blankets on the windows were just one more phase in Dinny's master plan—to create a physical barrier between the Johnsons and the outside world, a symbolic testament to the limitlessness of his power over the family. Day or night, the Johnson house remained in the shadows, no light penetrating the airy rooms of the Johnsons' River Oaks home.

Seth, Kaleta, and Joan were living in a tomb. They would live this way for four years.

There was one attempt to save the Johnson family, but it was quickly extinguished. An intervention among Joan's Del Monte

Drive neighbors, who had stood by and watched the physical transformation of the house coincide with the disappearance of the Johnson family, was organized, with Sharon Bryan and Olabelle Hall, neighborhood crusaders, leading the way. They hadn't been able to get close enough to Joan in months, couldn't find a way to talk to her in private, to see if she needed help of any sort. Sharon and Olabelle waited to catch Joan's car pulling into the driveway, to see if she would come out to check the mail or walk the dog—a good chance for them to catch up and maybe, inconspicuously, ascertain a bit of information about what was happening. But they never got that chance: Dinny and David kept Joan so busy, tag-teaming for her attention that she forgot all about her friends.

Late in 1998, after the ominous black tarp had been guarding the Johnson home for a few months, a group of Joan's concerned friends stopped by to see their neighbor Nancy Atlas, a federal judge. They were there to ask advice: Could anything be done to help Joan, to remove her from what was obviously a bad situation? Though Judge Atlas was obviously sympathetic to Joan's predicament, she regrettably, but correctly, told Sharon Bryan, Olabelle Hall, and the other neighbors that there was little anyone could do. Judge Atlas urged neighbors to document the comings and goings of the Johnsons, to record any suspicious activity—a task that Olabelle Hall and Sharon Bryan would keep vigilantly for four years, eventually testifying for the Johnsons in 2008. But for the present, everyone would have to learn to live with the sleeping monster on Del Monte Drive.

As bad situations often go, Joan Johnson's was about to get worse. She had failed to protect her children from Dinny and David's heavy-handed punishments. She had failed to protect herself and her family from the slow isolation that Dinny and David had orchestrated. She had failed to reach out to her friends or neighbors for help. And now, emboldened by the power they had seized, by their ability to convince Joan of anything, Dinny and David were about to advance an attack on Joan herself—physically.

It was spring break of 1999, exactly one year after Kaleta's brutal whipping in Palm Beach. The family had decided to explore the West coast for a bit, heading off to Santa Barbara, California, with David and Dinny of course. They checked into the oceanfront Four Seasons Biltmore. Again, Seth slept in the same room as Dinny, as was now protocol. David Collie slept on the couch, while Joan and Kaleta shared a room down the hall. And as usual, Joan managed to combine their annual family vacation with a more practical matter: scouting colleges for Wirt. Wirt was still in exile at Rocky Mountain Academy and would be graduating at the end of the spring term. They were looking for a university where Wirt could matriculate without coming home to Houston during the summer.

In between touring the many universities in southern California, the family found time to make the rounds, visiting Alcatraz, the Muir Woods National Monument, and the redwood forest. After one particularly exhausting day of sightseeing, the group was driving back to the hotel, looking forward to a hearty dinner. And just like the events that led to Kaleta's beating in Palm Beach, problems started in the car on the drive back and would erupt once David and Dinny had the family safely secured behind closed doors.

David Collie was behind the wheel, with Dinny riding shotgun. Seth sat in the middle of the backseat, sandwiched between Joan and Kaleta. There was little foresight in this seating arrangement because, as Seth described at the 2008 trial, another spat with his sister was brewing in the backseat.

Seth: "We had just come back from looking at colleges. My sister and I were just doing what a brother and sister does who are two years apart. We were poking, teasing, calling each other little names while Mr. Shah and Mr. Collie were up front talking. We got loud. They would tell my mom to tell us to be quiet. She would. We would start doing the same thing five, ten minutes later."

But after repeatedly ordering Joan to quiet her children, Dinny had had enough. Without warning, he reached into the backseat and slapped Joan across the face. Once wasn't enough for Dinny—he closed his fist and began beating Joan, punching her in the head, the face, the arm, wherever he could reach. Shocked, Seth and Kaleta looked on as Dinny continued his assault on their mother.

Kaleta's recollection of the event matches her younger brother's story; she later told the court that this was the first time she remembers Dinny or David beating Joan.

Kaleta: "Dinny was reaching back from the passenger seat and hitting my mother, pulling her hair and hitting her. I remember she tried to jump out of the car, and she tried to get David to help her. She kept saying, 'David, help me.'"

David Collie responded to Joan's cries for help by reaching into the backseat—he was sitting in front of Joan—and locking her car door. He made it clear that Joan wouldn't escape this time; she was up against both of them. After Dinny was winded from this sudden burst of activity, the five of them drove on in silence. But once they reached the Biltmore, it was clear that this nightmarish vacation wasn't over. It had just begun.

Kaleta and Seth were ushered into the room that Dinny and Seth shared. David Collie set them in front of the TV and told them to stay put. They wouldn't see their mother for the rest of the evening, but they heard plenty.

Meanwhile, Dinny led Joan into her own room and locked the door. He began slapping her around again, this time with little restraint: He wasn't concerned, as David had been with Kaleta, to carefully place his blows on parts of her body that couldn't be seen. Joan's screams echoed down the hall. After securing the kids, David Collie joined the two in Joan's room to watch.

Dinny raged on, his own screaming and yelling drowning out Joan's cries. She was pushed into the bathroom, where Dinny forced her head under running water in the sink. When that wasn't enough, David and Dinny pulled her up and dunked her head in the toilet. They flushed repeatedly, their own unique brand of waterboarding.

The children, meanwhile, sat in the hotel room alone, frozen in terror. Though the abuse probably lasted ten or fifteen minutes, the seconds ticked by in terrible agony. David Collie would come in to check on the kids intermittently, trying to keep them in check and under control.

Seth: "Every time you could hear a scream or a shout or my mother crying, he [David] would turn up the volume [on the TV]."

Attorney: Describe for us how that made you feel."

Seth: "I was scared. I felt helpless towards my mother, and I just held my sister's hand and sat right next to her on the edge of the bed."

Attorney: "Describe the defendant after that. I mean, after he comes out and you have heard this, describe the defendant's demeanor."

Seth: "He [Dinny] came out calm as could be. He got down on one knee and he told me and my sister that what he had done was righteous and that my mom had deserved it and that we should have no sympathy for her."

Dinny and David calmly dressed for dinner, and took the children downstairs to eat without Joan. It was a somber meal, the children staring at their plates, picking at their food. All the while, Dinny lectured them about that evening's events: *You should have no sympathy for your mother. Your mother deserved what happened. I did the right thing,* he told them.

Joan was upstairs in the hotel room. Dinny had locked her in there.

———————

Curiously, Dinny and David have little recollection of the events that occurred during this trip to California. In fact, the two couldn't even recall going to California with the Johnsons, much to the frustration of the Johnsons' trial team.

Attorney: "Do you remember a discussion about trying to locate an appropriate college in California for Wirt?"

David Collie: "No, sir, I do not."

Attorney: "Do you have any memory of driving with Joan Johnson from the Biltmore in Santa Barbara to San Francisco?"

David Collie: "No, sir."

Attorney: "And you have no memory of a trip to California where the Johnsons and Shah traveled by air and you drove out there? You don't—you don't remember that, do you?"

David Collie: "No, sir. I did not drive out there, sir."

Attorney: "And, of course, you have never shoved or hit Joan?"

David Collie: "Never."

Attorney: "Never put her head in a toilet?"

David Collie: "No, sir."

Attorney: "You never helped Shah do that?"

David Collie: "Never."

Attorney: "You never held her head under running water in a sink?"

David Collie: "Never."

Dinny seemed to have the same sudden amnesia that David Collie had while on the stand, categorically denying every accusation about the events that happened in Joan's room at the Biltmore.

Attorney: "You did go to California with the Johnsons in the spring of 1999 to look at colleges for Wirt, didn't you?"

Dinesh Shah: "I did not."

Attorney: "You stayed at the Biltmore Hotel in Santa Barbara with the Johnsons at that time, didn't you?"

Dinesh Shah: "I did not."

Attorney: "And isn't it true, sir, that you beat Joan in the Biltmore Hotel room with the children next door with David Collie?"

Dinesh Shah: "That is not true. It didn't happen."

Were all three Johnsons—Seth, Kaleta, and Joan—making up the events of their California trip just to win the sympathy of the jury? Were they pulling out all the stops, trying to incriminate David and Dinny for a crime that never happened? It's unlikely that the Johnsons lied under oath about this particular event—David and Dinny did go to California with the Johnsons in 1999, and it's likely that Joan did have her head shoved into a toilet. But the Johnsons were lacking a key piece of evidence that could have clinched their case: a police report.

The stars must have been aligned against Joan Johnson on that terrifying night in the Biltmore; no one, it seemed, heard her screams, not even any of the other hotel guests down the hall. There wasn't even a courtesy call from the front desk to uncover the disturbance happening in that hotel room. Joan would later admit that she never called the cops, didn't reach out to anyone. She could have run downstairs to the hotel's lush lobby, screaming at the top of her lungs that she had just been viciously beaten by two men—but she didn't.

Upon their return to Houston, Joan remained quiet about what happened that night in the Biltmore. Surely Sharon Bryan or Olabelle Hall could have been reached for help. It would have only taken a phone call or a stroll across the street. There's no rational reason that anyone—not even Joan herself—can give to justify her silence in the matter. For the next four years, Joan would choose to suffer in silence, dragging down both Seth and Kaleta with her.

The Gardener Sees It All

Dinny was happy. The family was now safely locked away from prying eyes. Seth, Kaleta, and Joan went about their daily lives in the darkened rooms of the Johnsons' River Oaks mansion, living as mere shadows of their former selves.

While the neighbors could not quite understand the changes that were occurring in the Johnson home, there was one person who still had access to the family. He saw Dinny Shah and David Collie hang the tarps that obscured the house from the street, and the sheets and quilts and blankets and towels that darkened the rooms inside. But the tarp and the shuttered windows were innocent-looking actions compared to the things that Jose Luis Moran, Joan Johnson's longtime gardener, witnessed behind the locked doors.

Starting back in 1994, Moran, who went by his middle name, Luis, was hired by Joan Johnson to take care of the property: mowing the lawn, taking care of the pool, and doing whatever handiwork that Joan needed. On Mondays, Wednesdays, and Fridays, Moran would show up at 2933 Del Monte Drive early in the morning, working through the summer and winter alike. On

Tuesdays and Thursdays, he worked across the street at Sharon Bryan's house. For years this arrangement left everyone happy: Moran had a full-time job, but Sharon and Joan only had to pay for a part-time gardener. The two neighbors would even coordinate Moran's schedule together, swapping days if one of them needed Luis for an urgent repair.

Moran had a good working relationship with Joan until, of course, Dinny and David showed up. By the time the shutters were closed and the tarp hung around the perimeter of the property, Luis Moran had been employed at the Johnson residence for more than four years. But as early as 1996, he'd already noticed small changes in Joan's demeanor, changes that were imperceptible to anyone who didn't see Joan every day. At first, Moran didn't think much of it when Joan stopped speaking Spanish to him on a regular basis: He thought she was just being polite, speaking only English whenever Dinny and David were around. As soon as they left, she'd revert to her normal self, speaking Spanish with ease, asking questions and giving instructions for the lawn.

And then, around the same time the house was cordoned off from the outside world and the family members became Dinny and David's personal punching bags, Moran was abruptly barred from entering the Johnson's house. In the days before Dinny and David took over, Moran had enjoyed a comfortable relationship with his employer, often letting himself in and out of the house as needed. But in 1998, soon after the men's arrival, Dinny sat Moran down one day and explained the new rules: Moran was no longer allowed to walk through the back door of the house whenever he wanted. He was to complete his outdoor chores and then go home with minimal contact with the family. Moran followed Dinny's request to the letter; even during the steamy Houston summers, he would cross the street to Sharon Bryan's house every time he needed a drink of water or a brief reprieve from the sweltering heat.

Why such strict rules for the handyman? Luis Moran made Dinny nervous: Moran was an outsider, with easy access to the family. He was the only person left that Dinny hadn't successfully driven away, the only person standing in the way of total domination over the Johnsons; surely, if Moran ever saw something outrageous take place in the house, he would report it immediately. In Dinny's mind, there were only two options—get rid of Luis or buy him out. He failed to convince Joan to fire the meddlesome gardener—one of the few times Joan refused to blindly follow Dinny's will. As a last resort, he decided to try to hire Moran full-time—perhaps as a way to grasp a little more control, to keep his enemies close, and to make sure that Moran didn't tell his other employer what was happening in the Johnson home.

That's when Dinny began making calls to Sharon Bryan.

Sharon Bryan had seen Dinny Shah coming and going from the Johnson home at all hours; she'd stood by as Joan Johnson and her children faded from sight, becoming nothing more than memories and shadows behind the curtains. It's not surprising that she was instantly suspicious when Dinny called her, but she was civil. She listened patiently as he made his request: He wanted Sharon to find her own gardener. It seemed that, according to Dinny, Joan suddenly needed Moran's services full-time.

Sharon calmly explained to Dinny that his proposition was unacceptable: The Bryans needed Moran twice a week, and she wasn't willing to give him up. This was, of course, not the answer that Dinny wanted to hear. He made another call, this time taking his appeal to Sharon's husband, Chip.

Chip Bryan was the former chief financial officer at Sterling Bank before he set off on his own, founding the Houston-based Republic National Bank. Chip was about to open a new Republic National branch on the day Dinny Shah called him at work. Dinny told Chip that Joan really needed Luis Moran at the house full-time, and he needed Chip's wife to agree to the arrangement. Like a sensible husband, Chip deferred to Sharon's decision: She was in charge of the house, he said, and she could work everything out with Joan. Sensing that the Bryans were not willing to budge, Dinny changed his tactics. Ever the manipulator, he casually suggested that, if they could come to terms over Moran's working schedule, Dinny might consider depositing a sizeable sum of money—the same money that Joan had gifted him—in Chip Bryan's new bank branch. Sick of Dinny's hardball tactics, Chip told him to take his money and deposit it in another bank—he certainly didn't want any part of Dinny's money—and hung up.

In a desperate, last-ditch effort, Dinny approached Moran directly: He promised Moran a bigger paycheck if the gardener would agree to quit his twice-weekly visits to the Bryan home. Moran refused; he didn't like Dinny. He later told Sharon Bryan that he was afraid that if he signed on full-time with the Johnsons, Dinny would later fire him in order to finally get rid of him. That's when Sharon Bryan put in a counteroffer, suggesting that Moran quit working at the Johnsons' and work for the Bryans. According to Sharon, Moran refused this offer too—he didn't want to leave Joan alone; he wanted to be there if anything really bad happened.

Moran knew a lot—he knew too much, really, for Dinny's comfort. Moran testified in 2008 that not long after the tarp went up around the house, he started noticing bruises on Joan, mostly on her legs. Whenever he asked about the bruises, Joan would dismiss them, telling Moran that she had fallen. But she'd never been that klutzy before.

Even though he'd been ordered to stay outside while he performed his duties, and even though he couldn't see what was going on in the house through the layers of shutters and curtains and blankets, Moran heard plenty. And he had a pretty solid suspicion that the fighting that reverberated from inside the house had something to do with Joan's bruises.

That suspicion wasn't alleviated on the day that Moran found Joan and Seth locked in the garage. After a screaming match over some issue, Dinny shoved the two in the garage and locked it from the outside. And Moran had seen the entire thing, making his testimony invaluable.

Attorney: "Did you, sir, ever see the defendant, Dinesh K. Shah, shove Joan Johnson and Seth Johnson through this [garage] door, lock it, and then leave the property?"

Moran: "Yes."

Attorney: "Did you personally observe that?"

Moran: "Yes."

Attorney: "What did you do after you saw that?"

Moran: "I just take the keys and open the door and tell Mrs. Johnson if she want to get out of there."

Attorney: "What did you say after you opened the door, unlocked it from the outside, and offered her the opportunity to come out after Mr. Shah had left?"

Moran: "Unlocked the door and she said just lock the door and leave me here."

Attorney: "Did she say she wanted to stay locked inside until Mr. Shah came back?"

Moran: "Yes, sir."

Attorney: "Despite the fact that you had unlocked it and gave her the opportunity to leave? Is that correct?"

Moran: "Yes."

Attorney: "Did she seem afraid of Mr. Shah?"

Moran: "Yes, yeah."

And she was afraid. To Joan, a few hours locked in the garage seemed like a small price to pay compared to what could happen if she angered Dinny further. When cross-examined in 2008 as to why she allowed herself and her young child to be locked away like that, this was Joan's only defense:

Attorney: "Well, if Mr. Moran came and testified that he unlocked the door and opened it for you, why would you not exit, ma'am?"

Joan: "Because I felt that the aftermath of doing something like that would be much, much worse for me and Kaleta and Seth than to just stay there and stay in the building."

Attorney: "What do you mean?"

Joan: "I was afraid of the retribution that Mr. Shah would inflict on us or could inflict."

Attorney: "What kind of retribution?"

Joan: "Beatings, maybe killing me, drowning me like he told me about. He told me how he could kill me in my swimming pool and how to do it. He told me all about how to kill someone and make it look like a drowning and I never thought about it, but it makes total sense. Do you want me to describe someone killing someone in a pool and how to make it look like a drowning? He told me how to do it. It's really horrible."

Perhaps Joan really was afraid for her life, so afraid that she couldn't act, couldn't protect herself and her children. But one would have to imagine that, by 1999, after the brutal beating that Joan endured in the Biltmore, and after having seen David and Dinny raise their hands to her children, a brief flash of courage on Joan's part could have saved her from years of additional abuse: a call for help, a police report, even just packing up the kids and running away—she had the money to do it, after all. And, of course, she had legions of lawyers at her beck and call.

As for Moran, he was one of Joan's few hopes: a careful watchdog, an onlooker from the outside. A humble man. A simple man. He noticed the changing moods and demeanor of the family as if they were seasons, slowly degenerating into winter. He didn't trust Dinny. He wanted to be around to help Joan and the children in any way he could.

But like so many others—Sharon Bryan and Olabelle Hall in particular—he'd keep his mouth shut for years, not quite sure how to reach out and help Joan, allowing this cycle of isolation, control, and abuse inside the Johnson home to move forward unimpeded. Even Moran couldn't penetrate the thick walls that Dinny, and to a lesser extent David, had built around the family like a fortress: The interior of the house was completely off-limits to Moran. With the Johnsons now tightly sealed off from the outside world by means of a black plastic tarp, David and Dinny went to work on the home's interior. The house, despite Dinny's efforts to restore some type of organization, was still overstuffed with antiques and furniture, even some Blaffer family relics. The need to control not just the family but also his environment was so strong that the Johnsons were soon to become more like guests in their own home.

The Man Who Must Not Be Named

In 1995, the year of Luke Johnson's mysterious death, Seth Johnson was only seven years old. Memories of his father were growing fuzzier as the years passed. And by 1999, the few memories that survived were locked away, never to be spoken of again—especially not in the presence of Dinny and David. Seth refused to even utter Luke's name, referring to his father only as "the man who must not be named." Dinny and David had made it clear that the family wasn't allowed to mourn or reminisce: By 1999, the Johnson home had been purged of any trace of Luke Johnson.

According to Joan, it was David Collie's idea. As if to finally murder the memory of Luke Johnson, the men ransacked the house, throwing away anything they could that reminded the family of their deceased husband and father: tearing out book inscriptions that Luke had penned, removing family photographs of Luke, and throwing out any mementos, Christmas gifts, and sentimental trinkets that were linked to Luke.

Even the grand portrait of Luke as a young man, a painting that had always hung proudly and conspicuously at the top of the stairs, was gone. Poof—it just went missing one day. The way Joan tells it, she was out running an errand when the portrait disappeared:

Attorney: "What happened to [the portrait]?"

Joan: "Dinny and David took it. They took it off—I went away to do an errand. When I came back, Dinny and David had taken it and they told me they took it for safekeeping."

Attorney: "But why didn't—if they took the painting of your husband, the father of your children, off the wall in your house, without your permission—why didn't you do something about that, ma'am?"

Joan: "Because I was—I didn't want to have a confrontation with them. I'm by myself. I have two very young children and I'm not going to go against two great big men."

And later in the same testimony:

Attorney: "What about just pictures of Mr. Johnson? Mr. Johnson around the home, Mr. Johnson perhaps with the children?"

Joan: "There were pictures of Luke at the—just all his life. And David went through and found where they all were. Actually, I have a photo album at home with pictures and they were old-fashioned, I had glued them in with rubber cement. Someone systematically went through and tore out certain pictures."

———————————

It seems that, to some degree, David Collie had succeeded in erasing all of the family's lingering memories of "the man who must not be named." With all the physical remnants of Luke Johnson's life removed from the house, the darkened rooms gathered an even more ominous, pressing gloom—no past or future lived there, only the fearful present.

And despite all of the warning signs, despite the fact that her whole life—and Seth's and Kaleta's—seemed to be disappearing, Joan did nothing. Joan's failure to act is one of the most mysterious aspects of the story. In fact, it was a central theme in the 2008 civil trial: Why had she allowed David and Dinny's abuse to continue for years and years? Many of Joan's explanations were confused and muddled, as if even she didn't fully understand how she allowed it to happen. Under normal circumstances, if an outsider entered your home and removed precious family treasures, it would be considered theft. But during this time, the Johnson household was far from normal: Joan's personal property got about as much attention and protection from David's and Dinny's greedy hands as her children did.

Once the physical reminders of Luke Johnson were disposed of, Dinny and David began changing the Johnson home to suit their tastes—doing anything that made them feel comfortable, no matter what Joan and the children thought. The TV was moved from the living room to the garage apartment that had once been Wirt's— that was Dinny's request. The garage apartment was then locked, and Dinny had the only key. The family wasn't allowed to watch television unless Dinny said it was OK—he claimed that it was for the children's sake; he wanted them to do their homework and take more of an interest in sports. And when Dinny did allow the apartment door to be unlocked, there wasn't much discussion as to what they would all watch: This wasn't a democratic system. So while the rest of the world was watching popular shows like *Survivor* or *Who Wants to Be a Millionaire?*, the Johnsons had to be happy with classic films—usually starring Cary Grant and especially Rock Hudson—that Dinny loved so much.

During this same time, Joan, Dinny, and David went on another cleaning spree, just as they had in 1996. But things were different now—this time, it was Dinny who took control of sorting and organizing the rooms piled high with collectibles and antiques. Dinny's detail-oriented, methodical approach to housekeeping was what made him so good at restoring order to Joan Johnson's piles and piles of financial documents in her home office. So as he began cleaning out Joan's attic, he decided to document exactly what Joan had stored away. Dinny began making lists—many, many lists—

keeping meticulous inventories of Joan's property. And while these lists serve as concrete examples of Dinny's ultra organized, Type A ways, they also hint at a more sinister side: According to Joan, Dinny Shah was shopping.

At least seven pages of numbered inventories were submitted into evidence at the 2008 trial—all of them in Dinny Shah's handwriting, though he wouldn't admit to writing them. These lists enumerate hundreds of Joan Johnson's possessions, which ranged from the mundane: ashtrays, ice buckets, Christmas ornaments; to the decadent: silver Tiffany frames from the 1930s, chandeliers, humidors, and several American prints and paintings; to the bizarre: top hats and tuxedos. The clothes—some of which were antique, some of which belonged to Luke Johnson—take up four pages of the inventory. In his notes, Dinny documents more than fifty pairs of pants, twenty sport coats, and heaps of other outdated fashions: smoking jackets, capes, country suits, and pocket watches. According to Dinny's testimony at the 2008 trial, Joan wanted a record of these items because she wanted to sell them and clear out the attic.

But in some places, the lists appear to be more than simple inventories. While many pages do appear to be catalogues of Joan's valuables, the documents also contain to-do lists, reminders, and personal notes—all in Dinny's hand. These other entries cover a broad range of topics: Ordinary household tasks—like a reminder to repaint Seth's room—are juxtaposed with financial notes, presumably part of Dinny's plan to sort out Joan's finances. The inventory includes entries like "Sell Allen Park Inn—$750,000," "Sell Bank—$2,000,000," and "Sell 502—$8,000,000." While these entries are relatively easy to explain—Dinny was constantly monitoring Joan's finances, shuffling money and selling stock— some of the other notes read more like Dinny's personal wish list. Numbers 16 and 17 of one two-page inventory are "Plane: Twin-Engine King Air 200" and "Lear Jet Gulfstream V," both of which Dinny claimed Joan wanted to purchase because she didn't like flying commercially. Joan would later claim that she had no intention of buying a private jet. These notes, she said, were solely Dinny's. There are also the names of many exclusive clubs included on the lists—Forest Club, Bayou Club, New York Yacht Club—all of which it is likely Joan wanted to look into. Ever since her family had ceased membership with the River Oaks Country Club, Joan longed to belong to an elite, upscale social club reserved for only the wealthiest, pedigreed families. Other clubs on the list seem as if they are meant mostly for Dinny, like the New York Stock Exchange Luncheon Club and the India Club—organizations that Joan certainly would have no interest in.

There would be a little more breathing room in the Johnson home after this cleaning and categorizing escapade. On June 9, 1999, Joan carted some of her more dispensable items down to Hart Galleries, an upscale consignment store in Houston. The furniture was mostly just odds and ends—a breakfast table, a few sets of armchairs and wingbacks. Totaling a little over $6,000, Joan's spring cleaning consignment items amounted to a measly sum compared to the millions of dollars worth of valuables gathering dust in the attic.

As Dinny and Joan set about taking inventory and sorting Blaffer treasures, Dinny was making an inventory of his own; several of Joan's heirlooms had caught his eye. On May 11, 1999, just a month before Joan's furniture was taken to the consignment shop, Joan signed a series of affidavits gifting three guns to Dinny. Similar to the affidavit that granted Dinny the $1.2 million, the typewritten series of letters say that Joan wished to gift Dinny the following items: a 20-gauge shotgun made in Belgium, a 1925 rifle with the initials "JHB" —a family heirloom once belonging to John Hepburn Blaffer—and another 20-gauge shotgun with the initials "DB." Joan was an avid gun collector and a crack shot with a pistol, so it was unusual that she would want to give any of the precious guns in her collection to Dinny. Interestingly, a month before, Joan had already given Dinny another valuable pistol—an antique from World War I that had belonged to her father—as well as a rare

American wingback chair circa 1700. In the affidavit concerning the World War I pistol, Joan says:

> *I know the value of this pistol may be significant, but this does not concern me because I wish this gun to be given to Mr. Shah.*

It's probably true that the actual value of the gun didn't matter much to Joan. She had plenty of money, after all, but how could a person give up something that held so much sentimental value? When cross-examined in 2008, Joan gave the only answer that she could: "I was scared and didn't want to—but I did." The typewritten "affidavits" where Joan signed over her heirloom guns may have been coerced out of her, with Dinny breathing down her neck, forcing her to sign. But affidavits have to be notarized and sworn to before an unbiased third party, in this instance usually a notary at a nearby bank. No outcry was made to the notary. The names of at least three experienced, reputable notaries appeared on the many affidavits Joan signed: J. C. Latour (commissioned in 1985), Patricia V. Ledbetter (commissioned in 1982), and Sharon A. Marsh (commissioned in 1983). Notaries are required, by the Texas Notary Handbook, to refuse to notarize a signature if he/she "feels the act is: for a transaction which the notary knows or suspects is illegal, false or deceptive; or for a person who is being coerced; or for a person whose demeanor causes compelling doubts about whether the person knows the consequences of executing the document. . . ." Three experienced notaries looked Joan in the eye over the years, found nothing amiss, and notarized the affidavits. The notaries did their duty. Joan was a good actress on those occasions. But Dinny was always nearby and perhaps that is a mitigating factor. Joan testified that she would hand the notary her affidavits while Dinny sat comfortably in the background, munching on the bank's cookies.

What's more, Joan gave Dinny three of the guns in May 1999— *after* the beating that left her with a broken rib and after the terrifying night at the Biltmore in California. No rational person would give a gun—let alone four—to someone she was afraid of, a person who had punched and pounded on her just a month or two before. Joan did. And she'd find out, in 2001, just how much she would regret giving Dinny the guns. If she was scared of Dinny in 1999, her fear was only going to intensify in the coming years.

"Mommy, Don't!"

As bad as things were for Joan, life was significantly worse for Seth and Kaleta. The children lived in constant fear, and with good reason: In the Johnson household, the tiniest infraction—an unauthorized snack, a messy room, or even a typical brother-sister spat—could end in punishment at the hands of Dinny Shah or "No Mercy Dave" as he would soon be known. Seth and Kaleta did their best to fly under the radar, whispering to each other in the home's darkened hallways and tiptoeing past Dinny's office (he was prone to fits of rage if disturbed while he was "working").

Unlike most children their age, Seth and Kaleta didn't play outside. They didn't ride their bikes down Del Monte Drive and they didn't have sleepovers or run around with the other kids in the neighborhood. Seth and Kaleta lived like prisoners: They only left the house to attend school or for family outings; they were all but forbidden to have friends or any social life outside of the house.

This fearful existence would be too much for almost any child, and it's nearly impossible to imagine any parent turning a blind eye to this kind of emotional and physical abuse. But during this time, Joan Johnson would admittedly be less than protective of her children. In fact, it seems that Joan did more than simply ignore the abuse: There is ample evidence that she contributed to the violence—and the accompanying cuts, bruises, and bumps—that Seth and Kaleta were growing accustomed to.

One of the most compelling pieces of evidence submitted by Dinny's defense team is a memo from Seth and Kaleta to Joan. It is dated February 21, 1998—when Seth and Kaleta were just eleven and nine years old, respectively—and it serves as a painful and sad testament to the abuse that Kaleta and Seth suffered at the hand of their own mother.

The document, titled "Things for Mom to Work On!," is written in uneven, childish print and reads like a wish list of sorts, a numbered petition that details the children's grievances. The memo seems to be organized in descending priority: The last item on the list is a request that Joan sign Kaleta's schoolwork promptly. Oddly, items #3, #4, and #5 on the list are concerned with Joan's mouth: "don't talk too much," "keep your trap shut," "don't talk too much on the phone." It's unclear why Seth and Kaleta were so concerned about Joan's talking: Perhaps the children felt that Joan spent too much time chatting with friends, or maybe they felt badgered by her. Or maybe this criticism was a product of Dinny's influence—Shah often chastised Joan and the kids for talking too much, and it was certainly in his best interests to keep the Johnsons quiet.

At worst, the latter half of Seth and Kaleta's list makes Joan out to be a distracted, forgetful parent—chatting on the phone and letting Kaleta's schoolwork fall by the wayside. On their own, these gripes are hardly damning evidence. But the top of the list paints a darker picture: The first item on the memo is "don't scream"—a reference to the fact that, according to Dinny, rather than disciplining her children, Joan often engaged Seth and Kaleta in screaming fights more suited to a sibling than a parent. But it is the second item in the memo that is the most jarring: "no violence/kicking."

It seems that Dinny and David weren't the only ones to take out their rage on the children: Joan Johnson, too, had learned the art of carefully placing blows so that they left no visible marks.

―――――――――――

For their part, Seth and Kaleta told the court that they had no memory of writing the list. While neither denied that it was written in Seth's hand and signed by both of them, they did deny having any memory of why or in what context they wrote it. During Dinny Shah's civil trial, the defense team went in circles with Seth and Kaleta, trying—and ultimately failing—to get the children to open up about Joan's suspected abuse. According to Kaleta, the list was probably something that Dinny had encouraged them to write. "I must have written it but I just don't remember. Seth and I were, you know, we were encouraged to tease our mother and to vilify our mother," Kaleta said. "He, you know, at a certain point he told us not to call her 'mom' anymore. The defendant wanted us to call her 'Delta' because he said that delta was a Greek symbol for chaos and he says that my mother would turn everything into chaos."

Seth, too, named Dinny as the catalyst for the "Things for Mom to Work On!" memo. When cross-examined by the defense counsel in 2008, Seth could think of only one explanation as to why he would write the memo:

Attorney: "What did you mean when you put 'no violence/kicking' [in the letter] to your mother in February of 1998, please?"

Seth: "I don't know what that means. I have a feeling that's dictated to me."

Attorney: "Dictated to you? That's the first we've heard of that. Can you tell us, did you just make that up?"

Seth: "Did I just make that up? I have no memory of that letter, sir. But I do not think that is something I would write on my own unless someone encouraged me to write that. I do not write lists like that today."

It was frustrating testimony: On the stand, both children sidestepped questions that should have had simple, direct answers. As the plaintiffs in this case, it was to Seth and Kaleta's advantage to make Joan appear as a good mother and a weak woman; someone who, though she loved her kids, wasn't strong enough to stand up to the evil forces of David Collie and Dinny Shah; someone who was beaten regularly, much like Seth and Kaleta themselves, to the point of absolute surrender. The jury would be led to think there were three children in the family.

But as the "Mom" memo illustrates, Joan did not act as an ideal mother. She sometimes engaged in physical abuse of both children— even admitting to it openly at the 2008 civil trial.

The trick is, according to Joan, to slap or kick your children just enough so that it hurts but not hard enough to leave marks. Dinny's trial team slowly developed this theme and then one day late in the afternoon Joan began to unravel. Her admission and detailed explanation of how to discreetly abuse a child—without leaving evidence—stunned the courtroom into silence:

Attorney: "How did you learn the skill of kicking your children without leaving marks?"

Joan: "By not kicking hard enough to leave a mark."

Attorney: "Well, I understand that . . ."

Joan: "I mean, you know, there's a slap and then there's a—harder. I'm not, you know, I mean, if a football players kicks somebody as hard as they can, it would be devastating to the person they kicked. But I have never kicked the children as hard as I could and with big old boots or shoes. You normally wear flip flops or tennis shoes."

The origin of the "Mom" memo may never be clear. Was it an honest cry for help? That's certainly plausible, considering that even Joan admitted that she often hit or kicked her children. Or was it, as Seth claimed, written under duress—the product of Dinny Shah's campaign to control the children and paint Joan as the source of the chaos and violence.

While it's impossible to know exactly how the "Mom" memo came about, it is interesting to compare the memo with another letter that surfaced during the civil trial. The letter, which Dinny submitted, presumably as evidence of the children's behavioral problems, was a letter of apology, written from Seth to Dinny.

Seth's apology letter stretches on for a little more than a page. While the letter is not dated, the large, careful handwriting and recurrent spelling mistakes suggest that this is the work of a very young Seth Johnson. However, the syntax, vocabulary, and high level of reflective thought seem like the work of an adult—probably Dinny—dictating to Seth. Seth had always struggled in school; the letters he wrote home from camp, even the Christmas cards he addressed to Joan and Dinny, were brief and barely legible. The wordy and effusive apology letter, in contrast, makes a strong case that Dinny probably did tell Seth what to write.

The letter begins with an admission of guilt, and it reads like a detailed confession of Seth's wrongdoings:

> *I did not do my math worksheets for three weeks. . . . I misbehaved in Mrs. Liviere's Spanish class. . . . I scratched Dinny's Patek Philippe on purpose because I did not get a laptop computer because of my grades and my actions.*

The end of the letter takes a bizarre turn, both in content and in tone. After spending nearly a page listing his various offenses, Seth switches gears, heaping praise on Shah:

> *It was not fair of my [sic] to scratch your watch just because I was mad that I was not getting a laptop computer. It was not your fault after all you have done for me like buying the new penny loafers [sic], dress shirts, costomade pants [sic], some of the food I eat, the books I read, and taking me places, and telling*

me very important things so I could know more about places
not to go to when I am older and more experienced [sic] in life.

The conclusion of Seth's letter reads less like the handiwork of an elementary school student and more like a regurgitation of Dinny's words (and inflated sense of self). Much like Joan's extremely generous affidavits—for the guns and priceless antiques she signed over to Shah, as well as the $2.5 million in cash and stock she gifted Dinny for his "helpfulness as a family friend"—Seth's letter sounds stiff and stilted. Knowing Dinny's personality—his sense of ego and his need for control—it is very likely that many of the Johnson family's personal letters and affidavits were the result of Dinny's coercion.

Dinny was obsessed with documentation—in the six years that he lived with the family, he had Joan write hundreds of affidavits and memos detailing every aspect of the Johnsons' lives, from Joan's financial transactions to who was allowed to watch the house while Joan was away on vacation. Perhaps the children picked up Dinny's strange habit of writing letters and memos; it seems they were often forced to do it by Dinny anyway. Or perhaps writing a letter to their own mother was Seth and Kaleta's only way to get her attention. Regardless, the differences between the "Mom" memo and Seth's apology letter are striking: The frankness and simplicity of the verbiage in the "Things For Mom to Work On!" note—so different from Seth's apology and Joan's affidavits—reads more as an authentic letter of appeal from Joan's children than a falsified plea coerced by Dinny.

———

Seth and Kaleta weren't the only ones who felt that their mother had things to work on. Dinny was critical of the way Joan disciplined her children: During his trial, he recounted several instances in which she crossed the line. He told the court about one particularly brutal incident in which he had felt compelled to step in, pulling Joan off of Seth and saving the little boy from a beating: Joan became increasingly annoyed at Seth at a backyard barbeque. When she'd finally had enough of his antics, she picked Seth up and slammed him down on the concrete edge of the pool. Seth and Joan began to wrestle—again, more like siblings than a mother and her son—until Joan managed to pin him down. As she raised her hand, ready to smack Seth across the face, Dinny broke up the fight.

Joan's relationship with Kaleta, Dinny claimed, was even more volatile. Dinny believed that Joan paid much more attention to Kaleta than she did Seth, constantly berating and picking at the little girl. Dinny told the court that they fought a lot, and that he had personally witnessed Joan strike Kaleta on multiple occasions. Joan's physical abuse, he said, was one of the reasons Joan insisted that the children stop seeing Dr. Farley, a local adolescent and pediatric psychiatrist. As early as 1996 or 1997, Dinny began taking the kids to see Dr. Farley in an attempt to get to the bottom of their obvious behavioral and disciplinary issues. Joan refused to participate in the sessions, allowing Dinny to drive Seth and Kaleta to their therapy appointments. After a few visits, Joan complained that Dr. Farley's services were too expensive, and that she wouldn't pay for any more visits. But according to Dinny, the appointments made Joan nervous—she felt the children were telling Dr. Farley too much, stories about how Joan regularly hit, kicked, and screamed at them. Embarrassed and afraid of any legal repercussions that might result from the visits with Dr. Farley, Joan put a stop to the children's therapy sessions.

Dinny's accusations make sense, in context: After all, Joan was a borderline alcohol abuser according to Dinny, although there is not much direct evidence to support that. She dropped in and out of Alcoholics Anonymous sessions, though she often drank at charity events and social gatherings with Houston's über wealthy families. Besides, she'd already had CPS called to come and investigate the well-being of Seth and Kaleta twice in their short lives—a third occurrence would happen in 2001—and she wasn't going to risk another report by Dr. Farley.

The first CPS report was made back in 1994, the night that Kaleta triggered the alarm system, inadvertently summoning police to Luke Johnson's Morgan's Point home. When the officers found the children without any adult supervision, CPS was called to investigate both Joan and Luke.

In 1999, CPS investigated Joan a second time concerning allegations that Joan was hitting and kicking Seth and Kaleta. A concerned teacher at St. John's School made the report, but Joan got off the hook with the help of her defense attorney, Earl Lilly of Piro & Lilly. Joan would use this firm again in 2001 when CPS stepped in a third time after Seth reportedly showed up at school with a bright red slap mark on his cheek. That incident, the family alleged, was Dinny's fault; he had slapped Seth and then instructed Seth to tell his teachers that Joan did it. Seth would later claim that he complied with Dinny out of fear, and blamed his mother when the authorities came knocking. Instead of telling the truth and pointing her finger at Dinny, Joan managed to convince the CPS investigator that the red mark on Seth's cheek was actually a rash. She avoided another close call with the authorities and failed to alert the CPS investigator to Dinny's abuses—again.

———

There is no denying that Dinny categorically isolated and terrorized the Johnson family for years. But in cases such as this, it's necessary to take a good, long look at who enabled Dinny to inflict so much pain on the family—a good, long look, that is, at Joan Johnson. Perhaps she was as terrified of Dinny and David Collie as she claimed to be; she had, in fact, been brutally beaten by them multiple times in the past and would continue to take the abuse until 2002. Perhaps that is the explanation. She said so.

The children were, quite literally, trapped. They were at the center of Joan's relationship with Dinny and David—their behavioral problems, their homework, their discipline were the things that provoked many conversations, and verbal and physical fights, between Joan and her companions. Many of the children's problems predated Dinny and David's arrival in the Johnson home, probably a combination of the turmoil that afflicted the household during Joan's divorce with Luke, the circumstances of Luke's sudden death, and, of course, Joan's occasional violent relationship with her children.

Curiously enough, Joan's parenting lapses were the reasons that David Collie gave for finally breaking off his relationship with Joan sometime in 1999 or early 2000. The kids were out of control, and Joan, he felt, did nothing but stand idly by. David Collie's testimony on this subject may have just been an easy excuse to bail out, to disentangle himself from a bad situation: By 2000, it seems that David had had enough of Dinny, too, and just wanted to get away from the whirlpool of abuse and violence that had built up between himself, Dinny, and Joan.

First Accusation of Sexual Abuse

The children may have been in their own small hell, but unfortunately, the physical abuse may not have been the worst of it. As early as 1996, there were hints that there was something far more sinister at play— evidence that Dinny, David, or both, may have been abusing the children from the very beginning of their relationship with the Johnsons.

In late 1996, Joan came to David with a confession: Wirt was plotting against him, was thinking about accusing David of molesting Seth. Once Joan heard the news from Wirt, she brought the issue directly to David. It's hard to know what David's reaction was to this, but what does seem clear is that somehow after the discussion, the subject of sexual abuse between David and Seth was dismissed, discreetly swept under the rug.

Why was Joan so dismissive about Wirt's accusations regarding sexual misconduct between David and Seth? Was it because she believed Wirt was making up stories? Perhaps this was the jealous invention of a cunning sixteen-year-old who wanted David and Dinny out of the Johnsons' lives. Like any teenager, Wirt could be manipulative; it also goes without saying that he probably resented the men's new role as disciplinarians in the Johnson household. Wirt, Joan claimed, had no evidence of sexual abuse; he had no proof. Or was Joan so desperate for an engagement ring that she would turn a blind eye to the truth? Whatever the reason, it seems that a few sweet words of denial were enough for Joan to put the idea of sexual misconduct out of mind, enough for Joan to turn against Wirt and believe David's version of the story.

Testimony from the 2008 civil trial suggests that, while the accusation of molestation may have been false in 1996, it wasn't far off the mark. After Wirt Johnson was shipped off to boarding school, the family alleges that David and Dinny's relationship with Seth and Kaleta began to cross the line.

For two people who claimed to adore Joan's two youngest children, David and Dinny had a funny way of showing their affection. According to the Johnson children's testimony, their relationship with the two men was based on constant criticism, sarcasm, and harsh punishments. Even light-hearted jokes and games turned hurtful. According to Seth and Kaleta, David Collie was particularly fond of games, and he even made up special ones for each child: Seth's game involved pliers, and Kaleta's involved creeping, prying, pinching fingertips.

Seth's game always started with an innocent round of tickling that quickly got out of hand. Seth alleged that David Collie would trap Seth in a scissor lock and tickle him until he couldn't stand it anymore. On one such occasion, Seth was pushed past his breaking point: He peed all over himself as a result of one particularly acute tickling assault. Soon after that, the hair pulling started. Seth recalled that occasionally, after he was pinned down, David Collie would pluck hairs from Seth's head, sometimes with his fingers, sometimes with a pair of pliers. During his oral and video deposition, David denied these accusations, though he did admit to tickling and horseplaying with Seth from time to time. Seth, however, remembered the painful, humiliating hair-pulling "games" vividly.

Kaleta's game was called "ants in the pants." It, too, started out innocently enough—with David Collie just horsing around, tickling Kaleta as she shrieked with laughter. But every round of "ants in the pants" ended the same way—with pain. As Kaleta put it, David "would pinch me very hard on my behind, the back of my legs and leave these little purple bruises" all along her backside. The hair-pulling and tickling incidents were two of the many "games" that eventually earned David Collie the nickname "No Mercy Dave" in the house.

David was very careful never to play the "ants" game in front of anyone else—not Wirt, not Joan, and not Lupe, the nanny that Joan hired to watch Seth and Kaleta from time to time. But it wasn't long before Lupe eventually noticed the many bruises and red marks on Kaleta, which were the result of multiple rounds of "ants in the pants." According to testimony, Lupe reported Kaleta's bruises to Wirt, who in turn told Joan. Perhaps this was the origin of Wirt's molestation accusations. Regardless, no action was taken by anyone to stop the "ants" game, and no evidence exists that Joan spoke to David about it or alerted the authorities. Her desire for David seemingly overshadowed her responsibilities as a mother; instead, she chose to ignore the questionable, abusive "game" that David engaged in with Kaleta.

Of course, years later, David denied ever hurting Kaleta while playing the "ants" game, though he did agree that it was a game they played often. It was just another form of "horseplay," like the basketball matches he and Seth would have in the family's driveway. He claimed that Kaleta loved the game—she would laugh when he tickled her—but the bruises that reportedly dotted her bottom and thighs, David said, were fabricated for the benefit of the Johnsons' case in court.

But according to Seth and Kaleta, the "games" didn't end with David Collie. Although Dinny never participated in the tickling games, he wasn't one to let David have all the fun. It seems that Dinny had games of his own—mind games that were less evident, more slyly circuitous. And though Dinny's games didn't leave physical evidence, the emotional scars he left ran deep. During the trial, both children recalled, in chilling detail, some of the "talks" they had with Dinny—mostly concerning their father.

According to Kaleta, the picture of Luke Johnson that hung prominently at the top of the Johnsons' stairwell served as a convenient conversation starter. Dinny told Kaleta (who was only about seven or eight years old at the time) that there were "things she needed to know" about her father—mainly about his homosexual affairs. And these "discussions" didn't end there: Seth and Kaleta testified that from 1996 to 2002, Dinny would torment the children about their gay father, speaking in a sexually graphic manner— totally inappropriate for children—and in a way that puzzled and confused them. All of this was on top of the constant barrage of insults that Seth and Kaleta already endured from their classmates after word of Luke's homosexuality leaked out at school.

Why the preoccupation with Luke Johnson's sexual orientation? In the 2008 trial, Dinny suggested that Luke had taught Seth about homosexual male activity, about "the things that men do together." Was this part of Dinny's plan to shield himself from the allegation of sexual abuse and to direct it toward the deceased father? According to Dinny, Seth was already exhibiting wildly inappropriate sexual behavior as early as age ten. Dinny recalled one evening when the family was dining at The Stables, an upscale Houston steakhouse, when Seth reached over and grabbed their waiter's crotch. According to his testimony, Dinny was flabbergasted, but Joan simply dismissed the behavior as something that Seth "learned from his father."

In court, Seth vehemently denied Dinny's suggestions, claiming that it was Dinny, not Luke, who taught Seth—firsthand—about homosexual activity. Dinny introduced the topic to Seth by discussing "man love," an ominous lead-in to what would become more horrifying behavior.

While no formal investigations were ever made, the 2008 trial often focused on Seth's and Kaleta's claims of abuse—sexual, physical, and emotional—at the hands of Dinny and David. But the Johnsons' accusations—however compelling—were undercut by one thing: Joan Johnson's failure to protect Seth and Kaleta from their alleged abuser, to blow the whistle.

Joan couldn't claim innocence regarding Writ's accusations against David Collie: She was the first person he told about the purported sexual abuse. But either Joan didn't know about the subsequent incidents—like the conversations with Dinny about Luke's homosexuality, or David's "ants" game and hair-pulling incidents—or she did, and her desperation to secure David's heart and Dinny's financial "expertise" allowed her to turn a blind eye to what was happening right in front of her.

Who Lies to Her Diary?

On one particularly boring afternoon in 1997, Seth did something that he shouldn't have. He was rummaging through his mother's things, when he came upon a slim green diary. And of course, he couldn't help but read it. As he flipped through the pages with the mischievous curiosity of the ten-year-old he was, he came across the following entry:

Sunday, November 17th

Writ's false accusations of David has led D. C. [David Collie] to believe that Wirt will accuse him of molesting Seth. He [David] went so far as to say "who knows what a jury would say in this country?" Would a jury believe D. C., or a plot between Wirt and Seth. David thinks that Wirt will bribe Seth.

Wirt's accusation could be very grave and if D. C. never calls back I wouldn't blame him. Of course, at this point he [illegible] us and beat W. D. J [Wirt Davis Johnson]. All he has to do is _ _ _ _ _ their mother. So easy but I bet he won't. He will take the "sensible" path of least resistance.

I wish David would ask me. I saw a strange heart-shaped box. I asked if I could open it. He said "no." I have a notion he

was contemplating presenting me with a ring in it. That has less
chance of happening now.

Like most of the other elements of the 2008 civil trial, the
story surrounding Joan's diary is clouded with finger-pointing and
accusations; the truth, not surprisingly, is hard to pin down. But
what most everyone can agree on is this: After Seth found the diary
entry in his mother's bedroom, he did something else he shouldn't
have—he showed it to David. And David did not take it well.

Although Joan had told David about Wirt's potential molestation
accusations back in 1996, the diary entry gave David an insight that
he hadn't considered before: In the world of the ultra wealthy, there's
no such thing as "keeping up with the Joneses." When money can
buy you anything you could possibly want—aside from David's
ring—accusations of misconduct and inappropriate behavior are
often used to manipulate, to get a leg up on another person.

As David read the entry, it all suddenly became clear to him.
Could Joan have meant, "In order to make this scandal go away,
all he has to do is _m a r r y_ their mother"? Whether or not this
is the correct interpretation of Joan's muddled thoughts, it's the
interpretation that David adopted; David believed that Joan had
planned to use her own children as pawns to blackmail him, to trick
him into marrying her in order to avoid a public scandal.

According to Dinny Shah, this diary entry is proof that Joan
had cooked up a classic case of entrapment. And it's true that Joan's
diary reads less like the words of a concerned mother and more like
the pining of a melodramatic teenager in love. Joan doesn't seem
overly worried or concerned about Seth, and she appears unfazed
by the idea that her lover might be a child molester. She didn't call
the police, and she certainly didn't take any special precautions to
keep David away from the children. In fact, the diary entry reveals
that she seemed more concerned about her relationship with David
Collie than any kernel of truth that may have been hidden behind
Wirt's accusation.

Shocked that Joan had been a part of the molestation accusations, and with what he believed to be tangible proof of the blackmail plot, David and Dinny rushed to copy the entire contents of the diary in Joan's home office. Twelve years later, these copies, along with the diary itself, would be submitted as evidence in the civil trial. But it wasn't Joan who supplied the information; in 2008, the diary was in Dinny's possession as part of his role as custodian of the family records, along with thousands of other documents that would be made public as part of the "discovery" process.

But are all of the back-and-forth allegations true? Would Joan sink so low as to use her children as pawns, to keep this information as backup in case David didn't want to marry her? Certainly, her next action does her no credit, especially if her children were actually being abused. Joan was so willing to keep David and Dinny in her good graces that she completely panicked when Seth showed David the diary. One can almost imagine her pleading with the two men, promising to make amends.

And those amends were quickly forthcoming.

Right after Dinny and David discovered the diary entry, Joan and David went down to the notary's office. There, she signed a series of rather shocking affidavits. Dated February 19, 1999, Joan confesses her plan to blackmail David:

> *I am in love with David Wade Collie and when I am mad at him, I often use wrongful tactics and make untrue statements about his character and Mr. Shah's character. On one such occasion I lied about Mr. Shah's and Mr. Collie's intention with my daughter, Kaleta Johnson. I implied that there was sexual misconduct on the part of Mr. Collie and Mr. Shah. This accusation and statement was a lie by me. Mr. Collie refused to marry me and I stupidly thought that I could entrap him, Mr. Collie, into marriage by lying about his intentions and Mr. Shah's intentions.*

It's unclear why the affidavit mentions Kaleta, when the diary entry specifically states that the accusations involved Seth, but it may indicate that there had been discussions involving the possible abuse of both children. This affidavit was followed by two less shocking but still telling affidavits on the same day. These affidavits gifted Dinny the antique World War I pistol that had belonged to Joan's father, as well as an eighteenth century wingback chair—the same pistol and chair that Shah had picked out for himself while helping Joan clean and organize her overstuffed house that spring. It's hard not to speculate that these gifts were meant to help ease Dinny's wrath—"make up" presents for Joan's bad behavior. David, it seems, didn't receive any gifts on the day these affidavits were signed, nothing more than the peace of mind that the signed affidavits canceled out any possible accusations of sexual impropriety between him and the Johnson children.

Yet despite her desperate attempts to placate David and Dinny, things would soon get worse—not better. Dinny and David were just getting warmed up.

Joan's scheme to trap David by getting him to marry her—if that is what it was—had, indeed, backfired. And Seth and Kaleta would pay the price. Joan would soon realize that the tables had turned completely and that she, herself, had become the victim of entrapment. It would happen sometime in early 2000, when Dinny officially moved into the house at 2933 Del Monte Drive.

Moving Day

What Dinny did with the millions of dollars that Joan gifted to him remains a mystery to this day. However, there is one indication of how he spent some of that money. Being the financial whiz that he is, Dinny decided to invest part of his haul in real estate: He became a homeowner. Moreover, he became a River Oaks homeowner, a member of one of Houston's most exclusive and posh neighborhoods.

The house at 67 Tiel Way just off Kirby Drive, is modest compared to some of its more ornate and extravagant neighbors: a three-bedroom, three-and-a-half-bathroom, mid-century home hidden behind a mask of trees and shrubbery. In 2008, the property was valued at $1.4 million. But in 1998 when Dinny Shah was house hunting, he bought 67 Tiel Way for a song at around $900,000.

But even though Dinny was a brand-new homeowner, he never moved in. The denizens of Tiel Way waited anxiously to meet their newest neighbor, but he didn't materialize. The house sat unoccupied, no furniture inside, for years. But it was not unkempt—Dinny never would have let his investment deteriorate and fall to pieces. Instead, he sent Luis Moran, Joan's trusted handyman, to mow the lawn and look after the place once a week.

Thanks to Joan's generous gifts, Dinny had effectively "arrived": He was a millionaire, a homeowner, and, most importantly, he had a highly valued River Oaks address. But the four miles that stretched between Del Monte Drive and Tiel Way was just too much distance for him. He had already become the financier and father figure that the family never had, and he wanted to retain that position, to keep his watchful eye on the Johnsons. So instead of moving into his new house, Dinny decided to make his relationship with the Johnsons a little more intimate: In 2000, he moved into their home on Del Monte Drive.

———————

Dinny's official move into the Johnson home warranted yet another affidavit, signed by Joan on February 16, 2000. Like most of the Johnsons' affidavits, this one is long and rambling; in it, Joan paints a glowing picture of Dinny as a helpful friend and father figure. And like most of the other affidavits, this one feels slightly stiff and stilted, as if Joan were taking dictation rather than expressing her own feelings:

> My name is Joan Blaffer Johnson and I am a resident of Houston, Texas. I reside at 2933 Del Monte Drive in Houston, Texas. D. K. (Dinny) Shah is a family friend. He has known me and my children for many years. I asked Mr. Shah to move into a spare bedroom of my home. My husband, Luke Johnson, Jr., died in 1995, and Dinny has helped me with my children tremendously.
>
> I feel that it is important to have a nice young man in my home to call upon in any type of situation. In addition, Mr. Shah, in the event of an emergency or my incapacitation, is the guardian for my minor children, Seth C. B. Johnson and Kaleta H. H. Johnson. Mr. Shah will and should have full access to my home at ant [sic] time. Mr. Shah is also fully informed of

all of my business activities and in fact knows every aspect of my financial and business affairs. In the event that something should happen to me or should I become incapacitated in any way or form, Mr. Shah should be relied upon as the parent of my children and as a counselor and true family friend. Mr. Shah manages his on [sic] portfolio and has his own business activity. He is completely up-to-date on all of my business activities.

On the stand at his 2008 trial, Dinny claimed that he had never seen this affidavit, that Joan wrote it of her own accord. It's difficult, however, to imagine Joan penning an affidavit like this, especially at this point in her relationship with Shah. According to the Johnsons' testimony, by 2000, the "nice young man" had been beating and berating the Johnson family for two years—since the day Dinny and David flogged Kaleta on the family's vacation to Florida.

Did Joan really believe that Dinny was a true friend? Was he really that helpful with the children? And most importantly, had she forgotten about the broken rib she had suffered at his hand, about her terrifying night in the Biltmore, the broken rib she would later have x-rayed at River Oaks Imaging?

———

Shortly after Joan signed this particular affidavit, Dinny Shah became the man of the house, the unofficial head of the household at 2933 Del Monte Drive. And from the beginning, he made one thing abundantly clear: From now on, he was calling the shots.

Although there was, as Joan's affidavit indicated, a spare bedroom in the Johnson home (Wirt's old room), it didn't meet Dinny's particular, peculiar standards. For whatever reason, Kaleta's bedroom—decorated with pink walls and pink curtains, a little girl's room—was the only bedroom that would work, Dinny decided. It was as simple as that. Dinny would take Kaleta's room, Kaleta would move into Seth's room, and Seth would take Wirt's old bedroom. It was an intricate chess move, with clothes and furniture and personal articles being carted up and down the hallways of the Johnsons' second floor until Dinny had positioned everyone right where he wanted them.

In 2008, neither Kaleta nor Seth had any real memory of the details surrounding Dinny's moving into the Johnson home. There had been no family discussion, no opportunity for questions: Dinny just moved in one day and took over Kaleta's bedroom. Like a grand conquistador, Dinny brought his things and claimed his pink-curtained territory, giving the children no choice but to obey his commands. And he did it all with Joan's complete cooperation, or at least her lack of objection.

There was no real reason for Dinny to move into the Johnson home: After all, he had his own house just minutes away. And even if he had insisted on living with the Johnsons, he could have stayed in the garage apartment, which had been renovated nicely and had remained unoccupied since Wirt had been dropped off at boarding school and told never to return home. The garage apartment would have offered the privacy befitting a young bachelor and would have been a more appropriate place for him to sleep, rather than just down the hall from Joan's young children.

But privacy wasn't an issue for Dinny—not when it came to Joan and the children. With Dinny in the house (rather than in the garage apartment), it was virtually impossible for any of the Johnsons to have any privacy of their own: They couldn't move, speak, eat, or breathe without his knowing. In Kaleta's bedroom, he could have total control over what went on in the house. And the fact that the room shared a wall with Seth's didn't hurt either.

Dinny often made jokes about becoming Seth's father, about replacing Luke through adoption. Occasionally, Dinny would take his "jokes" a step further and introduce the boy as "Seth Shah." It seems that Dinny's preoccupation with Seth had increased to disturbing proportions, but Joan apparently did not notice, or perhaps had reconciled herself not to care. Over the next two years of his cohabitation with the Johnsons, the temptation of the cute, blond little boy in the bedroom next door would only fester inside Dinny's mind until the day when—Seth claims—Dinny managed to orchestrate his own obsession's tragic and unfortunate climax.

As most people were celebrating the arrival of the new century, the year 2000 marked another event for the Johnsons: a point of no return. The Johnson home, the drive still wrapped tightly by the black tarp that forbade curious eyes from peeking in, became Dinny's private kingdom. He would be the catalyst for many of the dramatic and bizarre events surrounding the Johnson family through the end of 2002; family squabbles would continue, Joan constantly fighting with her sisters over their joint property while Dinny gently cultivated her finances. Wirt would be further excluded from the family as Joan tried to lock him out of her will and his own trust. And Kaleta, Seth, and Joan would suffer unimaginable horrors—increasingly cruel physical abuse and the initiation of Dinny's perverse sexual abuse. Dinny would place the family under house arrest: Mail and phone access would be restricted, friends would be cut off, and even the family's clothes would be handpicked by Dinny. Every day, depending on Dinny's mood, was a crapshoot: Would it go well, or would Dinny fly off the handle again?

Even David Collie, Dinny's right-hand man, would jump ship. By 2002, he'd manage to find his own way out of the trap that Dinny had created—much to Joan's dismay.

Heartbreak

Attorney: "Did you tell her you loved her?"

Collie: "Yes"

Attorney: "You discussed marriage?"

Collie: "We discussed it, yes."

Attorney: "The relationship, the romance, cooled at some point after six months. Is that fair to say?"

Collie: "I can't remember when it cooled. It cooled after the Seth incident with the Game Boy when Joan was teaching Seth to lie and steal."

Attorney: "And that's the incident that caused you to think, 'hmm, maybe I don't want to marry this woman?' Is that right?"

Collie: "Yes."

There had been talk of marriage between Joan and David Collie as early as 1996; just six months after David met Joan, he hinted that perhaps—while he was away with Dinny on some sort of "business trip" to New York City—Joan might fill up her time by doing a little engagement ring browsing. In Joan's mind, it was as if David had already proposed to her, an idea that she wouldn't give up for years. All of this talk of weddings and rings and happy futures came right in the midst of the tumultuous events of 1996, after Wirt accused David of sexually abusing Seth, but before Seth discovered Joan's diary entry and showed it to David and Dinny.

To Joan, David Collie represented a second chance at romance, a replacement for the romance she had but lost during her marriage to Luke Johnson. Being married to David would put an end to loneliness, the frustration of being a single parent. Being married to David would mean possible access to the River Oaks Country Club set and the social standing that came with it.

There was no way for her to know that in less than a week, David Collie would change his mind. Thoughts of engagement would be over by the time David returned to Houston.

Interestingly, as abusive as David and Dinny allegedly were, it was Joan's incomprehensible parenting that David cited as his reason for finally pulling away from the relationship: According to David, Joan showed her true colors when Seth come home one afternoon with a new Nintendo Game Boy.

The incident occurred when David and Dinny were in New York; Joan noticed that Seth had a toy she'd never seen before, and she knew that David and Dinny hadn't purchased it. When she asked Seth about it, she found out the truth: Seth had stolen the Game Boy from a classmate.

He'd unzipped the unsuspecting owner's backpack and slipped the Game Boy into his own bag—and he'd gotten away with it. Not surprisingly, word quickly spread from Houston to New York: Joan, who wasn't used to making decisions on her own, called Dinny and David for advice. David said that Seth needed to return the Game Boy to his classmate and apologize—publicly—for taking it. But Joan, perhaps not wanting to embarrass her family name, had other ideas: She told Seth to simply return the Game Boy, to slip it back into his classmate's backpack without saying a word.

In the 2008 trial, David recounted disagreeing with Joan over the matter:

Attorney: "What happened in the case with Seth when he made, when he stole a Game Boy?"

Collie: "This happened when Shah and I were in New York . . . when I talked to Joan, I told her, I said, 'Well, Joan, you just told Seth that it's OK to lie and steal.' What Ms. Johnson did was to tell Seth to put the Game Boy back in the kid's backpack without even telling him. And when Seth—when I got back home, I talked to Seth about it, and I said, 'You can't do this, otherwise you're going to grow up with no friends . . .'"

On the surface, it seems like an extreme reaction, to break a relationship over a Game Boy—especially a relationship that was at the point of an engagement. Maybe David Collie really did see a defect in Joan's personality—her drinking, her childish naïveté, her lack of responsibility—and was simply cutting his losses before he married her and really got himself in trouble.

A few months later, a letter from Joan to David on October 25, 1997, indicates that David was ready to end his romance with Joan. Joan, however, seems desperate not to let him go. The letter reads:

> *Dearest David,*
>
> *Please do not forsake us. We need yours and Dinny's help. You have contributed so much to our lives over the past year. . . .*
>
> *I am so sorry I keep making mistakes and annoying you. It is not intentional. Please believe me.*
>
> *It may all be lost if you pull out so soon, now. There is a bumpy demon waiting to devour us. Return; help us build a house of stone against him. We cannot do it without your help. . . .*
>
> *Much love, Joan*

Perhaps the plea worked, because although David and Joan don't seem to have had much of a romantic relationship after 1997, David was certainly still involved with Joan's life. He went on family

vacations—like the memorable trips to Florida and California—
with the Johnsons. And Joan, for her part, continued to rely on his
help.

For instance, just before Thanksgiving in 1998—two years
after the Game Boy incident—Joan signed the following affidavit:

> *I am away on a trip for the Thanksgiving holiday. I have given*
> *complete and full permission to David Wade Collie to house-sit*
> *for me at 2933 Del Monte in River Oaks. Mr. Collie can act*
> *on my behalf for any emergency and any nonemergency. No*
> *one else has permission to enter my home at 2933 Del Monte*
> *without David Wade Collie's permission. David Wade Collie*
> *is also in charge of my business affairs while I am away on this*
> *holiday.*

This would be the first of several documents regarding the keys
to her home over the upcoming years. Every affidavit, starting in
1998 and ending in the summer of 2001, explicitly stated that David
Collie would be house-sitting for her, and that her own son, Wirt
Johnson, was not allowed in the house under any circumstances: Her
relationship with Wirt had degenerated to the point where he was
not allowed to come home during his breaks from college. By early
2000, Joan trusted Collie more than her own son, and in several of
her signed affidavits, Joan states that Wirt would be prosecuted if
he showed up unannounced on Del Monte Drive.

In the aftermath of their broken romance, Joan also still relied
on David to help her with the kids and the finances and everyday
errands. Both David and Dinny were named godparents of Seth and
Kaleta—for the second time—in June 2000. And in September
2000, Joan signed another slew of documents giving Dinny power
of attorney on all sorts of real estate and financial matters, including
medical power of attorney, again. David Collie—who claims that he
broke up with Joan four years before these documents were signed—
is listed as the alternate agent to Dinny. Either Joan wouldn't face

the truth about her waning relationship with David, or perhaps David never made it clear that the romance was over. She could have had anyone—one of her numerous lawyers, for example, or Sharon Bryan or another trusted neighbor—fill in as executors on her accounts, but she didn't. She wanted David—and if she couldn't have him as spouse, if she couldn't have all of him, at least she could have a part of him on the power of attorney's signature block.

In the years following their supposed breakup, David seems to have been continuing to participate in "disciplining" the children. At the 2008 trial, Kaleta recalled a particularly unhappy memory regarding David Collie. It was the summer of 2000, and David and Dinny were driving Kaleta home from somewhere—perhaps school or a quick shopping trip. According to Kaleta, once they pulled up to the Johnson home, Dinny left the car in the driveway with the key still in the ignition, the engine running. Kaleta noticed Dinny's mistake but didn't say anything. After monitoring the car for a half hour, Kaleta finally decided to take action, to do what any normal person would do: She turned off the car and returned the keys to Dinny.

This, however, was the wrong thing to do. Dinny was livid. Kaleta shouldn't have touched what wasn't hers. According to Kaleta, Dinny and David hauled her upstairs to her room. David fashioned a large, pointy dunce cap. Kaleta was forced to sit stock still in her room with the dunce cap on her head, her mouth taped shut for good measure. Of course, David and Dinny denied ever treating Kaleta that way, but the children had a different story: "No Mercy Dave" was continually berating them, calling them "stupid" and things of that nature, and the dunce cap punishment had happened on more than one occasion.

Collie was also still playing sidekick to Dinny. In December 2000, Collie accompanied the entire Johnson clan, along with Dinny and Henry Dyches, on Christmas vacation to Newport, Rhode Island. The family often vacationed there, staying in various bed and breakfasts. It was during this trip that the family alleges that Dinny went on a rampage: He beat Seth with a belt and hit Henry Dyches over the head with a book.

These documents, and his continued involvement with the family, suggest that Joan believed that Collie would be in her life for years to come—and that the possibility of marriage still existed.

And indeed, Joan was correct.

On June 2002, David finally decided to marry. Unfortunately for her, David didn't marry Joan. In fact, according to Joan, he didn't even tell her about his impending marriage, didn't invite her to the wedding.

When Joan finally found out—as Dinny described it—it was an almost unbearable humiliation: While at a River Oaks party, Joan was gossiping with some girlfriends. She mentioned something about eventually marrying David Collie. That's when she was politely informed that David was recently married to another woman by the name of Melinda Stuart. David had met and started dating Melinda, a retired banker from New York, sometime in 2000. For two years, Joan had been unaware that Collie was seeing anyone else, still holding on to her dream marriage, until that bubble was burst in a very public way.

It's unclear exactly how Joan was kept in the dark about Melinda: Dinny, for instance, knew that Collie was dating another woman, but he never told Joan. Even Seth and Kaleta met Melinda when she moved from New York to Houston in February 2001 to be closer to David. She was working at Schumacher's, an interior design firm, when Dinny and David stopped by with the kids. (Interestingly, Seth remembers Dinny introducing him to Melinda as "Seth Shah.") Neither one of the children, though, really understood what David's relationship with Melinda signified, especially not for their own mother. Perhaps they assumed that Melinda was just another friend of David and Dinny, so no one said a word to Joan.

Regardless, after meeting Melinda in January 2001, it was clear that David quickly became disinterested in the Johnson household and in Dinny. So David cut him loose, too, sometime in 2001.

Attorney: "I want to make sure we understand. Are you friends with Shah today?"

Collie: "No, sir."

Attorney: "But you were friends and good friends previously?"

Collie: "Yes, sir."

Attorney: "Did you trust Shah?"

Collie: "At the beginning, yes."

Attorney: "But not at the end, right, not by May 30, 2002?"

Collie: "Trust? Hmm. Did I trust him? No."

As the wedding bells for David and Melinda were chiming in early 2002, David finally took steps formally to disengage himself from the Johnsons, even though he hadn't been a regular visitor to the house on Del Monte Drive for more than a year. Indications of David's slow disengagement from the Johnson household are intangible; it happened almost imperceptibly, even for Joan. During the 2008 civil trial the focus of the testimony slowly shifts starting in the year 2001; David is rarely mentioned after this point. There are no more documents giving him the keys to Joan's house while the family was on vacation, no real indication of David's presence in the house or in the family's lives. The last mention of David Collie's interaction with the family is a single good-bye letter to Joan dated May 30, 2002. The letter, not surprisingly, is brief and void of emotion:

> *Dear Joan,*
> *I have enjoyed helping you and the children out over the years. I am sure the children will continue to grow and do well in school. I feel as though I have become a godfather to Seth and Kaleta. I wish you and the children all the best.*
> *Sincerely Yours, David Collie*

Perhaps David had forgotten that he actually *was* the legal guardian and godfather to Seth and Kaleta, in addition to holding Joan Johnson's medical and financial power of attorney. A few months later, David apparently remembered the power of attorneys; a terse letter to his and Joan's mutual Merrill Lynch broker would sever these ties with the Johnsons forever. His final letter regarding the Johnsons ends with: *Please remove me effective immediately as I thought I was no longer power of attorney on Joan B. Johnson's account.* That sentence encapsulates David's entire relationship with Joan, Seth, and Kaleta: A one-time father figure turned tormenter, Joan's one-time lover, was now just a distant memory. There is another potential reason for his distancing act: Perhaps he feared that Dinny's manipulation of Joan's bank accounts and brokerage account could be laid at his doorstep. It would not do to have power of attorney in that event. David Collie, Dinny's eager wingman, would sense impending danger. To protect himself from legal liability once suit was filed he would retain excellent legal representation. He would escape the clutches of a jury trial. He would settle his case. A rich kid survivor.

Capitulation: She Buys Her Underwear at Walgreens

Joan Johnson had given up almost all of her autonomy. Dinny made every household decision, from family finances to the children's education to how the Johnsons spent their free time. In fact, by the time Dinny had settled in to his new digs at Del Monte Drive, Joan had control over exactly one thing: her underwear.

Once a month or so, Dinny would accompany Joan (she wasn't allowed to go out by herself, if Dinny were around) to Walgreens, where they'd stock up on things for the house—soap, shampoo, toothpaste. While they were there, Joan would also stock up on the cheap cotton panties sold in packs at the drugstore. It must have been an unimaginable humiliation: one of the wealthiest women in America—granddaughter of the founder of Exxon—buying her underwear at Walgreens.

Those plastic packs of underwear were the only thing that Joan was allowed to buy without Dinny's input, the only thing she could choose for herself without fear of criticism, or worse.

Dinny had already had his way with Joan's home, rearranging the furniture and reassigning bedrooms as he saw fit. He was already picking out fabrics and ordering custom draperies to suit his tastes.

It wasn't long before he decided that the home wasn't the only thing in need of a few updates.

The Johnson family was about to get a makeover—in the way they looked.

In 2000, Dinny informed Joan that she and the children would no longer be getting their hair cut at Estevan's, the Greenway Plaza salon they had frequented when Luke Johnson had been alive. After a little research, Dinny decided that Joan would now be going to Urban Retreat River Oaks, a trendy salon and spa on Westheimer.

So for the better part of two years, the routine was the same: Dinny would drive Joan to her appointment at Urban Retreat. Joan would sit quietly until her hair was finished, staring absently into the mirror and avoiding all but the most inconsequential small talk with her stylist: She was afraid that if she said too much or spoke out of turn or offered her own opinions, word would eventually get back to Dinny. And she was terrified about what he might do. After paying the bill and saying a polite good-bye to the staff, Joan would wait for Dinny to pick her up from the salon.

Joan later testified that she complied with Dinny's choice in stylists because she knew that it was easier to do exactly what he said than to try to fight with him—especially over something as silly as her hairstyle.

But the makeover didn't stop with Joan's hair. While Dinny had always taken pride in his eye for expensive fashion, Joan didn't share Dinny's flashy taste; she was, after all, the same woman who chose to drive a Ford when she could easily have afforded a Mercedes or a BMW. Joan's clothing was well-made but far from ostentatious. Dinny, however, felt that Joan didn't dress the part of a River Oaks woman. On a vacation to New York, he took Joan to an Armani boutique, where he acted as if he owned the place, ordering salesclerks around, picking out suits for Joan, and having them tailored for her to his specifications. In Houston, Dinny would take Joan to fashionable dress shops in the Galleria, River

Oaks Shopping Center or Highland Village and pick out clothes for Joan to wear. It was here that Joan bought an Ann Taylor suit. Joan, for her part, never offered an opinion; she wasn't allowed to have one. She just tried the clothes on and paid for the items Dinny deemed acceptable.

———————

Dinny Shah cultivated his fashion sense from the classic styles of Old Hollywood. According to the Johnsons, Shah studied antique fashion magazines and old books and movies for inspiration. He himself often dressed in an oddly formal style reminiscent of the 1930s and 1940s. He still dresses this way today: If you saw him on the street, he would most likely be wearing a tailored blazer and pleated trousers, a pair of suspenders, and either a bowler or a Casablanca hat to complete his look.

And while Joan—middle-aged, distinguished, and wealthy—could actually pull off Dinny's taste in clothes with a modicum of dignity, Seth and Kaleta could not. Especially not in 2000, when both children were attending junior high.

Luckily for Kaleta and Seth, uniforms were mandatory at their private schools. Otherwise they might never have survived the taunting and bullying and humiliation of the clothes that Dinny insisted they wear, especially not Kaleta

On the stand in the 2008 trial, Kaleta explained that Dinny was obsessed with the Kennedys; he admired the easy style and grace of the Camelot years. He studied Jackie's wardrobe, the tailor-made suits and custom-fit gowns that she was known for. When the inspiration struck him, he'd take out a pen and paper and design his own interpretation of a Jackie-O dress—always very formal and much too old-fashioned for a preteen.

But Dinny didn't care. He'd take his designs to his trusted seamstress, Samantha Scott Cooper, where he would fuss over fabrics and cuts. Sometimes, he'd arrive with Kaleta in tow; she was subjected to numerous fittings before each dress was finished. It wasn't long before the teenager had a closet full of expensive, high-quality dresses, tailored to Dinny's exact specifications.

And she never wore them—not even once.

For the children, it was relatively easy to avoid wearing Dinny's bizarre, Kennedy-inspired creations. After all, Kaleta never had any occasion to wear her Jackie-O dresses; it's not as if Dinny would have allowed her to go to a formal gathering. Seth and Kaleta, however, couldn't escape the humiliation of the "casual" clothes that Dinny outfitted them in every weekend—designed, of course, by dear Dinny himself.

Attorney: "Did the defendant ever get to the point where he would tell you what type of clothes to wear?"

Kaleta: "Yes."

Attorney: "How so?"

Kaleta: "He would take both Seth and I to a tailor and he would have pants and shorts made for us, but they were very strange. They were, you know, the full trouser pant leg with the pleat and cuff and, you know, it wasn't something a little girl would ever wear. And he had us wear that all the time with a polo shirt and—"

Attorney: "What do you mean, it wasn't something that a little girl would wear?"

Kaleta: "Well, I was dressed almost like a boy. It was like he wished for me to dress as a boy."

Dinny's behavior in wanting Kaleta to dress like a boy is not only bizarre but frightening in light of subsequent events involving the children. Did Dinny want two little boys around?

Anyone who's ever been a teenager knows exactly how confusing that time can be, how hard it is to navigate the world, to try to fit in with your friends and distance yourself from your parents. But to survive junior high dressed exactly like your older brother in outdated fashion is just one more burden that Kaleta had to bear throughout her formative years. And it wouldn't be the last humiliation she'd suffer—Dinny would ridicule her throughout her adolescent years, making fun of her changing body and using Kaleta's fluctuating weight as an excuse for a beating.

Whenever the family went out to dinner or a movie or shopping, they were a sight to see: pressed and starched in their tailored duds, looking as if they had stepped out of a black-and-white movie, Joan in her tailored suit and the children in their matching collared shirts and trousers.

And Dinny, the top-hatted, strutting, surrogate father figure, couldn't have been more proud.

———————

Though the family had been given a new look (no matter how out of fashion it was), everything remained the same inside the house. If anything, Dinny's temper and his controlling tendencies got worse after he moved into the Johnson home. The family had felt stifled before, but they were about to experience the suffocating loneliness of true isolation from the outside world.

A few months after he moved in, Dinny instituted a new rule: All personal communication between the Johnsons and the outside world would stop, immediately. If Joan or one of the children wanted to call a friend or mail a letter or even surf the Internet, they had to clear it with Dinny first.

It was after Dinny moved in that all of the phones in the house started disappearing—except for the phone in Dinny's office. He unhooked the phones in the kitchen, the study, the spare bedrooms, everywhere. Kaleta and Seth, now at the age when talking on the phone should have been a vital part of their burgeoning social lives, knew better than to ask if they could have a phone installed in their rooms. Dinny never would have allowed it.

Joan Johnson was the only person to ever answer the phone. But she wasn't allowed to answer the phone without Dinny sitting by her side. If the telephone rang, Joan would answer and immediately put the caller on speakerphone so Dinny could hear every word of the conversation. Often, he'd whisper in her ear, instructing her on what to say, how to respond. This was standard protocol, no matter who was on the phone—one of Joan's lawyers or financial advisors, a teacher from Seth's or Kaleta's schools, even personal phone calls. Of course, by this time, personal calls were scarce: Joan didn't have many close relationships with family or friends, no one that would call to just check in on her.

On the rare occasion when Seth or Kaleta received a phone call from a friend or classmate, the routine was the same: Joan would answer the phone with Dinny by her side. She would then call in Seth or Kaleta, and they would have their conversation via speakerphone, Joan and Dinny listening the entire time.

And for Kaleta, the monitored phone conversations could be humiliating.

It was the fall of 2002, and Kaleta was in eighth grade. A friend of hers—a male friend—called to invite her to a movie one weekend. When Dinny heard this, he instructed Kaleta to decline the boy's offer, which she did. But crushing the boy's hope of taking Kaleta to a movie wasn't enough for Dinny: Once Kaleta hung up, Dinny picked up the phone and hit callback.

When the boy answered, Dinny gruffly demanded to speak to his father. When the father answered, Dinny let him have it. He didn't bother with small talk or introductions; he went straight into yelling and screaming: *How dare you let your son call this house? Kaleta can't go out. She's too young. She won't ever go out with your son, how dare you let him call her?*

Needless to say, the boy's father was startled and confused. The next day at school, Kaleta apologized to her friend, but she didn't bother explaining exactly why Dinny had flown off the handle, had chewed out his father. Who could ever understand Dinny's motivations, unless they had to live with him? Like the phone, Dinny needed to have complete control over any mail that came in or went out of the Johnson household. He didn't need to bother himself with the mundane task of actually checking the mail himself; he'd let Seth or Kaleta or Joan go down to check the mailbox. But once the mail was in hand, they had to walk it straight into the house and up the stairs, surrendering everything to Dinny. He was the only person allowed to open and read the mail, and sometimes he'd dole out letters after he'd perused the contents. The Johnsons, Seth and Kaleta especially, knew how particular he was about the mail, and they didn't want to test his temper: They'd collect the mail without even looking at it, too afraid of what Dinny might do if he saw them flipping through the sealed envelopes.

Kaleta was the first to discover just how serious Dinny was about the mail: She had kept up a correspondence with one of her former nannies, Alma. Most of the time she just wrote short letters—nothing scandalous or unusual, just general musings from a sixth-grader. As she went to collect the mail, Kaleta would have her letter to Alma in her pocket, and she'd discreetly leave the letter in the mailbox to be delivered to Alma.

But that stopped in 2000, when Dinny, watching from an upstairs window, saw Kaleta deposit the letter in the mailbox. Her punishment: a spanking as soon as she got up the stairs.

By 2002, Dinny's paranoia and his compulsion to control the Johnsons had become unmanageable. It was October, just two months before he was forcibly removed from the Johnsons' home. A deliveryman knocked on the door, and Joan signed for the package as Dinny watched from the hallway. As soon as she closed the door and put the package down, Dinny kicked Joan in the leg.

Confused and in pain, Joan asked for an explanation. The kicking, Dinny said, was her punishment for "being too friendly" with the deliveryman.

These accusations about the phones and the mail, of course, were denied by Dinny at the 2008 trial. To his knowledge, he could never recall regulating the mail or monitoring telephone conversations during the six years that he was acquainted with the Johnsons.

To circumvent Dinny's chokehold, the family often had to use devious tactics for the simplest things—they could rarely, if ever, leave the house without him. Of course, violating any of Dinny's rules risked subjecting yourself to one of Dinny's spasms of rage. This was particularly true for Joan and Kaleta.

On one occasion not long after Dinny moved in, Joan and Kaleta made an unauthorized purchase. The two went out shopping at the River Oaks Shopping Center on West Gray. It was a secret shopping trip; they had to sneak out of the house to avoid Dinny's inevitable questions. But while they were out, they made a grave mistake: Joan bought her daughter a bracelet—a bracelet with little purple beads, something that had really caught Kaleta's eye.

It wouldn't go unnoticed by Dinny. Later that night, as the four set out for an elegant dinner at Anthony's, Dinny noticed Kaleta's new bracelet. That's when the questioning began: *Where did you get that? You haven't had that before. Where did it come from?*

Trapped in the car with Dinny, and with no quick excuse that would satisfy Dinny's questions, Kaleta was forced to spill everything about her secret shopping trip with Joan.

The betrayal was too much for Dinny to handle: How could they have gone shopping without him by their side, without him telling them what to do and what to buy? In one quick, brutal motion, Dinny slapped Kaleta for her insolence. He reached over and snapped the new bracelet from her wrist. Then he rolled down the car window and tossed it out, where it landed in the gutter. He continued to rage as he drove on, telling Joan and Kaleta that neither one of them deserved to go out to dinner with him. They were, in his eyes, badly behaving children.

As Kaleta described the incident in court, she showed a maturity beyond her young years. She understood Dinny, could see through his lies better than Seth and better than Joan, which is probably why Dinny often treated her with the most contempt. Recalling the bracelet incident, Kaleta testified that "you know, he would get furious any time we did anything that he hadn't told us to do or that he hadn't controlled."

But if Dinny was so concerned about keeping a low profile—about not letting anyone get close to the Johnsons, not allowing the Johnsons to get too far out of his reach—he certainly wasn't very good at controlling his temper around other people. Sharon Bryan and Olabelle Hall, Joan's neighbors, were already greatly concerned and suspicious of Dinny's relationship with the Johnsons. As his controlling tendencies toward Joan, Seth, and Kaleta grew deeper, he started showing his true colors, started erupting in front of more and more outsiders. This sent warning bells to everyone that happened to cross Dinny's path—from the neighbors on Del Monte Drive, to Joan's own lawyers and financial advisors, and, above all, numerous administrators at Seth's and Kaleta's schools.

The Reverend George Aurich, Memorial Hall's headmaster at the time Seth Johnson was attending the school, recalled a "meeting" with Joan, Dinny, and David. In an interview documented in February 2002, Aurich recalled the incident vividly—and the strange power David and Dinny seemed to wield over the Johnson family:

"Rev. Aurich stated that it was obvious that Mr. Shah and Mr. Collie were in charge, did all the talking, and if a question was asked of Ms. Johnson, either Mr. Shah or Mr. Collie would answer. Rev. Aurich said that it was apparent to him that Mr. Shah and Mr. Collie dominated both Ms. Johnson and Seth Johnson. It appeared to Rev. Aurich that Ms. Johnson was incompetent to make any decision and that all decisions were to be made by Mr. Shah and Mr. Collie."

Surveillance

As Dinny was busy playing house and dress-up with the Johnson family, Wirt was living his own story and becoming more and more estranged from the family. After graduating from Rocky Mountain Academy, Wirt went directly to college without even returning home for a visit. His first stop was Whittier College in Whittier, California, just a few miles southeast of Los Angeles. It was at Whittier that Joan began surveillance of her own son—and tipped their relationship past the breaking point.

———————

The California-based detective that Joan hired, Ellen A. Gold of Paula Drake Investigations, was paid to follow Wirt and feed Joan information about what he was doing, where he went, and who he was hanging out with. Gold's "reports" to Joan included the most mundane details of Wirt's life—what Wirt was wearing (usually shorts and a T-shirt), how many books he was carrying, when he left his dorm room, and where he went (he never seemed to go anywhere titillating—usually just to the student union building and back). Forty hours of surveillance and thousands of dollars during that summer led to nothing more than the workaday, commonplace information about Wirt's life that could have been garnered from a simple phone call. But Joan felt that she couldn't trust her son; their relationship had been strained for too long. Letters regarding Wirt's surveillance, one dated September 18, 2000, show just how far Joan and Dinny would go to keep tabs on Wirt—and to find any reason at all to cut him out of the family fortune:

> *Dear Ellen,*
>
> *Thank you for your report. I am sorry that I have not been in touch with you but I have been very busy with my two younger children. Can you please find out which dorm room number Wirt is living in and who his roommate is? I have sent a check to you for your services. As far as having an ongoing surveillance of Wirt: I think that watching him on the weekends would be the best bet. I would like to know what he does on the weekends and who his friends are there.*
>
> *Sincerely, Joan Blaffer Johnson*

Joan and Dinny, it seems, had so little contact with Wirt that they didn't even know his dorm room number and, it would seem, had absolutely no idea what he was doing out in California aside from attending school, let alone how his grades were. To say the least, it was not the typical behavior of a mother who'd just sent her firstborn son away to university.

Reconciliation seemed to be far from Joan's game plan: It seems that the only contact between Joan and Wirt during this time was a battle over Wirt's legal documents. For some reason, Joan refused to send Wirt his Texas driver's license, birth certificate, and Social Security card. In 1997, Wirt had been shipped off without any of these documents; he didn't need them at Rocky Mountain Academy anyway, but now, as a nineteen-year-old, his lack of identification would bar him from something as simple as applying for a credit card or applying for a part-time job.

An undated letter from Wirt to Joan— most certainly written during Wirt's college years—shows Wirt's frustration with Joan:

> *Dearest Mother,*
>
> *. . . Now, on the birth certificate, WHY ARE WE ARGUING OVER A STUPID BIRTH CERTIFICATE? CAN'T YOU EVEN BE A NORMAL ENOUGH $*$%$%* PARENT TO SEND ME MY BIRTH CERTIFICATE. I will contact the Texas Records Department and get my own copy, since you forget that I am a Texan, am from Texas, and Texas is my home state. I told you things are going to change, no I am not telling you what to do since you seem to be very sensitive about me doing that, but I am merely restating that this ridiculous arrangement/relationship is going to change. I have patiently bided my time and done what I said I would do out here, patience for these games is wearing thin. I really can't figure out what your game is, do you think that by continually pissing me off, you are accomplishing some greater good, hopefully you at least get some kind of entertainment out of this.*

Soon after, Wirt did what any silver-spoon-wielding trust fund baby would do: In 2000, he hired a lawyer, Miami-based Christopher Boyett of Holland & Knight LLP, to protect his interests. After Boyett was hired, most of the communication between Wirt and Joan went through their respective lawyers, including a letter sent from Boyett to Lacy, Joan's lawyer at Andrews Kurth, requesting that Wirt's driver's license be returned to him.

All subsequent communications, however, weren't going to be pretty. Wirt was going to use his new lawyer to take control of his own finances that had previously been guarded by both Joan and Dinny.

At some point after his relationship with his mother had crumbled, Wirt started asking questions about money. He was under twenty-five years of age, and therefore, under the provisions of his trust, unable to access any of the money himself. The trustee on his account was—naturally—Joan Johnson, his mother.

But because of the animosity that had cropped up between the two, Wirt had his lawyer order a request of accounting for both of Joan's standing trusts. He wanted to know that his money was being protected—and he wanted to know exactly how much of the family's fortune was rightfully his.

But Wirt's strong-arm methods to receive an accounting of the Johnson family trusts would be blocked by Joan's lawyers at Andrews Kurth. A letter from Douglas E. Clarke at Andrews Kurth to Wirt's lawyer stated these facts:

> *In conclusion, it is Mrs. Johnson's position that:*
> 1. *The statements [regarding Joan's two trusts] not be turned over to Wirt.*
> 2. *Wirt has not requested an accounting.*
> 3. *Wirt is not entitled to an accounting.*
> 4. *If Bessemer decides, as Trustee, to provide him with an accounting of Trust A, then Wirt should have to pay for it in advance and said accounting should be done by Reed Jordan and no account statements should be provided to Wirt in the accounting.*

Clarke argued that Wirt was not a beneficiary of Joan's trusts, not even as a lineal descendant of Joan. Neither were Kaleta and Seth—though Joan would soon make provisions to carve portions of her trust into new trusts for Seth and Kaleta. Wirt, however, was entitled to only a small portion of Joan's Trust A, but only for educational purposes—nothing beyond that.

What's more, Joan started taking steps to lock Wirt out of any of the family's money. Wirt did have his own trust—the Wirt Davis Johnson trust—but Joan was determined not to let him have a penny of it. There's no real explanation as to why Joan's reaction was so severe: Was she just used to fighting tooth and nail with family members—as in the case of her sisters—over money? Or was she simply following orders—doing what Dinny demanded without stopping to ask questions?

In a 2000 letter to Andrews Kurth, Joan's more vindictive side appears. In the letter, Joan states, quite plainly, that she would like to appoint a part of her trust to both Seth and Kaleta, but that:

> *I have no reservations nor any misgivings about leaving my older boy, Wirt Davis Johnson, out of this appointment. My older boy, Wirt Davis Johnson, has benefited much more financially in the past and the fair thing to do is to give [it] to my two younger children, Seth and Kaleta Johnson. Furthermore, for many years now, Wirt has demonstrated that he will never change and he has caused great problems for me and my two younger children. He continues to cause a great many problems and no matter how hard I have tried to keep him on a good path, he just wants to do wrong. . . . I am sure that I desire and want to make this appointment to Seth and Kaleta and I have absolutely no reservations about leaving Wirt Davis Johnson out and not participating in these trusts.*

It's unclear what types of "problems" Wirt was causing for his mother, especially since he was living thousands of miles away, in California. Was she simply annoyed that Wirt had requested an accounting of the family's trusts? Was she upset that Wirt didn't trust her judgment and her position as an executor over his finances? He had, obviously, been a violent and disrespectful teenager; perhaps Joan just refused to forgive and forget her son's bad behavior from years before.

In any case, Joan wasn't going to stop there. Joan was adept at combative legal and financial matters—and she had legions of lawyers and Dinny Shah at her fingertips, all willing to help. She had been involved in numerous legal battles with family members— her own sisters, mainly—for years. Not only was she locking Wirt out of her trusts, she tried to dissolve Wirt's trust. A second letter to Andrews Kurth, dated just one week later on July 27, 2000, states that:

> *I wish for the assets out of Wirt Johnson's Article IVC Trust to be transferred to Seth and Kaleta Johson's Article IVC Trusts. I do not want nor do I desire for Wirt Davis Johnson to benefit from this trust any longer.*

The financial spat between Joan and Wirt raged on in 2001. By that time, Wirt had transferred from Whittier College to Southern Methodist University, to finish out the last two years of his college career. He was now much closer to Houston than he had been before—a fact that would cause Dinny some major anxiety—and he would be relentless in his continuous pursuit of the family money.

As 2002 rolled around, Wirt took legal action against his mother, filing a lawsuit against her in Harris County. The lawsuit states that Wirt's case concerned "a breach of trust between a mother (Defendant) and her minor son (Wirt)." Wirt still had not seen an accounting of his trust; indeed, he was dangerously close to having his mother divide his trust between Seth and Kaleta.

But there was more: In the lawsuit, Wirt accused Joan of continuously draining his trust for her own benefit. Among the accusations were:

> *Beginning sometime in 1987, when Wirt was only 7 years old, Defendant began using Wirt's assets to pay her debts.*

Although smaller withdrawals were made by the Defendant in the beginning, Defendant, realizing that she had unfettered control over Wirt's assets, began withdrawing much more sizeable amounts over time.

In 1992 and 1993, when Wirt was only 12 to 13 years old, Defendant purported to "loan" herself . . . over one million dollars in Wirt's assets. For example, when Defendant's automobile dealership, Luke Johnson Ford, was in financial trouble, Defendant "loaned" Luke Johnson Ford, without a written agreement, collateral, or interest, at least two hundred thousand dollars ($200,000) . . . Defendant also wrote herself over eight hundred thousand dollars ($800,000) in checks . . . None of these over one million dollars in "loans" have been repaid.

Wirt, effectively, was suing his own mother for what he claimed was the entirety of the money that Joan had taken out of his trust over the years.

If Wirt's relationship with his mother was tense, his relationship with Dinny was outright adversarial. Wirt had long blamed Dinny for many of the problems that existed between him and his mother: It was Dinny's influence that caused Joan to take a stand against the spoiled, rebellious teenage Wirt. And Wirt had always blamed Dinny—perhaps rightfully so—for Joan's decision to send Wirt to boarding school. Wirt's contempt for Dinny wasn't a secret. And, for Dinny, Wirt was a dangerous wild card: The oldest Johnson sibling was beyond Dinny's control, so Dinny did everything in his power to separate Wirt from Joan, Seth, and Kaleta.

After his exile to Rocky Mountain Academy in 1997, Wirt's first trip back to Houston was in May 2000. The teenage son that Joan had packed off to Idaho was now a twenty-year-old man, a college kid who was beginning to take an interest in the family finances. Although Joan had made it explicit that he was not welcome at the Johnsons' Del Monte Drive home, he stopped by anyway.

Wirt did not receive a warm welcome. Wirt Johnson's home-coming began—and ended—with Wirt beating fruitlessly on the door of his childhood home. Although the family was home at the time, neither Dinny nor Joan opened the door to welcome him. In fact, immediately after her son's attempted homecoming, Joan wrote a letter to one of her lawyers about getting a protective injunction to legally bar Wirt from being anywhere near his mother and siblings.

Joan, however, never followed through on the suit. Her lawyer informed her that, since Wirt had not been violent toward the family, no legal protections could be put into play.

But Joan's attempts to shut Wirt out would have disastrous results: Older, wiser, and angry at his mother's rejection, Wirt Johnson set out to expose Dinny to be the lying, manipulative snake Wirt believed him to be.

That's why, in the summer of 2000, Wirt contacted Child Protective Services.

———————

Attorney: "When you came back to Houston for the first time in I guess what would be three years, in May of 2000, you said you believe the date was?"

Wirt: "That is correct."

Attorney: "Did you contact CPS, Children's Protective Services?"

Wirt: "Not immediately."

Attorney: "Did you contact CPS that summer?"

Wirt: "Yes, sir."

Attorney: "Why?"

Wirt: "I was concerned about the well-being of my siblings."

Attorney: "Why were you concerned about the well-being of your brother and sister?"

Wirt: "I had not seen them in three years. Upon returning home, I found out that none of their neighbors had seen them, none of their old friends had seen them, none of my mother's friends had seen my mother, drive by the house, the house looked like it was boarded up, curtains closed, general reasons to be concerned. I went by and visited with Kaleta's school headmaster at the time when she was in middle school and while he wouldn't tell me much, I could certainly tell that he had his concerns from the comments he did make."

Attorney: "You said you went by the house. Did you stop at the house or did you just drive by?"

Wirt: "Not the first time."

Attorney: "Did you notice anything—you said the house looked boarded up. There weren't boards on the outside of the house, were there?"

Wirt: "Well, figure of speech. The curtains were all closed, the shutters were shut. There was some type of black plastic tarp that was over the gate. It was certainly not the way I remembered the house."

Attorney: "Why were you concerned about your brother and sister at that point in time?"

Wirt: "Well, I was concerned for their well-being certainly because I had not seen them. That was also about the same time that I became aware [that] Mr. Shah was still there. The reason I know is because I saw his car parked in the back of the house one day."

Wirt, it seems, had been conducting his own type of surveillance on the Johnson family—and as he explained in his 2008 testimony, he didn't like what he saw. Certainly the altered appearance of his childhood home—the curtains drawn, the black tarp that obscured the house from the street—was disturbing to him. And while he was having legal problems with his mother, it was the knowledge that Dinny Shah was now living in the house that really set his blood boiling. Had he known any other details of his family's day-to-day lives—the regular beatings, the phone and mail restrictions, the new regime of fear and control that Dinny had instituted—he may have taken more drastic measures.

Wirt didn't know anything about what was going on behind the shuttered windows on Del Monte Drive—but he did know that he didn't like what he saw from the street, and he didn't like what the neighbors had to report. That's why, in the summer of 2000, he went to CPS to report his concerns regarding Seth and Kaleta.

The next time Wirt visited his mother's home was in the summer of 2002, on the occasion of his grandmother's death. Wirt said that he knocked on the door to drop off an invitation to Seth and Kaleta, but again, no one answered. Wirt knew, however, that someone was home—he could see the curtains moving upstairs as someone peeked out to watch him.

Around the same time, Dinny decided to take his part in the surveillance game. In the summer of 2002, Dinny made sure that he would be the first to know anything about Wirt's life in college—anything that might throw a kink in Wirt's legal battle against his mother or, more importantly, any fodder that could be used to blackmail Wirt.

He hired a Dallas private investigator, David Gillis, to investigate Wirt.

An investigative report of Wirt Johnson was submitted into evidence at the 2008 trial. In the report, which spans September 24, 2002, to November 18, 2002, David Gillis had been hard at work culling facts about Wirt's life: where he lived (a luxury apartment building in Dallas called The Travis), his home telephone number, driver's license number, and previous addresses where he had lived.

But the copy of the investigative report submitted into court had additional handwriting in the margins—a page and a half of notes, actually—all written in Dinny's hand. They were instructions to David Gillis about the types of information to gather. The list is a bizarre hodgepodge that ranges from the day-to-day—like whether Wirt was dating anybody—to the downright illegal:

1. *Need cell phone numbers that he has called*
2. *Credit report*
3. *Girlfriends et al. friends?*
4. *Grades SMU? Since he has been there?*
5. *What addresses shown on Texas Driver's License*
6. *Track home phone numbers?*
7. *Get somebody into apartment. Maintenance—set up bug. Take pictures of inside of place*
8. *Is there a maid? Maid service?*
9. *Car—license plate—picture of car*
10. *Pictures of Wirt*
11. *Credit cards—where is he spending money*
12. *We need to speak to neighbors at all addresses*
13. *Spanish maintenance men*
14. *Girlfriends, boyfriends, etc? Who are they?*
15. *Address books—phone numbers—probably on computer. Access drives on computer*
16. *What airline is he using—Southwest or Continental—to Newport?*

In order to avoid looking suspicious in front of the jury, Dinny countered testimony from David Gillis himself at the 2008 trial:

Attorney: "You know who Dave Gillis is, don't you?"

Shah: "I know that Dave Gillis is a former FBI investigator."

Attorney: "He's a private eye that you hired, yes?"

Shah: "I didn't hire him."

Attorney: "You hired David Gillis, a private eye, to spy on Wirt, didn't you?"

Shah: "No. Mrs. Johnson, your client, was interested in finding out about her son because they were in some form of lawsuit. So I think she wanted to get information about what was going on in his life."

That may have seemed like a plausible answer, but what about that list intended for David Gillis to investigate, written in Dinny's handwriting? Dinny's memory failed him at that moment on the stand: For every item on the list—sixteen in all, ranging from instructions on talking to Wirt's neighbors to having a private eye pose as maintenance to get inside and snoop around Wirt's apartment—Dinny's answer was similar. "That's your handwriting, isn't it, Mr. Shah?" the Johnsons' lawyer asked. "I can't testify to that. . . . I really can't testify to that," Dinny replied. "I'm sorry. . . . I don't know. . . . I'm not sure."

On the stand, David Gillis proved to be a reliable witness, directly contradicting everything Dinny said.

Attorney: "Isn't it true that Shah was a client of yours at some point?"

David Gillis: "It is."

Attorney: "In fact, Dinesh Shah still owes you about $4,000 for your investigative services. Is that right?"

David Gillis: "That's to the best of my memory. I don't remember the exact figure, but it was between four and five [thousand dollars]."

Gillis affirmed for the court that it was Dinny—not Joan Johnson—who hired Gillis to tail Wirt. It was Dinny who paid him for his services using a personal check. David Gillis had never even heard of Joan Johnson; he knew nothing of the drama that was unfolding between the mother and her son, nothing of the accusations that Wirt and Joan threw around so casually.

And he certainly didn't know anything about the accusations that would be brought against Dinny in 2008. He didn't care though; his testimony was a valuable victory for the plaintiffs.

Joan and Wirt's testimony concerning the private investigator reports that Dinny ordered had been suspect; they both had a vested interest in making themselves look good in front of the jury. But David Gillis, who directly contradicted Dinny for no apparent reason other than to tell the truth, exposed Dinny quite publicly as a liar.

In the years following Wirt's exile to Rocky Mountain Academy, no love would be lost between Wirt and Dinny. Though Wirt and Joan fought like cats and dogs, the animosity that had built between Wirt and Joan and Dinny resembled a contemporary version of Hamlet: Dinny, threatened by the young Wirt's temper and willingness to expose him as a liar and manipulator, did everything he could to rid the Johnsons' lives of Wirt. He was able to turn Joan temporarily against her own "bully son," helping her to freeze Wirt's access to his trust. But, as always, in the final act, Wirt rose victorious against Dinny.

Death Threats

Attorney: "Did you ever try to get Mr. Shah out of your house before December 14 [2002], when he was arrested?"

Joan: "No."

Attorney: "Why not?"

Joan: "Because he would have probably killed me or drowned me in the pool. I don't know what he would have done, destroy (sic) me."

Attorney: "Do you believe he was capable of that?"

Joan: "Absolutely. And then [he would have] said I drowned swimming by myself or something. He even told me that he would do that."

Attorney: "When was that?"

Joan: "The last year [Dinny was living with us]. That he would drown me out there in the pool and no one would know the difference. It is disgusting. He is not someone you go against."

As discovery in the civil trial progressed, the laundry list of Dinny's violent acts continued to grow: abuse, manipulation, lies, even theft. However, one of the biggest mysteries of this case is why Joan Johnson never just kicked Shah out of the house. That question hangs in the air even today.

It's hard to imagine a mother putting her children in harm's way, especially a mother with Joan's money and influence. Was this just an isolated example of poor parenting skills? Proof that she was too self-absorbed to notice Seth and Kaleta's suffering? In hindsight, it's easy to shift some of the blame to Joan, to view her inaction as negligence. And perhaps this is the case. Only Joan knows for sure. But perhaps, Joan was simply—and understandably—too afraid to go public about her situation. Her testimony at the 2008 trial suggests that, by the time Shah was arrested in December, she had lost all control. Dinny had taken everything: Joan's money, her autonomy, her sense of self, and her parental rights.

And, according to Joan's testimony, Dinny was willing to take something else, if necessary: her life.

Joan claimed that the first of the death threats centered on a dog carrier that sat vacant in the Johnsons' attic. Poor Prince, the family's dachshund, was dead (Joan, said Dinny, shot the dog in a fit of rage after he had nipped a family friend; she allegedly shot Prince with the same handgun that ended Luke's life). According to Joan, Dinny liked to remind her that that empty pet crate could come in handy if he ever had to kill her: He could simply stuff her body into the carrier and incinerate the whole thing; nobody would know the difference. Soon after, he told her that it would be easy to make her death look like a swimming accident. Of course, these death threats were never revealed to anyone until Dinny's criminal arraignment and bail hearings.

Perhaps that's because Joan really did believe that Dinny would act on his threats. One cannot overlook the potential reality of the "battered woman syndrome" at play here. It is a well-documented factor in prolonged instances of family violence. Why would Joan not reasonably think that death might be in Dinny's plans, given the physical abuse heaped on her? One threat in particular emerged during a dramatic day in her testimony. According to Joan, one of the antique guns that she had gifted Dinny in an affidavit eventually ended up pressed against her temple:

Joan: "He also threatened—he held my gun to my head and threatened to shoot me . . ."

Attorney: "When did he threaten to shoot you?"

Joan: "About two years ago [in 2000 or 2001]."

Attorney: "Was this before you had him moved into your home?"

Joan: "Afterwards."

Attorney: "This was before you gave him power of attorney over your children and guardianship?"

Joan: "Afterwards."

———————————

Because Joan was unable or unwilling, or both, to stand up to her aggressor, her children were left vulnerable to Dinny's attacks. Much of Seth's and Kaleta's testimony in the 2008 civil trial centered on Dinny's violent rage and its consequences. Like the time when, as Kaleta was sitting on Dinny's lap, she accidentally elbowed him. Dinny thought she had done it on purpose. Kaleta got a thrashing with a belt for the offense.

And then there was the time Dinny caught Kaleta picking a few decorative seashells off of a candle in the living room. Enraged, Dinny hit Kaleta repeatedly with a cardboard chair she'd made for a class art project. You couldn't move anything in the Johnson home without permission; Dinny would surely notice, and he wasn't going to like it. Kaleta recalled episodes where she could hear Dinny beating her mother, Joan intermittently crying out for help. The fear was so intense, Kaleta said, that her entire body would start shaking and she would pace in her bedroom. To pass the time, she would clean her room, making sure everything was in place, so that Dinny wouldn't be upset if he paid her a surprise visit. She would become Miss Perfect.

Seth, too, caught the wrong side of Dinny's temper on occasion: A conversation about his poor grades at Memorial Hall School resulted in Dinny beating him with a cane—Luke Johnson's cane, which had a decorative handle shaped like a dog's head. Seth told the court that, "I was being beaten in the office. I mean, I had bruises on my legs, my arms, my chest, even my face. I didn't go to school for almost a week and a half."

Seth claimed that his bruises were so severe that Dinny wouldn't let him out of the house until they healed. This was the daily reality for Seth and Kaleta, living in a circle of fear, abuse, and intimidation.

————————————

Although Joan Johnson couldn't—or wouldn't—try to stop Dinny, others did. As if by instinct, Sharon Bryan, an unknowing Good Samaritan, made one last attempt to save the Johnsons. She couldn't have known about Dinny's death threats, or about how he would beat Joan, Seth, and Kaleta when things didn't go his way. All Sharon knew was that the house had remained eerily quiet, the gate wrapped in an ominous black tarp, for years.

And then there was the strange man she had seen entering and leaving the premises—a man she believed was living with Dinny, a man she did not recognize.

Not long after Dinny moved in, Sharon called Joan. She pleaded with her friend and neighbor: Sharon wanted to get David Collie and Dinny Shah out of Joan's life.

Sharon's pleas, it seems, fell on deaf ears. According to Bryan, Joan Johnson never spoke to her after that phone call; even if they saw each other in passing, Joan wouldn't acknowledge her, wouldn't give a friendly, neighborly wave.

Olabelle Hall, too, had noticed what was going on in the Johnson household. She was with Sharon Bryan when, years before, they went to visit their neighbor, Judge Nancy Atlas, to see if there was any way to rid Del Monte Drive of Dinny Shah. Hall had seen the drapes close, the tarp go up, the children barred from playing outside. The only time she ever saw the Johnsons after Shah moved in, she said during the 2008 trial, was when the car was backing down the driveway.

But Olabelle Hall is not one to sit around idly. One night after Dinny moved in, she picked up the phone and called Joan.

When Joan answered, Hall launched into a series of questions, not wanting to beat around the bush: *What's wrong? I never see you. I never see Seth and Kaleta. Why are the drapes drawn? What is going on?*

What she got in response was a feeble attempt by Joan to skirt around the issue. Joan stammered, throwing out flimsy and bizarre excuses: It was just a rough patch in her life; she wanted to protect the children from being kidnapped for ransom, that's why they couldn't go outside; nothing was wrong at all. Still not convinced, Olabelle Hall asked Joan to make a lunch date with her. Joan agreed.

Not three minutes after Hall had hung up the phone, Joan called back. This time, it was Joan's turn to question Hall: Why did you call me? Did my family call you, are my sisters putting you up to this? A more intriguing question would have been: *Why did Joan call Olabelle back? Had Dinny been listening on the phone the entire time?*

Joan never kept the lunch date she had planned with Hall. This caused even more alarm bells to go off. Much later, as Olabelle and her husband, Gary, turned onto Del Monte Drive after an engagement party for a close friend, Hall saw her opportunity: Dinny, Seth, and Kaleta were walking Vicki, the Johnson's new dachshund, and crossing the street directly in front of the Halls' house.

As Gary started to pull into the driveway, Olabelle jumped out of the car and started running after the trio.

Hall walked right up to Seth, Kaleta, and Dinny and began to make small talk, trying to dig up information and determine the kids' demeanor. But she got very little. Dinny stood there, she said, with "a smirk on his face," listening intently the entire time.

Soon Hall's husband, Gary, joined the group with the couple's dog. Hall described the troubling outcome of her confrontation in great detail during the 2008 trial:

Hall: "And I think at that point we started to walk forward and Mr. Shah came up to me and, as he likes to do, got very close. He likes to get in your space. And [he said], 'Is that all you want to know?' Like that. And I said—no, excuse me. He said, 'Are you sure there is not anything else you want to know?' And I said no, I just wanted to see how the kids were doing, you know, just kind of acting."

Attorney: "All right."

Hall: "And then we walked on and got to the end of the block . . . once again he [Dinny] got right in my face and said, 'Are you sure that's all you want to know?' And I said, yeah, that's it, you know, lalala, and off we went around the block . . . we walked back around to our house so we didn't have to walk in front of their [the Johnsons'] house. Gary didn't want to run back into them again."

Weeks passed, but Hall never forgot Dinny's sinister questioning; the way he cringed when Hall approached the children; how he tried to intimidate her too, getting in her face, towering over her. On another occasion, Gary and Olabelle were walking their dog when the Johnsons' car pulled down the street. Dinny was driving.

"Hey, Gary, have you made any money today?" Dinny yelled out the window of the car.

"Not as much as you've stolen," was Gary's reply. Gary can dish it out.

That was too much for Dinny. The car went peeling down the street as Olabelle and Gary continued their walk. Dinny turned the car around in a neighbor's circular driveway, tires screeching. Soon, the car was pulling into the Halls' driveway, blocking them from entering. Dinny threw the car in park and jumped out.

Attorney: "What did Mr. Shah do then?"

Hall: "He ran over to my husband and took a posture, stuck his chest out. . . . He was right in my husband's face, screaming basically that 'You have a problem! Your wife!' and, oh, he said, 'Your problem is your wife.' He said, 'You don't have your wife under control; don't you know your wife is supposed to be under control?' And my husband said at that point, 'Look, buddy, I've been married to her for over twenty years, and there is no way that is happening.' And he [Dinny] said—screaming, spitting, and just, the whole time just right in his face, spitting and screaming—he said, 'Well, you need to get her under control, that's your job as a husband—to keep your wife under control!'"

Dinny continued the tirade, screaming at Gary Hall on the sidewalk of Del Monte Drive. Then Dinny turned on Olabelle. He was becoming more enraged. "I know all about you!" he yelled. He started making strange accusations; he knew, for instance, that Olabelle had gone to Lamar High School and that she had "bought her way into the River Oaks Country Club." It was a familiar intimidation tactic that Olabelle had seen before, so it didn't bother her. As far as she was concerned, Dinny was just raving gibberish.

To dispel the flaring tempers, Gary urged Olabelle to follow him, to continue their walk. Joan and the children had been witness to the entire incident, and there was little emotion on Joan's part:

Hall: "It was then when I walked around the car [to follow Gary] and I looked in the car, Joan, and I realized there was at least one and possibly both of the children were in the backseat. I didn't know they were in the backseat."

Attorney: "And how did Joan appear to you?"

Hall: "I told my husband as we walked around that corner that I thought she was drugged."

The altercation disturbed both of the Halls. Gary, who had been skeptical about his wife's concern over the Johnsons, who wanted Olabelle to stay out of their business, suddenly believed all of the things she had reported to him: The situation inside the house, with Dinny living there, was much more serious than they had previously thought. He told Olabelle to drop it, to not speak with the Johnsons anymore—Dinny was just too dangerous.

If you listen to Dinny's side of the story, Olabelle Hall was a River Oaks busybody, someone who was looking for any sign of trouble to get Dinny and Joan in trouble. Olabelle didn't like Joan, he claimed. Olabelle had long been a family friend of Luke Johnson—particularly Luke's mother and brother, Gary, two of Joan's enemies. To punish Joan, to humiliate her, Olabelle would throw elaborate tea parties and happy hours at her home and purposely not invite Joan. The two had a long, hostile relationship, he claimed, and that's why Olabelle Hall didn't like him.

But if that were true, why would Hall continue to try to intervene on the children's behalf?

———

That afternoon, Olabelle drove to the River Oaks security office and filed a police report against Dinny. The verbal and physical attack, she said, was completely unprovoked. But once again, Dinny would get away with it.

What Dinny didn't know was that Olabelle Hall hadn't quite given up, despite Dinny's best attempts at intimidating her. The altercation had only served to steel her nerves and to solidify her concern for Seth and Kaleta. Finally, someone realized there was a monster in River Oaks.

School Daze

Sylvia Bartz knew a thing or two about kids: In her thirty-nine years at St. John's School, Bartz—who taught middle school English before she became a Licensed Professional Counselor—had seen hundreds of students come and go. She'd graded countless essays and helped many students through rough patches—divorces, eating disorders, peer pressure. By the time Dinny's civil trial rolled around, Bartz had been retired for four years. But she remembered Kaleta very well. She would be a key character witness in the 2008 civil trial. Her presence in the courtroom would remind the jury of every high school counselor they had met. Short in stature with graying but neatly kept hair, impeccably dressed and calm, she would make a very credible witness to validate Keleta's recollection of those dark years.

According to Bartz, the phone calls started when Kaleta was in the sixth grade; it seemed Olabelle Hall wasn't the only person who sensed trouble at the Johnson home. Sometime in 2000, another one of Joan Johnson's neighbors—Jane Owen—called Bartz. Olabelle Hall is the quintessential River Oaks matron. She would recall, from the witness stand, her days as a young woman in River

Oaks, going to Lamar, knowing all the "right people," and living the life that would be the envy of any Houston teen. But Olabelle was more than just an observant neighbor. She, like Jane Owen, had the natural female instinct when something was not right. Mrs. Owen was concerned for Kaleta; she thought, mistakenly, that Kaleta's brothers may have been abusing her. Owen also recalled that two strangers were living at the Johnson residence, an arrangement that she felt was unhealthy and inappropriate.

Around the same time, Bartz received another call, this time from Joan's sister in Dallas. During this conversation, Bartz learned a little more about the "strange men" living with the Johnson family. According to what she learned, Joan had changed since Dinny had moved in; she'd severed all contact with her family, and she had abruptly cut ties with lifelong friends. By that time, Bartz was on the case. She was in the hunt for what had gone wrong with Kaleta. And she wouldn't let go.

Bartz asked Pat Krieger, Kaleta's gym teacher, to keep an eye on Kaleta as she changed in the locker rooms, to look for any evidence of physical abuse. After a period of careful observation, Krieger reported that she couldn't see any visible bruises on Kaleta.

Physically, there was nothing that pointed to abuse; at least not yet. But Bartz, who went out of her way to establish a rapport with Kaleta, did note that the sixth-grader "exhibited a flat affect, showed no emotion, neither smiled nor cried." This is, as any counselor knows, a very common trait in victims of abuse.

Bartz was one adult in Kaleta's life who wasn't manipulating, controlling, or abusing her, and Bartz would use every chance she got to chat with the young girl, trying to get Kaleta to open up. While Bartz continued to reach out to Kaleta, she eventually ran out of time: School recessed for the summer, and Kaleta was left to face her family alone.

When Kaleta returned to school in the fall, Bartz recalled, it seemed that things had taken a turn for the worse: In the summer between Kaleta's sixth- and seventh-grade years (the summer of 2001, one year after Dinny moved into the Johnson household), Kaleta lost ten pounds. It doesn't sound like much, but on a naturally slim thirteen-year-old—a thirteen-year-old who is still growing taller—the result was jarring: The Kaleta Johnson who reported to her first day of seventh grade looked emaciated and sickly—she was frighteningly skinny. Kaleta's appearance was so alarming that her friends and teachers approached Sylvia Bartz, concerned that Kaleta might have an eating disorder.

In October of Kaleta's seventh-grade year, Mrs. Bartz called a conference with Joan Johnson. Bartz suggested that Joan take her daughter to a doctor, just to make sure that Kaleta was growing normally. Joan, who remained strained and formal during the conference, agreed to take Kaleta for a checkup.

That's when the real trouble started. Bartz hadn't bargained for Dinny's outrage.

A few days after her conference with Joan, she received a phone call from Joan (the call was, of course, on speakerphone so Dinny could listen in). Bartz could hear Dinny whispering in the background, coaching Joan, who did all the talking and tried her best to ease Bartz's concerns: The women in the family are just naturally slender, she said. Kaleta had been to the doctor; everything was normal. But Bartz wasn't going to back down that easily. State law required all students to have a physical, she told Joan. Kaleta wouldn't be allowed to return to school until she had a physical examination form, signed by a doctor.

Soon after that call, Kaleta showed up to school with a signed physical examination form. Sylvia Bartz had, to an extent, won the battle. But in the process, she had piqued Dinny's ire.

———

Eric Lombardi was one of those natural teachers—the kind of teacher that goes out of his way to learn every student's name and be the friendly face in the school hallway. He had a reassuring demeanor and was well-liked by faculty and students. Lombardi came to St. John's in 1996 as a Spanish and history teacher. The students liked him, not only because he resembled Jerry Seinfeld, but because he was just as funny. And as it turned out, he was a good fit for the school: By 1998, he had been promoted to headmaster at St. John's Middle School.

As headmaster, Lombardi still makes it a point to know his students. Every morning, he stands at the carpool line that snakes around the St. John's grounds and greets students and parents before class. It was in the first few months of 2000 that he first noticed Dinny Shah in the carpool line. Dinny was violating carpool etiquette, driving aggressively through the parking lot at speeds higher than Lombardi thought were safe. As he testified in court:

"I had occasion to speak with him [Dinny] about the carpool line. The primary concern for me is the safety of the kids. We have rules about speed. . . . And I had occasion to ask him to drive more carefully, follow more of our expectations as he went through that line."

Unbeknownst to Lombardi, he had gravely offended Dinny. One afternoon in the spring of Kaleta's sixth-grade year—just about the same time that Bartz was receiving phone calls from concerned neighbors—Dinny Shah, Joan Johnson, and David Collie stormed onto the campus and demanded to speak to Lombardi. Dinny wanted to speak his mind about how Lombardi ran the carpool at St. John's.

Lombardi: "I was given a lecture [by Dinny] in a loud voice, oftentimes standing over me, about how to run a carpool, about how perhaps I could use the help of the Marines, which he [Dinny] had been a part of—"

Attorney: "Wait. Let me stop you there. The defendant said he had been a United States Marine?"

Lombardi: "Yes, sir."

Attorney: "And he said what about the Marines?"

Lombardi: "That he had friends in the Marines who could help me run a carpool line since I clearly didn't know how to run one."

During that visit, Dinny made other bizarre claims: He had been a student at Kinkaid, he told Lombardi, which had an excellent carpool line. The clothes that he and the children wore had been tailored by the Queen of England's personal tailor. Dinny continued his strange blend of veiled threats and outlandish fibs, yelling and causing a commotion until Sylvia Bartz (whose office was next door to Lombardi's) barged into the office to see what was going on.

When Dinny, Joan, and David left, Mr. Lombardi was admittedly shaken up. Dinny's shouting, combined with the silent, hulking figure of David Collie who crossed his arms like a Ninja warrior and stared menacingly the entire time, had intimidated the peaceful headmaster. He recalled telling Bartz that Dinny "seemed to me the kind of person who would potentially tap a phone or blow up a car." Lombardi alerted the rest of the administration about his meeting, and he told the maintenance division to be aware of Dinny Shah, to keep a sharp eye out for his car.

Things remained quiet for some time. Aside from Bartz's conversation with Joan and Dinny about Kaleta's physical examination form, the administration didn't hear anything further from Joan Johnson or Dinny Shah for a while. That's why, in December 2001—months since the incident in his office—Lombardi was surprised to get a call from Dinny and Joan again. The two had left a message with Lombardi's secretary, asking him to tea, of all things, at the Johnson home on a Saturday afternoon. Against the advice of Bartz, Lombardi accepted the invitation.

This meeting would go much more amicably than the first conversation the three had in Lombardi's office. But Dinny still had an agenda:

Lombardi: "I was being told to please limit the contact of Ms. Bartz and Kaleta. There was a concern that Mr. Shah was expressing about interactions that Sylvia Bartz had had and might have with Kaleta."

In return for reigning in Bartz and keeping her away from Kaleta—and out of Dinny's way—Dinny hinted that he was interested in writing a check to build some tennis courts for the school. But Lombardi didn't take the bait.

There was another item on Shah's agenda that afternoon in December: the upcoming Texas Heritage field trip. The weeklong trip, which takes seventh-grade students (and several teachers and adult chaperones) on a tour of the state's historic sites, is a St. John's tradition. But Dinny had concerns about Kaleta's safety.

Lombardi: "Mr. Shah was wanting me to know that Kaleta would not be able to go on this [field trip] because it would be dangerous for her, because of the possibility of people boarding our buses."

Attorney: "Possibility of people doing what?"

Lombardi: "Boarding the buses."

Attorney: "Boarding the bus?"

Lombardi: "And kidnapping her."

Attorney: "Did she go on the trip?"

Lombardi: "She did not go on the trip."

Dinny couldn't remember ever speaking to Lombardi about having his suits made by the queen's tailor. He also didn't remember the first meeting with Lombardi in his office at St. John's: "I met Mr. Lombardi for the first time at Ms. Johnson's home," he stated. And as for Kaleta not attending school field trips, Shah's answer was simple:

"Well, Kaleta did not want to go, as I recall."

———————

Meanwhile, Bartz didn't back off, and Lombardi never asked her to. If anything, she became closer to Kaleta. Bartz taught a weekly class that focused on themes like study techniques, human sexuality, drug and alcohol problems, and communication skills—and Kaleta was one of her students. During one session, Kaleta showed her a copy of a poem she had written for her English class. The first few lines, in retrospect, read like an account of Kaleta's personal suffering:

> *Their existence was too monotonous and unfair*
> *Their toils became so unbearable that in the end they just broke out into*
> *Open revolt.*

The title of the poem was "The Controlled."

It was only after Shah's 2002 arrest that Kaleta was able to open up to Bartz. In Kaleta's words, she had "felt like a prisoner in her own home" since the sixth grade.

Suddenly, the suffering that Kaleta had endured was thrown into full view. Bartz had seen the rejected field trip permission slips; Kaleta was never allowed to go, at Dinny's request. She had seen the hand-scrawled note at the bottom of the permission slip for Kaleta's school-assigned e-mail account and access to the school's Internet network: "I do not want for other people outside the school to know Kaleta Johnson's e-mail address. Do not give out her e-mail address over the phone."

Kaleta's restricted school activities were obviously the product of an overprotective—or perhaps paranoid—guardian. But it wasn't until Mary Craddock—yet *another* one of Joan's concerned neighbor's—called Bartz in December 2002 to report Shah's arrest that Bartz got the full view of Kaleta's extreme isolation.

On December 15, the day after Shah's arrest, Bartz pulled Kaleta out of class and invited her to lunch. As they ate at the Country Market that day, Kaleta showed Bartz her bruises and confessed her dark, sordid tale. She told Bartz how Dinny restricted the mail, phone, TV, and Internet access in the house; she told her how Dinny controlled their clothes, where they went to eat, and where they could shop (they were only allowed to grocery shop at Krogers.) The extreme isolation, she said, was the reason for her dramatic weight loss in the seventh grade—and because her appearance had drawn so much interest from people, Dinny would beat her. She told Bartz about the physical and psychological abuse that happened on a regular basis, about the name-calling that was constantly inflicted by David and Dinny, two houseguests who had never been invited.

On the stand at the 2008 trial, Kaleta's words show just how frustrated, sad, and oppressed the little girl had been; how she had tried to grow up in the shadow of a man who wasn't her father, cut off from family and friends, and the serious repercussions she often had to face:

Kaleta: "He [Dinny] wouldn't let me go on school trips. He wouldn't let me go to other events. You know, I didn't go to my friends' houses for years, didn't go out to different social things. I think one time, in sixth grade, he let me go to a birthday party at a friend's house. And from there, we went to a movie. I knew we were going to a movie but I didn't tell him that because I knew if I told him, he wouldn't let me go. When he came to pick me up, my friend's mother mentioned something like, "the girls had a good time at the movie." And he was furious that I had done that and not told him. He just, just going to a movie with friends, he said anything could have happened. He was furious, saying, 'You could have been kidnapped.' I received a beating for that."

Attorney: "You received a beating for going to a movie?"

Kaleta: "Yes."

Attorney: "In sixth grade?"

Kaleta: "Yes."

Dinny's Grand European Tour

The summer of 2002 was a hectic one for the Johnson family. Shortly after Dinny announced his decision to send Seth away, he dropped two more bombshells: He had planned a two-month European vacation for the whole family, bookended by stops on the East coast to check out a few schools in Connecticut, Massachusetts, and Maine.

And Dinny had found someone to take care of things at home, now that their onetime go-to house-sitter David Collie was no longer in the picture. While the Johnson family enjoyed their grand tour of Europe and America, Dinny's brother, Shyam Shah, would hold down the fort on Del Monte Drive.

Dinny had, of course, thought of everything.

Over two months abroad, far from home, with Dinny calling the shots. The idea had to be terrifying, especially to Kaleta.

According to Kaleta's testimony, Dinny's abuse had taken sadistic new turns. Early in the summer of 2002, shortly before Dinny announced the European vacation, he caught Joan wearing an unauthorized ensemble and forced Kaleta to help him mete out the punishment.

Kaleta: "She [Joan] was wearing an outfit that [Dinny] said was, you know, he didn't like it. . . . And he got furious with her for wearing it. And it was not a terrible outfit, but he became enraged and he ripped through her closet and he tore things out, threw them on the floor and he—there was a little antique table that she had and he, you know, hit her with it, broke it over her back and splintered it into little pieces. He was hitting her and yelled at her and he yelled at me to come into the room and he yelled, handed me one of the hangers and said, "'I want you to hit your mother with this.' I started crying. I didn't want to. I told him I didn't want to, and he said, 'Hit her or I'll beat you both up.' And so I kind of tapped her with the hanger. He said, 'That's not hard enough. You have to do it harder.' And you know, it took three or four tries before he said I hit her hard enough."

Even the humiliation of being beaten and berated in front of her daughter wasn't enough to make Joan reach out for help. She remained tight-lipped, either too embarrassed or too frightened— or perhaps simply ignoring it—to stand up for herself.

Instead, she turned her attention elsewhere, concentrating on the upcoming family vacation. It would, after all, be Seth's last hurrah; a chance for the family to enjoy some quality time before he left home.

But for the Johnsons, family vacations had never been that enjoyable. Kaleta and Seth still remembered listening in terror as their mom was beaten in a California hotel room. The trip to Palm Beach marked the very first time Dinny beat Kaleta with a belt. The Johnsons knew that, even if they weren't at home, even if they were out doing something fun or adventurous or relaxing, Dinny's anger never tempered.

Even Joan knew exactly what to expect from another vacation with Dinny. Just months before their summer tour, in January 2002, the family had traveled to New York City for a winter holiday.

While in New York, the family stopped for a bite to eat at a restaurant. Kaleta refused to eat her hamburger, asking for ice cream instead. Joan thought that was OK; perhaps, looking at Kaleta's skinny frame, Joan figured ice cream for lunch was an acceptable breach of protocol. But as Joan recalled, Dinny flew into a rage.

Dinny kicked Joan under the table, berating her for spoiling Kaleta. As they walked back to their hotel—the Waldorf Astoria, Dinny's preferred hotel—Dinny kicked Joan again on the sidewalk and then pushed her into the street. Luckily, Joan stopped just short of the oncoming traffic.

Joan took a memento home from that trip: an Ann Taylor suit with a bloodstain on the pant leg from where Dinny's shoe had split Joan's shin. For unknown reasons, Joan kept the suit and would show it to the Houston Police officers the day Dinny was arrested and she would testify about it in detail in the 2008 civil trial.

The children had witnessed the entire event transpire between Dinny and Joan—over a hamburger and ice cream. It's easy to assume that the thought of another trip with Dinny brought about strong feelings of apprehension and anxiety.

Dinny proposed a whirlwind of a trip, with a two-and-a-half-month itinerary touching major cities on both sides of the Atlantic: a week in Washington, D.C., a couple of days in New York City, then on to Paris, the south of France, and London. The family would then loop back to New York City before traveling up the New England coast to Connecticut, Massachusetts, and Maine (all to tour potential boarding schools for Seth). The bill, of course, was to be footed by Joan.

On the surface, it sounds like the trip of a lifetime: the Eiffel Tower, Buckingham Palace, the White House, the hole where the World Trade Center had once stood. In true Dinny Shah style, no expense was spared: They dined at the finest restaurants, stayed in the poshest hotels. But for Kaleta, who was becoming increasingly disenchanted with Dinny as she matured, the pomp and circumstance was nothing more than a sham:

Kaleta: "It was as if we were imitating, you know, trips to Europe that Americans would take in the '50s, just following World War II. Very elaborate trips. We stayed in elaborate hotels, and he wanted to go to all the nice restaurants and, you know, spend all of my mother's money on this trip."

And while Dinny acted out his fantasies, the family was expected to learn their roles.

Shah would run the show, while Joan, Seth, and Kaleta—dressed of course, in their odd, custom-made period clothes—played the parts of a happy, healthy family unit. The family ate when and where he said they could. They went where and when he said they would. And of course, Shah handled the sleeping arrangements: Joan and Kaleta in one room and, as always, Seth and Dinny in another. Joan and Kaleta weren't allowed to leave the room until Dinny came to get them:

Kaleta: "My mother and I would wake up in the morning and prepare to go out, but we didn't know what we would be doing that day. He was completely in charge . . ."

Attorney: "What were you doing in the hotel room until he came to get you?"

Kaleta: "We had to wait. My mother loves to swim every day and she, you know, she was sometimes too afraid to go down to the hotel pool and do her daily laps because if he had learned that she had left the room without him, he would have been very upset."

Despite the circumstances, it seems the family enjoyed their trip; Joan later told the court that it had been, in general, a good trip. Her daughter agreed—sort of.

At the 2008 trial, Kaleta would offer this statement:

Kaleta: "I have some fond memories, but, I mean, there were a lot of unpleasant things that occurred as well."

Psychologists tell us that abused children often feign fond memories of those who abuse them. There are numerous studies to support that position. It seems the abuser seeks to have the victim experience—and remember—the "good with the bad."

In the end, Seth and Kaleta would remember their grand tour as a brief jaunt through the annals of history, punctuated by fear, violence, and Dinny's tall tales.

Their first stop was Washington, D.C. Everyone was in good spirits, this being only the first leg of the vacation. Joan and the kids played along as Dinny cheerfully showed them around the city, pointing to the famous landmarks, including the building where he claimed to have once worked.

Attorney: "Did Mr. Shah show you where he served when he was in the FBI or Langley?"

Seth: "Yes. He showed us the FBI building. Then we drove out to Virginia. He showed us the driveway up to Langley and said that is where he used to work. And he drove us out to some random house and said that's where he used to live."

There is no record of Shah ever working for the FBI. Likewise, he never worked at Langley, where the CIA is reportedly headquartered.

Surprisingly, Dinny's temper stayed in check during the family's stay in Washington, D.C. He seemed calm and relaxed as they traveled on to New York City, then to Paris and the south of France. Perhaps the glitz and glamour of the Big Apple, the sophistication of Paris, and the pastoral charm of lavender fields dotting the Mediterranean coast had lulled Dinny into a more amiable state. This was, after all, the ideal trip for Dinny, who often imagined himself a cultured, educated man, the epitome of gentility, complete with a bowtie and suspenders.

And though the family tried to mind their p's and q's—wearing Dinny's clothes without complaint, holing up in their hotel room until he was ready for the day, following his lead, and swallowing his lies without question—they didn't always measure up to Dinny's high, ever-changing standards.

By the time the family reached London, Dinny was on edge. All of the double-decker buses and Westminster Abbeys and Towers of London in the world wouldn't calm the anger that was slowly brewing inside Dinny. But this time, most of the abuse was directed at Seth.

Seth: "We went to go see a battleship [in London]. I took off my—it was a sweater with a little hoodie on the back of it. I just basically tied it on my waist. I leaned up against something or I sat down, I can't quite remember. It got dirty. He got mad at me. He ripped it off. He hit me so hard in the back of the head that I fell down. Then he took the sweater off me and threw it in the trash can that was on the street."

After London, the family returned to the states via New York City. Now was the time to get busy: They had several boarding schools to check out in a short amount of time. Their tour of New England would take them to Boston, on to Connecticut, and as far north as Maine. And as the summer started to wane so did Dinny's patience. Stateside, Seth's beatings continued.

While on the stand, Seth related one such event that occurred at a Coast Guard museum in Massachusetts. While at the museum, Seth disappeared. Actually, he had just wandered out of Dinny's sight. Joan and Kaleta weren't concerned, but Dinny became very unsettled.

Seth: "And he got upset with me, said that I could have been abducted and kidnapped and stolen and stuff like that."

Attorney: "Did he beat you for it?"

Seth: "Yes, sir."

Attorney: "How so?"

Seth: "He knocked me around a few times."

Seth's description of the abuse—"he knocked me around a few times"—seems strangely casual, more suited to a brotherly spat than a depiction of abuse. Seth's demeanor on the stand, and particularly his feelings toward Dinny, were often complex and confusing. Though he was a plaintiff in the case, Seth sometimes exhibited ambivalence and even friendly regard for the man who had once terrified him, beating him repeatedly for the better part of his childhood. It was an ambivalence that would become even more disturbing as the court learned more about Shah's abuse. Seth's experiences would remind some jurors of the well-documented event that gave rise to a condition known as Stockholm Syndrome. Dinny wanted—and got—Seth under his thumb.

Meanwhile, the travel-weary family returned to Houston just in time to help Seth pack his bags for Westminster, the exclusive East Coast boarding school that Dinny had handpicked for Seth.

And that wasn't the only change Dinny had in store for the Johnsons. Always unpredictable, Dinny had more news for the family.

Shyam Shah would be living with the family permanently. The plan was for Shyam to move into Seth's room after Seth went to boarding school. Joan and Kaleta would now have two Shah brothers to contend with. The circle was getting tighter, smaller.

Seth's School Years

Kaleta: "I would say he [Dinny] was much more involved in Seth's school, schoolwork. Seth was severely punished many times for not doing well in school and, you know, I have thought, you know, that kind of frightened me into doing well. I saw what would happen to Seth if he brought home a bad grade. And, you know, it was very frightening."

Attorney: "What kind of things did you see happen to Seth if he brought home a bad grade?"

Kaleta: "I can't say that I always saw the beatings, but I would hear Seth and I would hear, you know, Seth being pushed around the room and I heard Seth crying out and I would see the bruises afterward and there were—and there were times Seth would stay home from school for days. You know, you could see it, he had such severe markings."

Kaleta wasn't the only young victim of Dinny's abuse: Dinny had taken particular interest in Seth early on, and had cast himself in the role of ersatz father figure, and disciplinarian, to the boy (and, as will be seen, far more than a father figure). But unlike his sister, Seth didn't have an escape. For Kaleta, school was a safe haven—St. John's School was safe and familiar; it was a place that was, to a degree, beyond Dinny's grasp. For Seth, school was just another source of turmoil and confusion.

From the time he started prekindergarten in 1989 until he graduated high school in 2006, Seth attended eight different schools. It's unclear why Joan chose to bounce Seth from school to school, but his records reflect a nomadic, haphazard academic life, punctuated by a four-year stint at Memorial Hall School. Seth attended Memorial Hall School from his fourth- to seventh-grade years. There was an implication that Seth needed special tutoring.

Seth had always struggled in school, and it was Dinny's personal mission to help the boy improve his grades. Dinny explored a number of avenues: He had Seth take several psychological exams, trying to figure out if he had some type of learning disability. Seth was evaluated by Dr. Rae Battin, from Houston's Battin Clinic, which specializes in evaluating learning disabilities in children and adults. Despite these extraordinary measures, there were no conclusive results about Seth's learning difficulties. Shah's only recourse was to transfer Seth from one school to another, to hire private tutors, and to tutor Seth himself.

Report cards and progress reports—all of which Dinny saved among the thousands of Johnson family personal documents, many of the offered into evidence—show that, despite Dinny's efforts, Seth's grades remained poor.

By the time Dinny moved into the Johnson home, he had all but taken control of Seth Johnson's education. Dinny generally only got involved with Kaleta's school when there was a problem—a slow carpool line, a nosey school counselor. But with Seth, Dinny openly communicated with the school (wherever Seth happened to be enrolled), asking questions about Seth's behavior and monitoring the quality of his work.

After Memorial Hall, Seth briefly attended Houston Christian High School in 2001. He was enrolled as a ninth-grader. Dinny wasted no time getting to know the staff at Seth's new school. Between October 2001 and the spring of 2002, Dinny contacted the school eight times—either by phone or by just showing up at the school, always eager to talk about Seth's grades. Interestingly, records from Houston Christian show that Shah used a variety of identifiers when he went to speak with the principal and teachers: On one parent contact form he is listed as Seth's father. On another, Shah is listed as stepfather. On yet another parent contact form, Seth's "parents" are referred to as "Mr. and Mrs. Shah" —referring, naturally, to Dinny and Joan.

The administration at Houston Christian was disturbed by Dinny's many fake claims regarding Seth, and so annoyed at his constant hounding about Seth's education that, Seth claimed on the stand, "They even forbid the teachers to speak to him [Dinny] anymore. He had to go speak to the dean of students." Though Dinny may have had good intentions regarding Seth's education, he inevitably wore out his welcome. Dinny's aggressive nature, combined with an eagerness to blame teachers and school administrators for Seth's gap in skills, was not well received. His relations with school officials quickly became strained.

Despite Dinny's involvement, Seth never quite caught up to the rest of his class. By the end of Seth's ninth-grade year at Houston Christian, Dinny and Joan were informed that Seth wouldn't be able to progress to the tenth grade. He'd have to repeat that year before continuing on. Dinny wasn't convinced that Houston Christian was doing all it could to help Seth.

For Dinny, that meant going back to the drawing board, trying to find a new solution for Seth's education. Dinny didn't think Seth could cut it at the public school down the street, Lamar High School. So, having exhausted most of the private schools in town, Dinny decided to try something new: boarding school.

Dinny chose Westminster School in Simsbury, Connecticut, because he liked the school's mission of "community, character, balance, and involvement"—a combination Dinny felt would benefit Seth immensely. Joan, of course, quietly acquiesced. In September 2002, Shah accompanied sixteen-year-old Seth to Westminster (Joan and Kaleta did not accompany the two), helped Seth carry his bags into his new dorm room, and said good-bye.

But it wasn't long before the administration at Westminster began making urgent phone calls to Dinny: Within just a few days, Seth was already having problems at his new school.

The complaints from Westminster weren't exactly news to Dinny or Joan: Seth wasn't doing his schoolwork. (Or perhaps more accurately, as Dinny said in court "I don't think he could do the work. I think it was too advanced for him at that time.") Seth wasn't waking up in the morning, and he wasn't attending classes. The school suggested Seth's extreme drowsiness was a result of breaking curfew and sneaking into the girls' dormitory with a few of his classmates.

Within three weeks of dropping off Seth at Westminster, Dinny was summoned back to Connecticut. The agreement was mutual: Westminster wasn't the best place for Seth. Dinny didn't want Seth in a place that couldn't discipline him or improve his study habits; Westminster didn't want a new troublemaker disturbing the peace. Dinny helped Seth pack his bags, and then he began shopping around for another school for Seth, a school where Seth could get the help he needed, and where he might have a shot at graduating.

Dinny first heard Chisholm Chandler's name from Michael Spence and Faith Howland, educational consultants that Dinny turned to for advice regarding Seth. He needed help finding the right school for Seth, and the Boston-area consultants suggested that he look into the Salisbury School, a very small, private college-preparatory school. The all-boys school, located in the quaint and pastoral northwest corner of Connecticut, had a century-old reputation of educational rigor.

Chisholm Chandler is a stocky man with a boyish grin and shock of well-groomed blond hair, educated at Brown University and with a graduate degree from the school of education at Harvard. He started working at Salisbury in 1991 as director of admissions. By the time he met Dinny Shah, Chandler had been promoted to assistant headmaster, where he was responsible not only for advising students about college and university options after their stay at Salisbury, but also fund-raising, external affairs, and recruiting new students for the school. And in the fall of 2002, it just so happened that Chisholm Chandler was in Houston, fund-raising for the school. Dinny called him up and invited him to tea.

Though the school year had already begun, Chandler agreed to meet with the Johnsons and Dinny at their house on Del Monte Drive; the meeting was a preinterview, to see if Salisbury would be a good fit for Seth. When he reached the home, Chandler noted the black tarp that covered the front gate, as well as the covered windows. As Chandler remembers, the family dynamic struck him as odd:

Chandler: "Ms. Johnson didn't speak at all. It was almost exclusively Mr. Shah speaking, which at the time I thought was, you know, a little odd. And I didn't have a lot of eye contact with Ms. Johnson either . . ."

Attorney: "So, you thought it was kind of unusual that the mother, Joan Johnson, was kind of disengaged and not participating like you would expect an average, ordinary concerned parent to be, correct?"

Chandler: "At the time, I did think that, yes, sir."

Later during his testimony at the 2008 trial, Chandler described how he understood Dinny fit into the family equation:

Chandler: "Mr. Shah really described his relationship as Seth's guardian. I had very little contact with Ms. Johnson after Seth enrolled at Salisbury as a boarding student. Mr. Shah was really kind of the parent or the point person in the family. And to be honest with you, he was as involved a parent or guardian as I ever remember."

The Johnsons' odd family dynamic apparently didn't affect Chandler's decision about Seth. The interview, by all estimations, went well. Dinny explained all of Seth's learning difficulties, pulling out report cards, progress reports, test scores, and psychological evaluations for Chandler to peruse. Chandler would later describe Seth as "a quiet student who demonstrated some learning style differences, but also a willingness to take direction and try to succeed." By the end of the meeting, Chandler assured Dinny that there was a place for Seth at Salisbury. Seth was packed off to Connecticut again in October 2002—accompanied, of course, by Dinny—for his second stint at boarding school.

There's a lot of disagreement about what happened after Seth made his way to Salisbury. It all depends on who you want to believe: Dinny Shah—who is not an ex-CIA agent or former Marine, who is not a Kinkaid or Rice University or Baylor University graduate, who is not even certified to work in the financial sector—or Chisholm Chandler—Ivy-league educated headmaster of a select school for young men.

Dinny claimed that Salisbury couldn't handle Seth; much like at Westminster, the concerned phone calls from teachers and administration started immediately. To Dinny, Salisbury wasn't fulfilling the promises that Chandler had assured him of during their meeting in Houston:

Attorney: "Did Mr. Chandler call you a few times or many times on the telephone?"

Shah: "He called me many times."

Attorney: "Do you believe that Mr. Chandler fulfilled his role as headmaster and fulfilled his responsibilities that he represented that he would fulfill to you?"

Shah: "No. I wanted the boy to have a good education, and I was frustrated with Chandler. I was really involved with trying to find solutions for Seth to make Seth's life better. And Mr. Chandler did not have solutions. He was looking to me for solutions 2,000 miles away . . ."

In short, Dinny wasn't seeing the results he expected, especially not for the $30,000 tuition Joan paid.

To the contrary, Chandler claims that he never called Shah. Rather, it was Dinny who called him—some twenty to twenty-five times between October and December 2002, both at the school and at home. This was in addition to dozens of calls that Shah placed directly to Seth's teachers. Shah's phone calls, over the weeks, became increasingly disturbing—all echoing the interactions that Shah had had with administration and educators regarding the Johnson children in the past:

Chandler: "He [Dinny] would call literally every five minutes for hours to the point where it was a little scary."

And Chandler wasn't the only one who found Dinny's behavior a little scary: The teachers at Salisbury were upset at Dinny's verbally abusive manner. Chandler described some of the phone calls that he and Seth's teachers received:

Chandler: "He used to say over and over again, 'I don't know what the hell you people are doing up there.' But it was just, you know, it was a lot of swearing, a lot of shouting on the phone, real anger. I mean, you could tell the guy had a real temper. And I think that's why so many of Seth's teachers were quite honestly afraid of this guy, because of how he spoke with them on the phone. . . . He was just a very unpredictable guy and it frightened a lot of people."

Dinny's behavior frightened at least one person a little too much: Seth's initial academic advisor at Salisbury asked to be replaced. He was unable to tolerate Shah's tirades and verbal abuse any longer

Dinny would be arrested only two months after Seth started attending Salisbury. But even with a court order directing him not to contact Seth, the staff at Salisbury would have several run-ins with Dinny over the subsequent months. Chisholm Chandler, in particular, would be in contact with the Houston Police Department, monitoring and reporting Shah's attempts to contact Seth after his arrest.

The threatening phone calls from Dinny Shah were about to get a lot more scary.

Shyam, the Keeper's Brother

Attorney: "You moved into the Johnson's house, didn't you, sir?"

Shyam Shah: "No, I did not."

Attorney: "Did you spend any time in the Johnson family home in the last six months of 2002?"

Shyam Shah: "No, I did not."

But according to police records, Dinny's brother, Shyam Shah, was the one to place the 911 phone call from inside the Johnson home on the night of December 14, 2002. He was there when the police arrived—Officer Suzanne Hollifield vividly recalled interviewing the nervous, shifty-eyed Shyam Shah that night.

And that certainly wasn't his first visit to the Johnson household. A family photo taken on Easter weekend of 2002 contradicts Shyam's claim that he'd only met the Johnsons a few times. The photo was taken in what is clearly Joan Johnson's backyard; in it, Joan, Seth, and Kaleta appear in their Sunday best, strained smiles spread across their faces. But there is a new addition to the household in that photograph: Shyam Shah.

Despite the overwhelming evidence to the contrary, Shyam stuck to his story. He did not live with the Johnsons, he insisted. He had no idea that Dinny monitored the family's phone calls or mail. And he didn't know anything about the sheets and blankets that kept the house on Del Monte sealed off from the rest of the neighborhood.

And more importantly, Shyam insisted that he'd never seen Dinny abuse Seth, Kaleta, or Joan. It seems that, in the six years that stretched between 2002 and the 2008 civil case, Shyam couldn't remember *anything*. His incredible denials, under oath and before a shocked jury, were the equivalent of a Holocaust denial.

The Johnsons, however, remember everything: According to Joan, Seth, and Kaleta, Shyam stayed in the Johnson home, taking care of the place and babysitting their daschund, Vicki, while Dinny took them on an extended summer vacation. And they all agree that, once they returned from their travels, Shyam never left.

It was surely Dinny's idea to have his brother move into the Johnson home: Perhaps he needed a partner in crime, a wingman, now that David Collie was gone. Or perhaps Shyam had some personal troubles and needed a little help to get back on his feet. Anyone's guess is as good as another.

Dinny had certainly worked out the particulars of Shyam's stay flawlessly: Once Seth moved to boarding school, Shyam would take over his room. It worked well—until Seth came back from Westminster in September, after just a few weeks of floundering while away at school. Seth would soon be shipped off to Salisbury, but in the meantime, suddenly, sleeping arrangements in the Johnson house were tight.

Aside from throwing a wrench in Dinny's plan, Seth's unexpected return did one more thing: It opened Shyam's eyes to Dinny's true nature and his true relationship with the family.

What Shyam discovered would soon turn him from wingman to rat. He was about to turn against his brother, and Dinny's carefully constructed house of cards was about to come crashing down.

In September 2002, Seth would bear the brunt of one final abusive incident from Dinny: It was a clear night, and Dinny, Shyam, Joan, and Seth were walking the dog. They were on Inwood Drive, just a few blocks from Joan's house on Del Monte. Seth was playing around and started running down the street, but as Joan described in 2003, Dinny didn't like that:

Joan: "Seth sort of ran by Mr. Shah, and Mr. Shah didn't like that, took objection to it, and started beating him up. Grabbed him by the neck, threw him down on the ground, and tore his shirt."

Attorney: "And did you see [Dinny] hit him?"

Joan: "Yes."

Attorney: "Where did you see [Dinny] hit him?"

Joan: "On his back, on his face, on his arm."

By the end of the altercation, Joan claimed, Seth was bleeding from the head. His shirt was ripped. And it was Shyam, Dinny's own brother, who finally intervened, pulling Dinny off of Seth and putting an end to the assault.

Luckily for Seth, this was the last assault that he would suffer after nearly six years of physical abuse. He would see Dinny only a few times after he left for Salisbury School in October 2002.

But Joan and Kaleta still had to live with Dinny every single day.

It seems that Shyam was supposed to act as a fill-in for Dinny, to be his eyes and ears while Dinny was off on trips to Connecticut to visit Seth. As Kaleta told the court, "[Dinny] would leave his brother sometimes kind of in charge of my mother and I."

But Shyam wasn't the best watchdog. Though he was two years older than Dinny, Shyam often followed his younger brother's lead. But not this time—Shyam Shah didn't share his brother's controlling and violent tendencies. He turned out to be much more lenient with the Johnsons, perhaps more lenient that Dinny would have liked.

With Shyam in charge, Joan and Kaleta had a little more freedom. They left the house on occasion, mostly just to go shopping or have lunch in nearby Rice Village—the type of innocent mother-daughter outings that were the norm in most River Oaks house-holds.

But Dinny's controlling tendencies—even when he was 2,000 miles away in Connecticut—often made up for Shyam's leniency. Once, Kaleta told the court, Dinny shouted at her over the phone for writing a letter to Seth without his consent:

"I had written Seth a letter at school. I don't remember exactly what it said," Kaleta said. "Dinny had found it in Seth's room, his room at [boarding] school. And, you know, he immediately became enraged and called me and said, 'Why are you sending your brother letters without my permission? I haven't told you you could do this.' He said, 'You're going to be in big trouble when I get back.'"

This event was the straw that broke Shyam's patience with his brother. He had already witnessed Seth's public beating and saw how his brother had turned the Johnsons into slaves, and the thought of Kaleta having to ask permission to write a letter to her own brother was much too creepy for Shyam's sensibilities. Shyam had had enough of putting up with Dinny's temper. He started debunking all of Dinny's lies, tearing down the façade and persona that Dinny had carefully built:

Kaleta: "Shyam said, you know, this had gone on, this is too much. This needs to stop. And he started unraveling his brother's lies."

Attorney: "What do you mean?"

Kaleta: "Well, it was from Shyam that we first heard that Dinny had not gone to Kinkaid or Rice, that he had not worked for Reagan or the CIA or the FBI, that he was not in position to be the ambassador to India. My mother and I were shocked at first that this was—it took a while to absorb this because we had been living that truth for almost six years. And Shyam took us out to his parents' house in Alief. Previously, Dinny had told us he was from Sugar Land, and he had driven by some mansion down in Sugar Land and said that was where his parents lived but we didn't go inside."

Sugar Land is one of Houston's bedroom communities, a suburban neighborhood of wealth and social prominence. It would be easy to believe that a former CIA or FBI agent or government ambassador would have grown up in Sugar Land, where basketball players and local politicians (notably Tom DeLay) live alongside the many millionaires-next-door and average citizens. Alief, on the other hand, is a much more middle-class neighborhood in southwest Houston, filled with hard-working families, a large Asian immigrant population, and its fair share of teenage gang violence.

Boastful Dinny had finally been exposed, and this emperor had no clothes; he was nothing more than a common, run-of-the-mill hoax.

Everything Shyam said reaffirmed what Kaleta had felt was true all along. Still, for the Johnson family, having the truth exposed in such a blunt manner was probably shocking. The knowledge that they had been living with a fraud, a complete sham, was slow to sink in.

Still, no one confronted Dinny. No one said anything about the lies. Kaleta and Joan went on quietly living beside their personal jailer and impostor, all under the passive but watchful eye of Shyam.

It seems that Shyam wasn't satisfied with simply exposing Dinny's lies to the Johnson family. He wanted to help them get out from under Dinny's thumb. He reached out to Reed Jordan, a CPA that Dinny had contracted years earlier to help with Joan's extensive finances and massive legal family issues.

On November 5, 2002, Shyam showed up unannounced in Reed Jordan's office. Dinny had sent him to drop off some of Joan's financial files. Shyam took the opportunity to speak privately with Jordan, but he wasn't there to discuss finances. What he said instead was a shock to Jordan:

Attorney: "What sort of tone of voice or demeanor was Shyam Shah exhibiting?"

Jordan: "He was in somewhat of a hurry. It was somewhat of a bizarre meeting, to be honest."

According to Jordan, Shyam said he was pressed for time because if he were gone too long, Dinny would become suspicious. Dinny knew exactly how long it took to drive from the Johnsons' home to Jordan's office, so Shyam was trying to beat Dinny's internal timer.

Suspicious that Jordan may have some sort of recording device in his office, Shyam indicated that he wanted to speak to Jordan in the hallway. So the puzzled CPA obediently followed Shyam into the deserted hallway.

Attorney: "What did he say, if anything, about the defendant, Dinesh Shah?"

Jordan: "He indicated that there were, that things [at the Johnson household] were not what they seemed."

Attorney: "Did he say specifically how things were not what they seemed at the Johnson house?"

Jordan: "He indicated that Mr. Shah's background was not what I had been led to believe, that his family background was not what I had been led to believe, and that there had been some abuse of the boy."

Jordan is a stocky, pleasant-looking man with something of the demeanor of Ed McMahon, Johnny Carson's sidekick. He is observant but quiet, befitting a CPA to the rich. Alarm bells went off in Jordan's head. Shyam's unexpected confession was certainly disturbing to him, but what could Jordan possibly do in that moment, with Shyam nervous and ready to leave? Jordan had an idea. He suggested that they hold a meeting with Ms. Johnson to fully assess the situation. Shyam left Jordan's office promptly. Jordan was suspicious but could not move forward without proof..

The follow-up meeting took place the second week in November. Shyam asked Jordan to park his car around the corner from the Johnson home so as to be as discreet as possible, just in case Dinny happened to show up unexpectedly. Jordan could not recall where

Dinny was that afternoon, but it's likely that Shyam and Joan set the meeting time deliberately so that there was little chance of Dinny showing up unexpectedly.

During their afternoon meeting, Reed Jordan would come to understand the relationship between Dinny Shah and Joan Johnson. He had known the two for nearly four years, and had never really questioned their interaction. Dinny would freely talk to Jordan about Joan's finances; in fact, in many of their previous meetings, Dinny would do most of the talking while Joan sat quietly in the corner.

But this time, it was Joan's turn to talk.

Attorney: "Was there any manifestation of physical abuse on Joan that was shown to you?"

Jordan: "She indicated that he had—she pulled up her skirt and showed some, what I would characterize to be minor bruises at the time on her legs and said that he had kicked her under the table."

Joan would go on to tell Jordan how Dinny had compartmentalized and controlled every aspect of her daily life. Abuse toward Seth was not discussed in great detail; incredibly, Jordan didn't probe, presumably because he wasn't sure if it was appropriate for him to know the details.

Jordan, however, is not a lawyer. He was simply the family CPA, the kind of guy much more comfortable crunching numbers than discussing intimate, personal details with his clients. He left the house with little accomplished, other than the general consensus between himself, Shyam, and Joan that something needed to be done. Joan, however, emphasized that she didn't want Jordan to take any type of action yet; she asked him to bide his time and, presumably, wait for the right moment. He obeyed.

As it turned out, Jordan wouldn't get the opportunity to do anything about Joan's Dinny problem anyway. Shyam would act before he did. And though Dinny would be forthcoming with Reed Jordan and the Houston Police Department, he wouldn't be nearly as obliging with lawyers during the 2008 civil trial.

To see Shyam on the witness stand would give a completely different understanding of his interaction with the Johnsons. Shyam was subpoenaed by the Johnson trial team to testify against his brother—and it was clear that he didn't want to. Perhaps he didn't want to implicate himself in any of Dinny's crimes. Perhaps he didn't want to get Dinny into any more trouble.

Or perhaps he was afraid of his own brother.

Attorney: "You don't want to be here testifying, do you?"

Shyam Shah: "No."

Attorney: "You don't want to testify against your brother, do you?"

Shyam Shah: "No, I do not."

Interestingly, during his testimony Shyam couldn't remember who Reed Jordan was. He denied being present at a meeting between Joan Johnson and Reed Jordan at Joan's house in November 2002. He drew a convenient blank.

Attorney: "Reed Jordan & Company, a CPA firm that your brother got to work for Ms. Johnson? Reed Jordan, you don't know who that is?"

Shyam Shah: "I don't know who Reed Jordan is."

Shyam, it seems, even had a hard time remembering how often he had met the Johnsons. He vehemently denied living at the family's River Oaks home. Perhaps lying is a common Shah brother's trait, because there was no evidence to back Shyam's testimony. In fact, Jordan's own testimony and the 911 call evidence seemed to discount Shyam's entire account—and the jury was listening. At best, his witness stand demeanor could be described as drugged or wooden. Monotone answers, no eye contact, no facial expression—those were the hallmarks of his testimony. What effect this had on the jury was unknown, but again, his testimony was the equivalent of Tiger Woods saying, under oath, that he was faithful to his wife.

Final Days at
2933 Del Monte Drive,
River Oaks

Perhaps, if Reed Jordan had taken immediate action (even against Joan's urging), or if Shyam had stood up to his brother earlier, things might have taken a different turn. Perhaps December 14, 2002, would have never happened, could have been avoided altogether.

Or perhaps Dinny never would have been forced out of the Johnsons' lives. And if that had occurred, who knows what the home—and its occupants—would be like today.

In his final few weeks at the Johnson home, Dinny Shah became more liberal with his money. In October 2002, he bought over $100,000 worth of Persian rugs—and listed his address as 2933 Del Monte Drive. He also began hoarding money. On three separate occasions between November 7 and December 13, 2002, Shah withdrew $60,000 from his Frost bank account (the money, of course, having been a "gift" from Joan Johnson). There's no indication of what Shah did with either the rugs or the cash.

The abuse continued, too. Joan and Kaleta would each report one last attack before the December 14, 2002, events.

On November 4, 2002, Joan was in the driver's seat of the car, returning home from an errand. In one of his particularly sour moods, Dinny allegedly became angry with Joan over something. He reached over and slapped the right side of Joan's face.

According to Joan, one of her teeth punctured the right side of her upper lip, leaving her lip bleeding from the force of Dinny's hand. He also inflicted a blow to Joan's thigh, leaving a bruise near her groin. Once they got home, Joan secretly photographed the red mark that still stung on her cheek. Though she was finally collecting evidence against Dinny, Joan failed to alert the authorities about the assault.

On Thursday, November 28, 2002, Dinny walked into Kaleta's bathroom. "Your sink is leaking," he told her.

Kaleta, growing tired of Dinny's games, losing respect for the man who had been exposed as a fraud, snapped back at him, saying, "Why were you in my bathroom?"

According to Joan and Kaleta, Dinny flew off the handle at Kaleta's disobedience. He started hitting Kaleta on her chest and back, going so far as to pull hair out of her head. This incident, like all the others, was never reported to the police.

And then, on the night of December 14, 2002, Shyam Shah called 911 after his brother beat Joan and Kaleta in the car on the way home from a movie theater, and then later after they reached the Johnson home. When Officer Nguyen showed up, a terrified Joan Johnson opened the door, insisting that no such events had occurred. Shyam Shah lurked in the shadows of the hallway, listening to the conversation.

After several minutes of coaxing, Nguyen finally convinced Joan to let him enter the home, and he and another officer got Shyam Shah talking. It was Shyam who explained what happened that night. The officers found Kaleta Johnson locked in the bathroom, hiding from Dinny. Later that night, Hollifield and Nguyen took statements from Joan, Kaleta, Shyam, and Dinny. They also took pictures of marks and bruises on Kaleta and bruises on Joan. As far as HPD is concerned, bruises don't lie.

Dinny was arrested and taken to jail, charged with injury to a child. Shyam Shah moved out that night, escaping any involvement with the assault or with the events leading up to the assault. His whereabouts after the civil trial in 2008 are unknown.

The HPD officers continued to interview the family over the next few weeks. Little by little, the Johnson family began unraveling their sordid tale. Joan submitted the pictures that she had taken after Dinny slapped her in the car in early November. She also showed them the Ann Taylor suit she'd worn on their first trip to New York City; it was still bloody from where Dinny had kicked her.

The evidence was stacked against Dinny. Hollifield, Bounds, and Nguyen were sympathetic to the Johnsons and would be instrumental in finally extracting Dinny from the Johnson home. But even with Dinny temporarily behind bars, he wasn't out of Joan's life. He didn't give up that easily.

Joan Takes Back Her Life and Home

For the first time in six years, Joan Johnson was in control. Without Dinny around to intimidate her and tell her what to do, she took charge of the situation.

The day after Dinny's arrest, a magistrate's order for emergency protection was issued to the Johnson family. The order, signed by Judge Larry Standley and dated December 15, 2002, prohibited Dinny from communicating with the Johnson family in any way. As an extra measure of security, Joan called a locksmith and ordered every lock in the home changed. On December 16—a Monday— Joan formally revoked Dinny Shah's power of attorney. In a written statement, Joan nullified "any authority, power, trust, and delegation that I may have previously made to Dinesh K. Shah," on all of her financial, legal, and medical accounts, including Seth's and Kaleta's accounts.

And with Dinny out of the picture, Joan finally contacted her oldest son, Wirt Johnson. The two made amends, forgetting all of the bad feelings that had built up over the years, including the lawsuits. Wirt rushed from his apartment in Dallas to join the family in Houston. This was the first time Seth and Kaleta would see their brother in nearly five years. Wirt would now take his place as the family's patriarch, supporting his mother and siblings through the tough times that were ahead. Wirt was beginning to grow up.

The next few days leading up to Christmas were hectic, as the Johnson family finally united into a single unit against Dinny Shah. But even after his arrest and physical removal from the home, despite the changed locks and the temporary protective order, Dinny continued to hound the family.

On December 20, 2002, Joan Johnson was taking a walk in her neighborhood when, she claims, Shyam Shah pulled up to her in his car. It was the first time she'd seen Shyam since Dinny's arrest. According to Joan, Shyam told her that she owed him a lot of money; after all, he reasoned, he had saved her life. He had been the one to place the 911 call, resulting in his brother's arrest.

Joan refused to pay Shyam anything. Perhaps she was finally learning to stand up for herself and her family. Or perhaps, as Shyam would insist, Joan had made up the whole story, hoping to stack more evidence against the brothers. On the witness stand, Shyam denied ever speaking to Joan—for any reason—after the events of December 14.

But Joan wasn't the only one who had run-ins with the Shahs after Dinny's arrest. Kaleta testified in 2008 that, despite the protective order, the family lived in constant fear of Dinny, who was keeping a watchful eye on the family.

Kaleta claimed that Dinny often cruised their neighborhood, checking up on the family. It intimidated them enough that they hired an armed guard to watch the house. In January 2003, Joan filed for a second, permanent protective order: The new provisions of the protective order stated that Dinny wouldn't be allowed within two hundred feet of Seth, Joan, or Kaleta, and that he wasn't allowed to contact the family in any way—ever.

In a signed affidavit, Sharon Bryan, the Johnsons' neighbor, verified Kaleta's claim. Specifically, Bryan noted that "after Shah was arrested in December 2002, I observed Shah driving in the neighborhood. On several occasions, I saw Shah's vehicle parked near the west end of Del Monte, with Shah sitting in his car looking towards the Johnson house. On several other occasions, I saw Shah driving very slowly down Kirby looking towards the Johnson residence as he passed Del Monte. I found these actions by Shah to be unsettling, particularly since I knew that he had been arrested and charged with violence at the Johnson home."

It seemed that no matter what precautions Joan took to protect her family, Dinny continued to harass the Johnsons. Kaleta told the court that even after the family changed their home phone number, Dinny managed to get the new number:

"He [Dinny] would also try to call. He somehow got my, my phone number. I got a new phone after this," she said. "He somehow had the number. I would answer the phone and say 'Hello?' and he would say, 'Uh-huh.' That's how he used to, he used to make that sound a lot as in, 'Look what you've done, I'm going to get you' type of a threatening sound." His smirk could travel down a phone line.

No doubt the immediate relief of having Dinny gone from the family's lives was soured by Dinny's constant, menacing phone calls. The family was finally able to talk on the phone, use the Internet, and go anywhere they wanted without having to ask Dinny and without the threat of violent consequences if they disobeyed Dinny's direction. The blankets and sheets were taken down from the windows inside the house, and the tarp that had encircled the front gate was finally torn down. But they still weren't completely free from Dinny.

Thankfully, the Johnsons received overwhelming support from friends and neighbors. Ms. Bartz, Kaleta's school counselor, took control of the situation at St. John's, even going as far as holding a meeting with a few of Kaleta's classmates, just to let them know that their friend had been through a rough time.

In the weeks following Dinny's arrest, Bartz noticed that Kaleta seemed overwhelmed and withdrawn, though much less so than before. Bartz did what she could to help Kaleta feel safe and comfortable as she transitioned to a normal life. Both Bartz and Mr. Lombardi took turns picking up Kaleta and taking her to school in the mornings until exams were over and the winter break started.

Kaleta wasn't the only one feeling overwhelmed: Even two thousand miles away in Connecticut, Seth was not safe from Dinny's threats. On December 14, 2002, Seth was still away at the Salisbury School, preparing to come home for the Christmas holiday. Dinny claims that he only contacted the Salisbury School once after his arrest: He called to let the administration know that he would not be escorting Seth home for the holiday, as he'd planned. At no other time, he claims, did he try to contact Seth. But the family and school officials tell a different story.

Chisholm Chandler was immediately contacted by both Joan Johnson and HPD. After learning of Dinny's arrest, he put the word out, instructing faculty and staff to take extra precautions to ensure Seth's safety. He immediately changed the phone number to Seth's dorm room, and campus security was put on high alert. Dinny would not be welcome on the Salisbury campus. As an extra safety measure, Chandler personally escorted Seth to the Hartford airport for his trip to Houston for the Christmas break. Seth would be met at the airport in Houston by members of the Houston Police Department who would escort him home.

But according to Chandler, Officer Hollifield, and the Johnson family, none of the school's extra safety measures were enough to keep Dinny out of Seth's life at Salisbury. Once he realized that Seth's phone number had been changed, Dinny began calling Seth's teachers and Chandler. Chandler reported that as Shah became increasingly frustrated at not being able to talk to Seth, his phone calls became increasingly threatening. "Shah would scream at me at the top of his lungs," Chandler recalled. "Shah also shouted at me, in a veiled threat, 'Do you know who I am? How powerful I am?'"

Chandler had experienced Dinny's fury before; he had been receiving threatening phone calls from Dinny ever since Seth started attending Salisbury in October 2002. But Shah's arrest meant that the Salisbury School had no obligation to speak with Dinny. Eventually, Chandler stopped accepting Shah's phone calls. Shortly after, Dinny switched gears: He wasn't getting anywhere with the Salisbury administration, so he decided to turn to the students.

"Faces" is the official telephone directory of the Salisbury School. It is handed out to all Salisbury parents at the beginning of each school year, and it contains the names, photos, and contact information (at home and at school) of each student at Salisbury, by grade level.

During their search of Dinny's belongings in the weeks after his arrest, authorities came across a copy of "Faces," thrown in among the family records that Dinny maintained. What "Faces" showed would chill even hardened HPD investigators. It showed signs of heavy use—more than a dozen students' pictures were circled in bold, black marker; a few of them had notes scrawled in the margins. All of the students, it turned out, were close friends of Seth. If the administration would not cooperate, Dinny would get to Seth through his dormitory suitemates.

Chisholm Chandler began receiving complaints from students soon after Dinny's arrest. As Chandler put it, Dinny had started contacting Seth's friends, urgently, ardently trying to speak with Seth, who, like his sister, had also acquired a new phone number. On January 9, 2003, one of Seth's friends received fourteen calls from Shah in half an hour, Headmaster Chandler reported. Dinny even tried to bribe some of Seth's friends, offering them money if they would put Seth on the phone. There was a monster in River Oaks.

Bribes, threats, coercion: Chandler's reports certainly reveal desperation on Dinny's part. But the most interesting testimony—and the most damaging to Dinny's case—was the recordings Wirt Johnson had captured.

Even in Dallas, Wirt was not excluded from Dinny's intimidating game of phone tag: Almost immediately after Dinny's arrest, Wirt began receiving threatening phone calls from Dinny. The calls came to his home phone and his cell phone, and they were more than a little disconcerting; the calls usually ended with Dinny whispering things like, "You better be a good boy or you're going to get it."

The calls were too much for Wirt. He bought a tape recorder and hooked it up to his phone. This way he could record any conversations he had with Dinny.

Eventually, Wirt felt he'd collected enough evidence. On February 19, 2003, Wirt filed a formal complaint with the Dallas Police Department against Dinesh Shah. The night before, on February 18, Wirt received a message from Dinny. In the recording, Dinny's voice is heard whispering, "Faggot, you're dead. You're dead."

After filing the complaint against Dinny, the threatening phone calls miraculously stopped. But the evidence was preserved. At the 2008 civil trial, the jury would hear the actual recorded conversations. The Johnson trial team, well funded, would persuade Judge Christopher to let each juror have a specially created headset so that each word could be heard. The jurors listened to the words spoken by Shah, the whispered threats hanging in their ears; "Faggot, you're dead" had their effect as the jurors looked briefly at Shah and then quickly away.

———

Sometime after Dinny made bail, he reached out to his former friend, David Collie. David Collie had moved on with his life: He was a recent newlywed, and he and his wife were now living in Florida. He hadn't heard from Dinny in months—and he certainly hadn't heard about his former friend's arrest. Dinny was trying to rally witnesses, but David wasn't buying it. Dinny told David the same story he had tried to feed Officers Hollifield and Nguyen: Joan had been beating Kaleta on the night of December 14 while Dinny was out walking the family dog.

But that's not the account that David heard—and his video deposition testimony in 2008 was damning for Dinny. David began talking to Tio Newton, a lawyer and personal friend of both him and

Joan Johnson, who offered David another version of the December 14 events: According to David, Newton told him that Dinny was arrested for hitting Kaleta and that there were visible bruises on the teenage girl. Surely this was no surprise to Collie: He had seen the effects of Dinny's punishments firsthand. Despite Newton's account, Dinny would not be swayed from his original story:

Attorney: "What else did Shah say to you about the events of December 14, 2002?"

David: "No more because I—I didn't want to hear it. I just said you know, that's your own problem."

Not only had Dinny's own brother Shyam turned on him but Dinny's best friend had lost the stomach to help bail him out of trouble again. Dinny wouldn't find sympathy from anyone, not this time.

Dinny had not complied with the temporary protective order issued on December 15, which was later extended by a judge on January 7, 2003. So, on January 22, 2003, a hearing was called to determine if the Johnsons needed a permanent protective order against Dinny. The hearing included testimony from Joan, who outlined the events that occurred between 1996 and Dinny's arrest in 2002. The court granted the permanent protective order to the Johnsons, explaining the reasons for the decision as follows:

"The court finds that the applicant and respondent previously lived in the same household. The court finds that family violence has occurred and family violence is likely to occur again. The court finds that respondent, Dinesh Shah, has committed family violence. The court finds that the following protective orders are for the safety and welfare and in the best interest of the applicant and are necessary for the prevention of family violence."

According to the order, Dinny would be subject to arrest if he were within two hundred feet of Joan, Wirt, Kaleta, or Seth.

He was also prohibited from contacting the family members by phone.

Perhaps Dinny realized that he was finally defeated—that no matter what, he would never gain access to the Johnson wealth and standing. Or perhaps he knew that he was in deep, deep trouble. The phone calls stopped. Dinny must have realized that the circle was tightening.

———————

Dinny denied everything at the 2008 trial. He had not, as the Johnson family would have the jury believe, stalked, followed, or placed threatening phone calls to the Johnson family in the weeks following his arrest. According to Dinny, it was the Johnsons' lawyer, Paul Clote, who contacted Chisholm Chandler at the Salisbury School. The only call Dinny admitted to placing was to Luis Moran, the Johnson's groundskeeper.

Attorney: "Did you tell Mr. Moran that you wanted him to tell Seth Johnson that you loved him? Did you do that?"

Shah: "Sure, because I love the kids. Sure. What would be wrong with that?"

Dinny was still trying the same old tactic of using "love" to make it all right. In the past, his abuse followed a predictable pattern: violence followed by an explanation that "he did it because he loved" Seth or Kaleta. There is no reason to doubt this is the explanation he gave Joan, too.

———————

The last the family would hear from Dinny was on February 21, 2003, when one of Dinny's lawyers at that time, Patricia Wicoff, wrote a letter to Joan, asking for Dinny's personal effects. After his arrest, Dinny had not been allowed back into the Johnson home, and he wanted his things back. Even this letter reflects Dinny's over inflated sense of self-importance, his puffed-up ego: "Mr. Shah placed his beautiful belongings in your home not only to fill major gaps but primarily for the benefit of the children so that their taste, education, and general outlook on life might be developed and enhanced."

Attached to the letter were more than ten pages delineating all of Shah's possessions and where they could be found in the house.

Among the many chairs, rugs, and oil paintings that Shah was requesting was a 1963 Lincoln Continental sedan in pristine condition—no doubt the Lincoln Continental belonging to Mrs. Glennis Goodrich. Also among the items requested were several photos of Shah and the children that were scattered about the house; clearly, he wasn't ready to give up that portion of his life just yet. He was living a dream, and if he could not have the children next to him in person, he would try for the next best thing: photographs. Clearly, Dinny still wanted the good life. And would fight to keep it.

Dinny's Not Too Guilty Plea

The legal system, as many people know, is like a slow-moving machine. There are tactics that good lawyers employ that can slow the legal process to an almost complete halt. Dinny Shah's case was no exception; after his arrest in December 2002, he hired two very good criminal lawyers, well-known throughout Houston: Mike DeGeurin and Paul Nugent of DeGuerin & Nugent. Mike was no stranger to high-profile cases, having represented Paul Fratta in connection with the Branch Davidian standoff near Waco, Texas, a confrontation that ended when law enforcement charged the group's compound. He is also well connected to the River Oaks community. He represented Vanessa Leggett, a journalist who came to national prominence when she refused to disclose her sources for a book about Houston's most famous River Oaks bookie, Robert Angleton, who was assassinated in the late 1980s. And when voluptuous eighteen-year-old Christine Paolia, known as "Miss Irresistible," was accused in a Clear Lake, Texas, murder, Mike would be available to serve as her counsel.

Though the Johnson family was granted a permanent protective order in January 2003, and though the Houston Police Department continued to collect evidence and interview the family on a regular basis, there would be no swift action regarding Dinny's criminal charges.

During the investigation, the Johnsons cooperated with the Houston Police Department. On the night of Dinny's arrest, HPD confiscated twelve pistols and shotguns belonging to Joan Johnson and Dinny, as well as the designer alligator purse that Dinny used to beat Joan over the head. Joan also provided the Ann Taylor suit with a bloodstain on the leg; it was the suit she was wearing when Dinny kicked her at a New York City restaurant. The family gave multiple statements regarding their long and abusive history with Dinesh Shah and the phone calls and stalking they suffered for weeks after his arrest. Officers assigned to the case were also in contact with Chisholm Chandler, who was responsible for Seth's safety at boarding school.

Copies of the investigative report show that the Houston Police Department were baffled by the case and took the Johnsons' complaints very seriously. A report issued on December 17, 2002, said:

> Sergeant Bounds stated this is one of the most unusual cases he has seen. From his conversations with Joan Johnson, it appears that the physical abuse of Joan Johnson and her three children has been going on for years and probably includes the sexual abuse of 14-year-old Kaleta Johnson and her 16-year-old brother who is in boarding school out of town. . . . Joan Johnson is terrified of Dinny Shah which is the reason she has not reported this abuse previously . . .
>
> Shah's motive for this abuse appears to be to control Joan Johnson and her vast wealth . . .
>
> Sergeant Bounds advised that Shah's brother (listed #1 witness Shyam Shah) was probably in on the financial misappropriation of Joan Johnson's money but Shyam apparently got a conscience and called the police. . . . Shyam Shah told

Sergeant Bounds that he believes Dinny would have eventually killed Joan Johnson . . .

Sergeant Bounds believes that Joan Johnson and the others he has spoken to are credible people and he also believes that these other allegations merit follow up investigation.

If the allegations against Dinny Shah were that serious—and if the police did believe the family's story over Dinny's version of events—what took so long to get Dinny's case to trial?

In cases such as this, the district attorney often works closely with the victims for a period of a few months, gathering as much evidence as needed before going to trial. However, if the victim expresses little interest in having the case tried in a criminal court, district attorneys are often forced to enter into lenient plea bargains with the accused.

It would take more than three years for Dinny to go to court and face the charge of injury to a child, one of the least serious criminal charges he could have received. His lawyers were earning their fee by convincing the district attorney to reduce various felony charges involving sexual abuse to a child to a much less serious "injury to a child." On February 13, 2006, the day after Dinny's birthday, a punishment hearing was scheduled in the 182nd Criminal District Court. But according to the court's Record, there would be no witnesses in court that day. Dinny had already pled guilty to the charge; the hearing would only serve to determine Dinny's punishment, and he got the better of the plea bargain—deferred adjudication.

To think that someone charged with injury to a child—and someone who had committed increasingly heinous crimes for many years—could walk about freely for more than three years without any type of punishment should horrify the public. Joan Johnson should have been horrified too; now was her chance to get back at Dinny, to testify and expose him for the monster he is, to have him locked up behind bars for the many abuses she and her children had endured.

To its credit, the Johnson family was in court on February 12, 2006, the day Dinny faced the judge. But the Record reflects that the actual participants in the sentencing were Dinny, his lawyer, Paul Nugent, Assistant District Attorneys T. Buess and Jane Waters, and Judge Jeannie Barr, who presided over the hearing.

Considering that Dinny was facing a third-degree felony, there seemed to be no interest in pressing for a trial. So Dinny walked out of the 182nd court with a slap on the wrist. His punishment is summed up succinctly in the hearing document:

> *Terms of Plea Bargain: 10 years probation, $3,000 fine, 500 hours of community service; Pay for Kaleta Johnson's counseling, psychological, anger management classes; Verifiable full-time employment; Letter of apology to Kaleta Johnson; Return of the 2004 BMW to BMW financial services by 2/14/2006, and settlement of that debt; No contact with Kaleta Johnson or the Johnson family.*

That was it: a small fine, ten years of probation, community service, an apology letter, and return of the luxury car. The terms of the agreement also stated that Dinny wasn't allowed to drink alcohol, carry a firearm, or enter any nightclubs or bars for the duration of his parole. The luxury car—the BMW—is troublesome. It was a 2004 model, meaning that Dinny came into its possession *after* the arrest. It was a lease car but the lease cannot be located. Why, therefore, would the BMW's return be part of the deferred adjudication? Who co-signed on the lease? And why would the car's return be part of the plea bargain?

All parties agreed to the terms. Documents were signed by Judge Jeannine Barr, District Attorney T. Buss, Dinny, and his lawyer, Paul Nugent. The accused child abuser was once again out in the free world. Later, DeGeurin and Nugent would tell friends, "We walked him." Indeed.

Dinny disappeared from the Johnson's lives, as per the terms of his deferred adjudication. This could have been the last chapter of the Dinny-Johnson family saga had it not been for one small matter: the $2.5 million and more that Joan Johnson had "gifted" Dinny during their six-year relationship, in addition to priceless furniture, art, and guns.

Perhaps Joan Johnson could have pressed the DA harder to force Dinny to a jury trial where a jury of his peers could hear all the facts. For reasons still unclear, that did not happen. But what did happen is that on the very eve the two-year statute of limitations for tort cases was to run out, the Johnsons would file a civil suit for money damages against Dinny Shah and David Collie in the Harris County civil court system.

Was Joan Johnson really the neglectful, uncaring mother that Dinny claimed she was? Whether or not that's true, one thing is clear: Actions seemed to say that what she wanted was not jail time *for* the perpetrator as much as money *from* the perpetrator. The millionaire wanted money for the crime, not time behind bars.

Where Justice Is Rendered

The Harris County Civil Courthouse, completed in 2006 at a cost of $119 million, is equipped with the latest technology, from visual aid projectors to advanced security systems to sophisticated, state-of-the-art sound equipment. The courtrooms themselves are spacious, large enough to accommodate a major trial—as this one promised to be—yet compact enough to permit the jury, the judge, and spectators to see and hear every word of testimony, every nervous twitch, every hushed pause. The structure is a wonder of modern design, with one exception: the "church pews" in each courtroom for spectators.

The Harris County Civil Courthouse's church pews seem oddly out of place juxtaposed against the high-tech gadgets and the bustling streets of downtown Houston outside. Straight-backed and rigid, the pews are a throwback to a bygone era, when court and church were intertwined. In modern courthouses, courtroom benches sometimes have cushions to make them more comfortable. But the long, narrow high-backed construction invariably makes them anything but comfortable. *Stay if you must*, the pews say. *But it may not be comfortable to do so.*

In any other setting, this combination of the modern and traditional, of contemporary design and old-fashioned craftsmanship might have appealed to Dinny Shah, the man-about-town decked out in his Humphrey Bogart hat and suspenders.

But in May 2008, there was nothing appealing about the court's nod to tradition, not to Dinny, in any case: In a surprising turn of events—and shortly after Dinny decided to plead guilty in 2006—Joan Johnson on behalf of Seth and Kaleta had filed a civil suit against their former father figure. And they didn't stop there: Although he hadn't had contact with the Johnsons since 2002, David Collie found himself tangled up in Dinny's affairs again, named as a codefendant in the suit.

Though she'd eventually take the stand and offer her own version of the events leading up to December 14, 2002, Joan Johnson was not a named plaintiff at the time of trial. As soon as the children attained the age of eighteen, the Johnson lawyers dismissed Joan's case so that the jury would not be asked to even consider awarding her a money verdict.

Why did Joan wait over four years before taking legal action on behalf of the children? Perhaps Joan was acting on the advice of her attorneys and accountants. For years, Joan's trusted advisors stood quietly by as Dinny Shah swindled Joan, milking her for millions. They would be involved in handling the transfers and filing the appropriate paperwork that was necessary when Joan transferred a small fortune to Dinny. Why did no one blow a whistle? Presumably, they were obeying Joan's wishes. Her many detailed affidavits provided cover for Dinny and, ironically, for her advisors.

It's also possible that Joan had finally gathered the strength to fight back, after years of living under Dinny's thumb. Maybe, for the first time in twelve years, Joan was finally stepping up and acting like a different mother to her children, lashing out at the person who had caused them harm. It's even plausible that this was Joan's way of exacting revenge on David Collie for jilting her years before.

Joan's motivations, whatever they were, will probably never be completely clear.

And David Collie never faced his day in court: He would retain famed Houston litigator David Berg, of Berg & Androphy, who would skillfully negotiate a high, six-figure pretrial settlement with the Johnsons. While the exact amount of Collie's cash payment to the Johnson family is still under court seal, what is clear is that David Collie escaped the probing of a jury trial, a trial in which his sordid role would be revealed. He took what remains of his inheritance and moved to Florida, where he lives with his wife, Melinda. While he was subpoenaed for an oral and video deposition, he would not stay around to help Dinny, but neither would he stay around to discredit Joan. The jury would see only his video deposition, an ironic ending for a man who once fancied himself a video production mogul.

Dinny, however, didn't give up that easily, and he would face the jury alone.

For four weeks and three days in 2008, the church pews of Houston's 295th Judicial District Court would be home to a cast of familiar characters: HPD Officer Suzanne Hollifield. Sylvia Bartz. HPD Officer Kenneth Bounds. HPD Officer P. D. Nguyen. Eric Lombardi. Chisholm Chandler. Olabelle Hall. Shyam Shah. Luis Moran. Wirt Blaffer. Kaleta and Seth. Joan Johnson.

Anyone who knew Dinny Shah knew exactly what to expect from him during the trial: Denial. Rage. Convenient memory lapse. Falsehoods. Rabbit trails.

But no one expected what would happen when Seth and Kaleta took the stand. Though eighteen people testified against Dinny, painting him as a liar, a manipulator, and a fraud, it was the children's emotional testimony—particularly Seth's—that would prove most damning.

The Legal Battlefield

At the time of trial, the 295th Judicial District Court was presided over by the Honorable Tracy Christopher. Christopher grew up in Dallas and attended Ursuline Academy, a private Catholic girls' school whose motto is: *Serviam*, meaning "I serve." She takes the motto seriously. A graduate of the University of Texas School of Law, where she was an honor student, she joined the prestigious firm of Vinson & Elkins upon graduation and later moved to a boutique litigation firm, Susman Godfrey. In her more than fifteen years on the bench, Judge Christopher has developed a reputation for being fair, cautious, and professional. But make no mistake, it is her court and she alone rules it with an iron fist, but from inside a velvet glove.

The courtroom is arranged around the bench where Judge Christopher presides. To her immediate left would be the court clerk, Jay Hicks, an intense, courteous young man, in charge of documents and routine court business. Seated farther to the left and at his own station would be the bailiff, an armed deputy employed by the Harris County Sheriff's office but on permanent assignment to the court. In the 295th, that role is assumed by Winfred Seawood, a barrel-chested fireplug of a man whom one would be ill-advised to cross. Seawood, a longtime veteran of the Sheriff's Department, kept a watchful eye in the courtroom, ready to intervene if—or, in Dinny Shah's case, when—the verbal sparring might turn physical.

The two primary litigants in the case, Seth and Kaleta Johnson, would sit at the counsel table next to their team of lawyers. The Johnson trial team could easily be called a Dream Team. Lead co-counsel Paul Clote resembles an intense Keanu Reeves. He would be a relentless cross-examiner with a mind like a steel trap. His co-counsel, Jim Perdue, Jr., is a folksy, persuasive attorney with a ready smile and an understanding way. The jury would love him. He was Mr. Everyman, Opie, all grown up. Together they would be the Johnson family's avenging angels. And they lacked for nothing when it came to technical support. As F. Scott Fitzgerald noted, the "rich are different than you and I." The Johnson trial team would be well funded from the start, even to having its own IT support staff on hand, always ready to throw a graph, photograph, chart, or other document onto several TV screens. When a recorded phone call between Dinny and Wirt was played to the jury, a simple speaker would not do. No, the Johnson trial team had arranged for each juror to have a private set of headphones, the better to hear Dinny's whispered threats.

Before the trial even started, weeks and weeks of work had already been poured into the case. Jury selection took several days. Preparing arguments, witnesses, and expert opinions would take hundreds of man-hours for both the plaintiff and defense legal teams.

As the trial got under way, court coordinator Jackie Struss and official court reporter Kimberly Kidd had their work cut out for them. The defense alone submitted over five thousand documents in response to pretrial discovery motions filed by the Johnsons: Report cards, financial statements, family photos, diaries, affidavits, and other highly sensitive documents would become part of the public domain, except for those sealed by the court. Joan would be surprised by the number of documents that Dinny came to possess and to keep track of over the years. Likewise, the Johnson team had assembled several thousand exhibits of its own. Ultimately, after lengthy pretrial motions were heard, only 254 documents were marked as exhibits and offered for the jury's consideration.

After lengthy pretrial matters, testimony started on the morning of May 22, 2008, six years after Dinny Shah was forcibly removed from the Johnson home that December night. Judge Christopher leaned forward and asked, "Are the parties ready for trial?" "Ready for the plaintiff," intoned the Johnson team lead lawyer. "Ready for the defense," echoed Shah's lead lawyer. Shah sat silently at the counsel table during the process of jury selection, known to the law as *voir dire.* That phrase means "to hear and to see." Hopefully the truth. Impeccably dressed in pinstripes and wingtips, hair slicked back, Dinny resembled a comfortable country squire more than an accused child molester. Seth and Kaleta were no longer children. Kaleta was now twenty and a student at Georgetown University; her brother was attending a private school on the East Coast. Joan Johnson, always expensively dressed and coiffed, resembles in facial features and mannerisms the actress Susan Sarandon. At first, the family was standoffish with one another, but as the trial progressed and the anguished story came tumbling forth, a noticeable change came over each family member. They would meet at recesses and at the end of the day in a conference room where there would be howls of laughter when they had made points and silence when not.

In particular, the change in attitude was most noticeable in Wirt. He is a handsome young man who faintly resembles Justin Timberlake but with good posture. A change came over Wirt as he sat through the trial. Hearing the enormous grief he caused his mother and siblings seemed to finally, at long last, make an impression on him. Perhaps his wastrel life caused him to think.

His adolescent behavior, his physically intimidating manner, and his irresponsible, spendthrift ways came crashing down on him as he listened to his mother pour out her heart to a jury of complete strangers, many the type to whom Wirt would not give the time of day. As the trial progressed, a change in attitude gradually came over him. He became protective of Joan, a confidante to Kaleta, a source of strength for Seth. And he would viciously curse Dinny's legal team, under his breath, when no one was listening, except Dinny. Steinbeck once wrote that a boy becomes a man when a man is needed. Perhaps he had someone like Wirt in mind, for Wirt seemed to undergo that transformation.

Kaleta Johnson took the stand almost three weeks after the start of the trial. She appeared in a simple skirt and blouse. Keleta is soft-spoken and appealing. One might say she resembles Carrie Fisher when she played Princess Leia in *Star Wars*. Kaleta would be a powerful witness. Her testimony was matter-of-fact, something attorneys are used to seeing from victims of abuse. The witness seems to almost step out of the body and testifies as if peering down from above. Kaleta was completing her junior year at Georgetown, where she excelled in academics.

Over the next few hours, Kaleta would finally speak out against Dinny, detailing all of the insults, cruelty, physical violence and humiliating treatment that had been doled out to her.

Kaleta claimed that Shah would force her to sit on his lap. And then there was the ominous comment that Shah had yelled at the young Kaleta on the night of December 14, 2002: "I've been living next to you, I could f—k you if I wanted to."

That threat was of particular interest to Kaleta's lawyers:

Attorney: "Was the night of December 14 the first night that he had made some type of sexual threat against you?"

Kaleta: "That was the first time he had explicitly said anything. 'I've been living next to you . . .' that comment. But he had in the past, he would talk about marrying me and he would ask how many sons I wanted to have with him. And there was another time I was in my room and he came in and sometimes he would try to tickle me or something. And I would sit down on the floor if he tried to do that because he has a hernia and he can't bend over and, you know, I thought that would end the tickling. . . . But on that occasion he grabbed my ankles and he pulled my legs up towards him off the floor and he was trying to pull them apart. I was very upset, said, 'Stop that, what do you think you're doing?' And he kind of leered at me with this smirk and he said, 'What do you think girls are for?' He has a lot of hatred towards females that I've seen. Their only role is, you know, procreation, very derogatory towards females, called my mother a weak woman, a dumb woman, very misogynistic."

Dinny would have his chance to rebut. But his short, staccato answers to the detailed instances Kaleta described wouldn't have the impact he wanted:

Attorney: "Isn't it true that you grabbed [Kaleta] by the crotch that night [December 14, 2002] and said "I could f—k you any time I want"? Didn't you do that?"

Shah: "Totally false."

Attorney: "When no one else was home, on other occasions you got Kaleta to sit on your lap and you asked her questions about her breasts, didn't you?"

Shah: "Totally false."

Attorney: "You told Kaleta you wanted to marry her, didn't you?"

Shah: "No, I don't think so."

Attorney: "Did you talk to Kaleta about having your children?"

Shah: "Never."

Kaleta stepped down from the witness stand after about four hours. To the jury, here was a girl who had her head screwed on right. She was a survivor, a modern and powerful woman, and a for-keeps girl for some lucky man. As she left the stand, her testimony had validated and corroborated testimony of Bartz, Hall, Chandler, Bounds, and many others who had testified about what they had seen. But in the eyes of a jury, the acid test is the impression made by the litigants themselves. Kaleta passed the acid test.

As for Kaleta's mother, one must pause to consider the stress she was under during these years. Her behavior would seem incredible to many mothers, but studies report that "battered woman's syndrome" does not apply only to married women. It is the *relationship* that develops between male and female that matters. If it becomes one of dominant to subservient, almost unbelievable acquiescence may become the norm, not the abnormal. When Joan's behavior is viewed in this light, perhaps many of the things she did or did not do to protect Seth and Kaleta are understandable. And Kaleta never, not once, criticized her mother. She forgave her mother, something the jury would undoubtedly consider when deciding what role Joan's behavior should play in deciding fault. Things were beginning to look bad for D. K. Shah as Kaleta's testimony ended and as Seth Johnson hesitantly approached the witness stand and in a quavering voice took the oath. "I swear to tell the truth, the whole truth, and nothing but the truth, so help me God."

———————

For the most part, Seth Johnson's testimony went well: Seth, now a strapping twenty-two-year-old, resembled photographs of a young Luke Johnson, with blondish hair and a friendly, appealing manner. He even smiled as he settled into his seat in the witness box. His lawyers were about to earn their keep.

The experienced trial lawyer works hours and hours perfecting his ability to conduct "direct examination," meaning questions to his own client. He must be careful not to lead the witness and not to make the jury think he is "selling" his case. He must conduct a conversation under the guise of questions and answers. By any criteria, Seth made a very impressive witness. The first series of questions was simple and straightforward: where he was born, where he went to school, his young years, sports, movies. Then the testimony moved to Dinny and David. Here, a perceptible change began to creep over Seth. He kept his composure even when the subject turned to the "ants" game, to the scissor locks, to the pliers that pulled hair—even to the beatings he endured and the beatings of his mother where he could hear her cries. He soldiered on without as much as a quiver. And then the questions turned to sexual abuse.

Attorney: "When Mr. Shah moved into the house, do you remember what year that was?"

Seth: "Roughly around 2000."

Attorney: "How old were you at that time?"

Seth: "Thirteen, fourteen."

Seth had already described for the court his relationship with Dinny: He was a sort of father figure for the boy, an educator. But when his mood shifted, Dinny turned into a tyrant—like the time he beat Seth so severely with a cane that Seth couldn't attend school.

The discussion turned to the sleeping arrangements at the Johnson home—and a secret that Seth Johnson had been harboring for nearly eight years. Seth had kept Dinny's sexual abuse from everyone, including his mother and siblings. It wasn't until he began seeing a therapist in Rhode Island while he was attending a private school that he finally got the courage to speak out.

According to Seth, the sexual abuse started when Dinny moved into the Johnson home. He described these instances stoically, as he was led gently and slowly by his lawyers:

Seth: "He [Dinny] did come in to the bathroom while I was showering a few times, and he said he was showing me how to take a proper shower. He took a wash rag and wiped me down from head to toe."

Attorney: "Did that happen more than once?"

Seth: "Yes, sir."

What's more, though Dinny had his own bedroom in the Johnson home, he rarely slept in it. Instead, he bunked in one of the two twin beds in Seth's room.

Attorney: "Did anyone know that he was sleeping in the same room with you?"

Seth: "My mother and sister did."

Attorney: "Why would he sleep in the same room with you, if he had a room in the front [of the house]?"

Seth: "To keep an eye on me."

After lights out, Seth claimed that Dinny would often converse with him about sexually charged topics.

Seth: "He taught me how to masturbate."

Attorney: "What do you mean?"

Seth: "He called me over to his bed, which he was sleeping on the right-hand side of the fireplace. Yeah, he was sleeping in that bed. He called me over and he showed me how to masturbate."

Attorney: "How did he describe it? Just what he was doing or teaching you? What did he describe he was teaching you?"

Seth: "He told me he was teaching me what a man has to do and what a man must learn."

The courtroom became as silent as a tomb. All action came to a halt. No paper moved. The judge leaned forward. The bailiff, sensing what was coming, stoically folded his hands. The jury was on the edge of their chairs. The spectators seemed frozen in place, and the women among them grasped one another's hands. Only the court reporter moved, her hands, silently tapping out the testimony on her steno machine.

Sobbing, Seth at long last described the instances of sexual abuse that happened on their family vacations, when Dinny made sleeping arrangements so that he and Seth shared a hotel room, with Joan and Kaleta down the hall:

Attorney: "Seth, when you went on trips in 2001, 2002, and the sleeping arrangements were as they were, was there ever occasion where Mr. Shah performed a sexual act on you?"

Seth: "Yes."

Attorney: "Can you describe it?"

Seth (crying): "He said it's what two men do when they're in love and he said it's—he told me to take a knee and to—and—and he took off my boxers and inserted my penis in his mouth.

Attorney: "OK. Are you OK?"

Seth: "No." (A short pause in questioning for him to recover)

Attorney: "What did he say that was?"

Seth: "He said—he said that that's what two men do who are in love, it's what—it's what guys do that are in love."

As the questions continued, Seth never regained his composure. The sexual abuse that he had hidden since the age of thirteen when Shah moved into the Johnson home in 2000—came flooding back to him:

Attorney: "What did he tell you about telling anybody?"

Seth: "He said that I shouldn't and that we should keep it between us and that I should never tell anyone because it's no one's business."

Like a good boy, Seth kept his promise: He never told a soul, not his mother, not his sister, not the police. It wasn't until just before the 2008 civil trial that Seth finally told.

During Seth's reexamination, the subject of sexual abuse came up one more time, exposing even more horrible truths:

Attorney: "Seth, given the questioning I feel like I need to ask you because you were just asked, other than just the oral rape, did he [Dinny] do anything else?"

Seth: "Yes."

Attorney: "Is it hard to talk about?"

Seth: "Yes."

Attorney: "Let me ask it as technically as I can, Seth. Did the defendant place his mouth on the sexual organ of you when you were under the age of seventeen?"

Seth (crying): "Yes."

Attorney: "Did the defendant, when you were under the age of seventeen, insert his sexual organ into your anus?"

Seth: "Yes."

Attorney: "Did that happen more than once?"

Seth (crying): "Twice."

Attorney: "Seth, let me ask you this: Do you feel shame?"

Seth (crying): "Yes."

Attorney: "No further questions, your honor."

"The witness may be excused," said Judge Christopher. There was an audible sigh. People began to breathe again.

———————

By the time Dinny took the stand for rebuttal, the jury was already swayed. The sheer emotional drama of his testimony made it difficult to believe that Seth had simply made up the whole thing. Dinny denied everything.

Attorney: "When Seth was thirteen years old, didn't you tell him you wanted to teach him to properly shower? Didn't you do that?"

Shah: "No. The showers in the house were not operating. The kids were taking a bath out in the pool when I got there."

Attorney: "Did you ever use a soap bar to wash Seth Johnson?"

Shah: "I did not."

Attorney: "Didn't you instruct Seth how to masturbate in his room at night?"

Shah: "That's ridiculous. Absolutely not."

Attorney: "You instructed him to masturbate until he ejaculated. You did that, didn't you?"

Shah: "Absolutely not."

Attorney: "Did you tell Seth that there are things that men do when they love each other? You told him that, didn't you?"

Shah: "Absolutely not."

Shah had the opportunity to explain himself many more times but would decline the opportunity. Most of the instances of sexual abuse that Seth had described took place either while the family was on vacation or while Shah was visiting Seth at boarding school in Connecticut.

Attorney: "Traveling outside Houston, you stayed in the same hotel room as Seth, didn't you?"

Shah: "We traveled as a family together."

Attorney: "I'm just asking, did you share a hotel room with Seth, traveling outside of Houston?"

Shah: "We always had separate hotel rooms. He stayed with his mother and sister. I stayed in a separate room."

Attorney: "Did you take him up to Salisbury School in Connecticut by yourself?"

Shah: "Yes, I did."

Attorney: "The truth is, Mr. Shah, isn't it, that when you traveled outside Houston and stayed in a hotel room with Seth, you inserted your penis into him? Didn't you do that?"

Shah: "That's outrageous and that's a lie and you know it. I have never done anything in that manner, never been accused. This is the first ever. It is an outright lie."

Attorney: "You used the hotel hand lotion as lubricant, didn't you, Mr. Shah?"

Shah: "You know that's a lie. I never did that."

During his testimony, Seth, Kaleta, and Wirt observed as if from a different galaxy. Joan would only stare at the floor. Dinny had perjured himself too many times. No one would believe him over the young Seth Johnson. When Shah stepped down from the witness stand, he'd be confronted by twelve stony-faced jurors.

In every jury trial there is a turning point just as there is in a football game, a war, a revolution, or a failed relationship. This trial's turning point occurred during Seth's testimony and was characterized by sobbing. But not all the sobs were from Seth who often was able to compose himself. No, the sobbing that truly mattered came from the worst possible place for Dinny—the jury box. Three of the female jurors had heard enough. Judge Christopher quickly declared a short recess, but the damage had been done.

The thousands and thousands of dollars spent by the Johnson legal team on exhibits, fancy diagrams, recording devices, lengthy depositions, and expensive expert witnesses would no longer be necessary. In two hours and eleven minutes Seth Johnson won the case for his attorneys with a simple, childlike recitation of what he remembered happening to him. The turning point in the case of *Seth and Kaleta Johnson v. D. K. Shah, No. 2006-38382, in the 295th Judicial*

District Court of Harris County, Texas had arrived. One must wonder what R. L. Blaffer would think as he looked down on this spectacle. He would be enormously proud of his great-grandson and great-granddaughter. But what would he think of those who let it happen? On this day Exxon Mobil stock closed at one of its all-time highs. Who in the family would notice?

The Jury Speaks

By the time the Johnson-Shah trial was winding down, almost four weeks after it began, court reporter Kimberly Kidd had nearly 1500 pages of typed testimony. The patient jury had heard from more than 20 different witnesses, including HPD Officers Hollifield and Bounds, and expert testimony from one of the plaintiff's psychiatrists, Dr. Arthur Farley. The jury had carefully reviewed the 254 exhibits.

The testimony was complete, all relevant exhibits admitted into evidence, and now it was time for the reading of the Charge of the Court. In Texas, the Charge is written by the judge and consists of three parts: First, there are general instructions given to the jury, "don't talk to the lawyers, don't do your own investigation, don't discuss the case outside of court." Second, the Charge contains legal definitions that the judge feels are appropriate. "Reasonable care" is defined, as is "proximate causation" and "burden of proof." Finally, and most important, the Charge contains a list of written questions—much like a high school exam—to which the judge asks the jury to decide disputed issues of fact. In this Charge, the jury would be asked thirteen questions ranging from whether Dinny intentionally inflicted emotional harm on the children to whether Dinny violated a section of the Penal Code by his treatment of Seth. While this was not a criminal trial, violation of the Penal Code would form the basis of punitive damages. And the jury is asked to decide how much money, if any, should be awarded. After the Charge of the Court had been read to the jury, the judge paused momentarily, took a deep breath and asked, "Are counsel ready for final summation?" After a month of legal war, it was the lawyers' last chance to explain, to persuade, and to influence.

First up was Paul Clote, lead counsel for the Johnsons. He asked the jury to examine pictures of Seth and Kaleta; pictures taken before Dinny Shah took over. In one picture, Seth is dressed in his Little League uniform, grinning at the camera, bat in hand. In another, Seth and Kaleta are sitting on the stairs of their home on Del Monte Drive, just goofing around.

"Seth looks like a happy enough kid, a normal enough kid," Clote said as the jury studied the images. "These children were so young; they were OK."

But, Clote concluded, because of the abuse both children suffered at Dinny's hands, these "normal enough" kids grew up to be cautious, emotionally damaged young adults, forever altered by the terrors of their formative years:

"These are scars you don't hide with clothing: Kaleta went through high school without ever having a boyfriend," Clote said. "Seth lives in Rhode Island because of the fear and horror of that house—he still can't go back into what is supposed to be his home."

Clote began weaving a bitter tale, connecting the dots for the jury into a heartbreaking narrative:

"[Dinny] ingratiated himself into the family. Then he began to isolate them. Then he began to make them wholly dependent upon him. Then he started to manipulate and control and abuse. And over time, it got worse."

In closing, Clote cautioned against falling into the same trap that had held the Johnsons captive for six years:

"Now, the defendant says, well, no, nothing like that ever happened, and nothing like any of the events described by the plaintiffs ever happened, what happened on December 14, 2002, didn't happen. Everybody is lying. The police, everybody. Except the defendant. That's his position.

"He has the temerity to come in here and make those perjured statements. . . . He's the most practiced liar I have ever, ever—in thirty-one years of law practice—seen.

"Now, how do you feel about his conduct? Let me tell you what's significant. He uses deception and lies to control people. So when he comes into this courtroom and continues with the deception, trying to perpetrate the deception on you, boy oh boy, he's trying to manipulate and control *you*."

As Clote and co-counsel Jim Perdue, Jr., skillfully reviewed the facts of the case, they offered the jury a suggestion for reparations in damages to be paid to Seth and Kaleta Johnson for their lost childhood. It was the same number that Dinny Shah claimed to have made for the family through his financial services: $40 million. "Not a penny less" was counsels' last admonition, else there would be no justice.

Rebuttal would not be easy for the defense counsel. Dinny Shah certainly was not a sympathetic character, not compared to Seth and Kaleta Johnson, and the facts seemed to be stacked against Dinny. The defense counsel's only strategy was to rely on the weakest part of the Johnson's case: the strange, almost unbelievable behavior of Joan; that had she put a stop to Dinny the first time, there would have been no subsequent abuse. He would argue that Joan Johnson's inaction as well as her lack of responsibility was as shocking as many of the things David Collie and Dinny Shah were accused of doing. Who was really telling the truth?

Lead counsel for the defense—Michael Phillips—summed it up as best he could, given the circumstances. He would submit to the jury that many inexplicable events occurred in the family's long and tangled history both before and after Dinny Shah and David Collie came on the scene. Many of them—abandonment, frequent school changes, forced attendance at preparatory schools, kicking/screaming by the mother—would be a probable source of mental anguish and physical pain that the children suffered regardless of what Dinny did or did not do. The accusations against Dinny were exaggerated, he would argue, in order to deflect jury attention from Joan's failure to blow the whistle, to resort to the legions of lawyers who looked after her millions, to respond to helpful neighbors. To do something, anything. Who could say what was more traumatic to a child: being kicked and screamed at by a parent or being hit and screamed at by a stranger? How could a jury separate the multiple strands of a child's mental anguish under these circumstances and assign to each strand a monetary value?

What, for example, became of Joan's diary and her plan to force David Collie to propose to her? Was this civil trial just a fabricated conspiracy against Dinny Shah, similar to the conspiracy Joan recorded in her diary about Wirt's accusations of sexual abuse against David Collie?

Was Joan Johnson really a battered, terrified woman so terrified of Dinny Shah that she failed to tell anyone about her situation for six years? Why didn't she say anything to any of her friends, family members, or professional acquaintances? Was the reason that Joan Johnson did nothing to stop Dinny from abusing her children because *she*, too, had neglected them as Seth and Kaleta's "Things for Mom Work On!" memo would suggest?

And then, perhaps the biggest unanswered question: If Kaleta and Seth had truly suffered the horrors described, why did Joan wait so long to file suit? Four years.

"There are holes after holes after holes in this case," he said. And this meant that the Johnsons' counsel hadn't fulfilled their obligations under Texas law; put simply, they hadn't carried their burden of proof.

"I hope you were looking at the family. I didn't see any rage. I saw son, daughter, sister, politely talking to each other, sometimes laughing out in the hall, laughing in the courtroom. Seth smiled at my client the first day of trial, big smile, a big smile. There is no pain and suffering, no mental anguish here."

Almost a full day had passed by the time the attorneys completed final summation. All were exhausted. Four weeks of testimony with major financial consequences for a historic Houston family had finally concluded.

It was now up to the jury.

Many experienced litigators—trial dogs they call themselves in private—think that waiting on a verdict is more difficult than the trial itself. There is nothing to do. Walk, drink tepid coffee, make long, meaningless phone calls, renew better relations with opposing counsel, urinate a lot, joke with the judge, flirt with court reporters, and try to work on other matters. In the Harris County Civil Courthouse, the jury indicates that it has reached a verdict by pressing a buzzer that is located next to the door inside the small and narrow Jury Deliberation Room, a room located a few steps from the Judge's Chambers. The Jury Deliberation Room is guarded by the bailiff during deliberations. Time crawled.

On June 11, 2008, the buzzer finally sounded. The judge quickly assembled court staff, the reporter, the attorneys, and their clients. The twelve jurors solemnly filed back into the courtroom. They had deliberated for eighteen hours. "Ladies and gentlemen of the jury have you reached a verdict?" asked the court. "We have your honor," said the jury foreman, a distinguished, middle-aged man. "Please hand it to the clerk," instructed the court. The judge silently read the answers, making certain to not let facial expression give away the jury's verdict. The verdict was then read aloud. It was not a happy ending for D. K. Shah. By a unanimous verdict, the jury found that Dinny had intentionally inflicted pain and mental anguish on the children, and had violated the Penal Code in the process thereby providing a basis for an exemplary damage award. And then the jury awarded monetary and exemplary damages of $20.75 million to Kaleta and Seth to be divided between them in accordance with the jury's assessment of damage to each. Seth would receive the largest share. As the verdict was read, some members of the jury closely observed the effect on Dinny. Others smiled at Kaleta and Seth. But to all on the jury, the verdict was their final say. They sent a message by their verdict. Dinny's lawyers could take solace only that the amount awarded by the jury would be just half of what the Johnsons' lawyers asked the jury to award, something that more than one courthouse wag would later call "a miracle in May."

Of course, Kaleta and Seth may never see the millions that they were awarded. Although Dinny got at least $2.5 million from Joan, no one today knows where the money is. Is it hidden? Is it in India? Will Joan's lawyers be able to find it? Everything he owned, every penny to his name, he owed to the vulnerable rich people he preyed on: He had pilfered from Glennis Goodrich's pocketbook, and had added to his wealth by manipulating Joan Johnson's generosity— from the $2.5 million she gave him, to the expensive antiques, clothes, and vacations Joan paid for—all given to him as tokens of appreciation for helping Joan manage her finances and raise her children.

The end of a complex jury trial is always anticlimactic. Once the jury verdict is read, there is a noticeable exhaling by all concerned. There is a period of silence, sometimes thoughtful silence, as the impact of the verdict sinks in. And then formality again takes its rightful place and the lawyers busy themselves with mundane tasks.

The hallway outside the 295th was deserted that bright morning when the verdict was handed down. After the verdict, it had taken the lawyers a while to pack their files, the bulging briefcases, and video equipment. Good-byes were said to court staff, embraces shared, lunch dates made. The litigants and their attorneys moved, almost as one, to the elevators, ironically the only time during the past month they had walked in unison. Their steps echoed in the dark hallway as they walked suddenly conscious that there was a victor and a vanquished. The Johnson trial team was understandably jubilant. Indeed, if there is one good thing to come from the trial it would be that the family was reunited. Years, perhaps decades, of disagreement and anger seemed replaced by understanding and cooperation. Perhaps the lasting legacy of the trial will be that a splintered family was rejoined. Great-grandfather Blaffer would approve.

The defense team was somber and downcast as it slowly moved to the elevator banks, each attorney on the team asking himself if something, anything, could have been done to have improved the odds, to have avoided the result. But the one member of the defense who was noticeably not as perturbed or downcast was none other than D. K. Shah. Unhappy of course, disappointed, but not devastated. Affable in fact. He would console the losing defense counsel, extending a kindness unexpected from one who has just been branded with a multimillion dollar verdict.

At street level, the lawyer and client parted on the crowded steps of the Harris County Civil Courthouse as throngs of lawyers, clients, judges, witnesses, jurors, and others swirled around them in the heat and humidity. In this circumstance the lawyer will always pause, deferring to the feelings of the client, seeking to ease the client's pain. But that was not necessary. D. K. Shah warmly shook the hand of his counsel, bounded down the courthouse steps, and then at the bottom paused momentarily to look back, flashed the confident smile he used so often on so many people, gave a jaunty wave, and melted into the crowd.

He is out there somewhere today.

Epilogue

On a sweltering June morning five days after the verdict, an aging Jaguar rolled through the ornate gates of Glenwood Cemetery, past towering statues and rows of neatly trimmed hedges, past the grave of Howard Hughes, former governors and power brokers to the final resting place of a famous Houstonian. The car's driver was a tall, lanky lawyer. He had come to pay respects to a man he learned to admire during the trial. The lawyer was there to visit the grave of R. L. Blaffer.

The marker itself is simple: R. L. Blaffer 1878-1942. There is no elaborate headstone or flowery engraving. It is almost as if the heirs knew even then that they could not and would not fill his shoes. Ever. The lawyer approached the grave hesitantly. As he stood under the canopy of oaks, many emotions swept over him, many desperate cries for help were remembered, many stories that shocked and dismayed would cross his mind. What was to become of the children? What would become of Joan? And most importantly, what would become of Dinny, the man seemingly nonplussed by the verdict, upbeat as always. Would there be more Glinnis Goodriches in his future? More Michael Holsteins? More Joans? More Seths?

As he pondered on what he had seen, one knee unconsciously dropped to the manicured turf and a Catholic Prayer for the Dead came to his mind:

God our Father,
Your power brings us to birth,
Your providence guides our lives,
And by Your command we return to dust.

Would this be the end of the story? He was momentarily depressed because these facts can be forgotten, swept under the memory rug. He knew from experience that the litigants would now go on with their lives, glad to have the ordeal over. The lawyers would have new clients to represent. The court would handle other cases.

But, he thought, is there not a lesson to be learned here? Is this not a story that may teach, remind, and caution? Isn't this more than just a story about River Oaks, about Houston? There has to be some good that comes from this sordid tale. Else, what occurred in the 295th Judicial District Court would be just another gossip column space filler. And it was at that moment a decision was made that the story would be told—fully and completely—so that hopefully others would learn the hard lesson: Victimization can creep up on you. Wealth, privilege, and social standing may be no protection.

Almost a half day had passed since he arrived at the gravesite so lost was he in his thoughts. Under the gently rustling oaks the lawyer—Dinny's lawyer in fact—slowly turned away and walked thoughtfully to his car.

About the Author

Michael Phillips is a graduate of the University of Texas School of Law. He currently resides in Houston, where he is a managing partner of a mid-size litigation firm. He is married and has two daughters. This is his first novel.

Febuary 21, 1998

Things for mom to work on!

1. don't scream

2. no vidence / kicking

3. don't talk to much

4. keep your trap shut

5. don't talk to much on phone

6. sign KKs work fast!

signed

KALETA & SETH JOHNSON

Kaleta & Seth Johnson

The controversial "No Violence" memo to mom.

CERTIFICATION OF VITAL RECORD

City of Houston, Texas

STATE OF TEXAS   CERTIFICATE OF DEATH   STATE FILE NUMBER

1. NAME OF DECEASED (a) FIRST	LUKE
(b) MIDDLE	JOHNSON, JR.
(c) LAST	JOHNSON, JR.
(d) MAIDEN	
5. SEX	MALE
3. DATE OF DEATH	MAY 5, 1995 found
4. DATE OF BIRTH	MAY 4, 1948
5a. AGE	47
8. BIRTH PLACE	HOUSTON, TEXAS
7. SOCIAL SECURITY NO.	465-72-3220
8. RACE	CAUCASIAN
11. EDUCATION	16
13. MARITAL STATUS	NEVER MARRIED
SURVIVING SPOUSE	NONE
14a. USUAL OCCUPATION	PRESIDENT
14b. KIND OF BUSINESS	AUTOMOBILE
15a. RESIDENCE STREET ADDRESS	311 BAY RIDGE
15b. CITY OR TOWN	MORGAN'S POINT
15c. COUNTY	HARRIS
15d. STATE	TEXAS
15f. INSIDE CITY LIMITS	YES
16. FATHER'S NAME	LUKE JOHNSON, SR.
17. MOTHER'S MAIDEN NAME	SHIRLEY ROACH

18. PLACE OF DEATH: RESIDENCE

19. COUNTY OF DEATH: Harris   20. CITY: Morgan's Point   21: 311 Bay Ridge

22. INFORMANT: SON   23. MAILING ADDRESS: 1904-C NANTUCKETT HOUSTON, TX 77057

24. METHOD OF DISPOSITION: BURIAL

25. PLACE OF DISPOSITION: GLENWOOD CEMETERY

26. LOCATION: HOUSTON, TEXAS   27. DATE: 05-08-1995

28. FUNERAL HOME: GEO. H. LEWIS & SONS, 1010 BERING DRIVE, HOUSTON, TEXAS 77057-2110

29. SIGNATURE OF FUNERAL DIRECTOR: JAMES E. ALLEN #9642   *James E. Allen*

30. CERTIFIER: MEDICAL EXAMINER

31. SIGNATURE & TITLE: Mahinder S. Natula, M.D. Assistant Medical Examiner, 1885 Old Spanish Trail, Houston, Texas 77054-2098

32. DATE SIGNED: 6 16 95   33. TIME OF DEATH: unknown M.

IMMEDIATE CAUSE: Close range gunshot wound of chest, through and through.

37. DID TOBACCO USE CONTRIBUTE: —   38. DID ALCOHOL USE: YES   39. DECEDENT PREGNANT: —

34a. AUTOPSY? NO   34b. AUTOPSY FINDINGS AVAILABLE: NO

40. MANNER OF DEATH: SUICIDE   41. DATE OF INJURY: found 5-5-95   TIME: unknown   INJURY AT WORK: NO   PLACE: home

41d. LOCATION: 311 Bay Ridge, Morgan's Point, Harris, Texas

41e. DESCRIBE HOW INJURY OCCURRED: Shot

42. DATE RECEIVED BY LOCAL REGISTRAR: JUNE 20, 1995   *R. W. Hanks*

U7967

2256722

STATE OF TEXAS, COUNTY OF HARRIS   CERTIFIED COPY OF VITAL RECORDS   DATE ISSUED 20 JUN 1995

This is a true and exact reproduction of the document officially registered and placed on file in the BUREAU OF VITAL STATISTICS, HOUSTON HEALTH AND HUMAN SERVICES DEPARTMENT.

R. W. Hanks — R. W. Hanks, Registrar, BUREAU OF VITAL STATISTICS

This copy not valid unless prepared on engraved border displaying seal and signature of Registrar. LAMINATION MAY VOID CERTIFICATE.

ANY ALTERATION OR ERASURE VOIDS THIS CERTIFICATE

DEFENDANT'S EXHIBIT DS 68

Official report, death by suicide.

CAMILLA D. TRAMMELL
2 BRIARWOOD CIRCLE
HOUSTON, TEXAS 77019

February 6, 1980

Mr. Luke Johnson, Sr. &
Mr. Luke Johnson, Jr.
3998 Inverness
Houston, Texas

Gentlemen:

I recently learned that my daughter Joan Blaffer Johnson is working toward a very considerable investment in the Luke Johnson Ford Agency of Houston. As you know, my daughter is very unsophisticated in business matters and emotionally involved with both of you, therefore I request that you cooperate with her retaining proper independent legal counsel in this investment.

While I understand you have retained your own legal advice, I do not believe that my daughter's interest in this matter is adequately served by this arrangement.

I would appreciate your cooperation in this matter and am available to work toward this end at your earliest convenience.

Sincerely yours,

Camilla D. Trammell

Camilla D. Trammell

CDT/rjb

Mother-in-law scolding Luke.

February 19, 1999

My name is Joan Blaffer Johnson and I am a resident of Houston, Texa

My address is 2933 Del Monte which is located in Houston, Texas

My phone number is 713-942-2322 I have three (3) children; Wirt Dav

Johnson, Kaleta H H Johnson, and Seth C B Johnson D K (Dinny)

Shah and David Wade Collie have been very close friends of my family

Mr Shah and Mr Collie came into my life when I needed much help

They have contributed to my life and my children's lives so much

In the past, I said many wrongful and untrue statements regarding

D K Shah and David Wade Collie I am in love with David Wade

Collie and when I am mad at him, I often use wrongful tactics and

make untrue statements about his character and Mr Shah's

character On one such occasion I l̶i̶/ lied about Mr Shah's and Mr

C̶o̶o̶// Collie's intention with my daughter, K̶l̶a̶t̶e̶a̶ KALETA Johnson I implied

that there was s̶e̶x̶u̶a̶l̶/ sexual misconduct on the part of Mr Collie

and Mr Shah This accusation and statement was a lie by me Mr Col

refused to marry me and I stupidly thought that I could entrap him,

Mr Collie, into marriage by lying about his intentions and Mr, Shah

intentions. I am very sorry about this behavior on my part Mr Shah

and Mr Collie have been nothing but gentlemen to me and my children

_____

JOAN BLAFFER JOHNSON

_____

NOTARY PUBLIC

Joan's 1999 false accusation affidavit.

June 22, 2000

Dear Terri,

Would you please draw up a General Power of Attorney for me and one for health also. I wish for David Wade Collie and D. K. Shah to be appointed. I would also like for you to draw papers concerning guardianship for Seth and Kaleta with the same persons appointed and the alternate persons being Mr.   and Mrs. Shah.

Sincerely,

Joan Johnson

Joan Blaffer Johnson
2933 Del Monte
Houston, Texas 77019
713-942-2322
713-807-8443 FAX

DEFENDANT'S
EXHIBIT
DS 33

Signing away her life and health and even children to David and Dinny.

Aug 22 06 01:30p   WDB
AUG-22-2006 12:57   MERRILL LYNCH   713 807-8443   p.7
                                                              P.16/19

7/12/2001
PlCASE ChECK

Dear Dave,

Please transfer the amount of $250,000.00 dollars from my Merrill Lynch account to D. K. Shah's account using my Exxon stock with the low basis. This is considered as payment to him. Thank you.

Sincerely,

Joan Blaffer Johnson

Joan Blaffer Johnson
2933 Del Monte
Houston, Texas 77019
713-942-2322
713-807-8443 FAX

XOM
Move   1177   SHARES   INTO   ACCOUNT   SR   53477.
Move   1177   SHARES   INTO   ACCOUNT   582-54R54
Move   58+   SHARES   INTO   ACCOUNT   582-44L16

7   0000000097

Joan's first $250,000 transfer to Dinny, one of many.

THE KINKAID SCHOOL

201 Kinkaid School Drive, Houston, Texas 77024
(713) 782-1640

April 4, 1994

Mrs. Luke Johnson
2 Briarwood Ct.
Houston, TX 77019

Dear Joan:

I am disappointed that Kaleta will not be continuing at Kinkaid in
1994-95.

Kaleta is able, promising, personable. We will miss her, students and
teachers alike.

I am disappointed that you presented me with a fait accompli, Joan.
Also I'm disappointed by your expressed reasons for withdrawing Kaleta,
namely, the unwillingness of parents to include Kaleta in a carpool and
classmates who are sometimes unfriendly. All of this sounds rather
childish.

Your Aunt Jane also visited me to express disappointment that a great
grandchild of one of the school's founding trustees should be mistreated
by the school. I was astonished at this, though I didn't let Mrs. Owen
know my feelings. I would be deeply disappointed if any child were mistreated by the school. But I don't know what the school can do about
adult relationships involving voluntary carpool arrangements. Nor can
the school really get involved in the personal relationships of students
beyond our teachers' constant efforts to promote good manners and equally
constant refusal to knowingly tolerate bad behavior among children. Of
course, we cannot legislate friendships among the children however much
we might wish to do so. On the other hand, sensitive, wise teachers
can and do help children to develop appropriate social skills, reduce
inevitable conflicts, and lessen the emotional pain that children
occasionally inflict on one another. But teachers are unaware too often
of problems between children and need parents' help in this.

Well, you must know that we'll do everything possible to assure that
Kaleta's final weeks at Kinkaid are educationally meaningful and
personally rewarding.

Best wishes always,

Glenn Ballard
Headmaster

GB:jb

Carpool controversy results in Kaleta's withdrawal from elite school.

Joan Blaffer Johnson

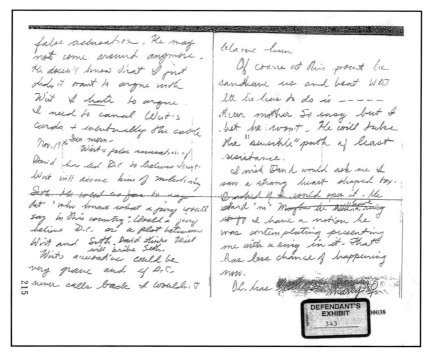

Joan's diary speculation of sexual abuse by David Collie.

June 21, 2000

Dear Terri,

I firmly believe that my son Wirt has lied to this attorney
that called you. My son came back to Houston in the summer of 1996
the year after his father had died. In the summer of 1996, he
obtained his driver's license at the age of 16. I also bought
him a brand new Jeep Grand Cherokee- Eddie Bauer Edition for
$42,000.00 dollars. That fall of 1996, he flunked out of Lamar
High School and he had tired of his Jeep and demanded a new Tahoe.
Wirt did absolutely nothing but sit in the house and demand more
and more expensive items. He picked on his little brother and
sister to the point where I had to take Seth to the doctor. My
sister Sarah advised me to send Wirt to a lock-up boarding school
where he could concentrate and receive his high school diploma.
After   running away several times from the boarding school,
he finally graduated and received his high school diploma. Every
step of the way, I have had to remain firm with Wirt; give him an
inch and he takes 200 miles. Wirt has blamed everybody for being
sent to boarding school but himself. Every person or individual
is responsible for his failures. He never blames himself for his
own misdeeds. I will not tolerate a bully son who is being used
by his two older half brothers to try to get money out of me and
my son. I question the integrity of this lawyer and I know for
a fact that Peter and Tracy are the individuals who hired and
paid the lawyer.

Joan Johnson

Joan's "My Bully Son" affidavit when sending Wirt away.

ORDER DEFERRING ADJUDICATION OF GUILT

CAUSE NO. **1040406**

THE STATE OF TEXAS
VS.

DINESH KUMAR SHAH
(Name of Defendant)
AKA

IN THE **182ND** DISTRICT COURT

COUNTY CRIMINAL COURT
AT LAW NO.

OF HARRIS COUNTY, TEXAS

Date of Order: **02/13/2006**   Date of Offense: **12/14/2006**

Attorney for State: **T BUSS**

Attorney for Defendant: **P NUGENT**   ☐ Defendant Waived Counsel

Offense: **INJURY TO CHILD** *under 15 Bodily Injury*

☐ A MISDEMEANOR, CLASS: ☒ A FELONY, DEGREE: **3RD**

Terms of Plea Bargain (In Detail): **10 YR DADJ/$3000 FINE, 500 HR COMMUNTY SREVS PAY FOR KALEETA JOHNSON'S COUNSELING, PSYCHDOGICAL, ANGER MANAGEMENT CLASSES VERIFIABLE FULL-TIME EMPLOYMENT, LETTER OF APOLGY TO KALEETA JOHNSON, RETURN OF THE 2004 BMW TO BMW FINANCIAL SERVICES BY 02/14/2006, AND SETTLEMENT SETTLEMENT OF THAT DEBT. NO CONTACT WITH KALEETA JOHNSON OR THE JOHNSON FAMILY**

(Make appropriate selection – N/A = not available or not applicable)

Plea to Enhancement Paragraph(s)	1st Paragraph N/A	2nd Paragraph N/A	Charging Instrument: Indictment
Findings on Enhancement(s):	1st Paragraph N/A	2nd Paragraph N/A	Plea: Guilty

Affirmative Findings:

Deadly Weapon: N/A	Family Violence: N/A	Victim Selected by Bias/Prejudice: N/A	Victim Younger Than 17 years: N/A *yes*	Controlled Substance Used to Commit Crime: N/A

ADJUDICATION OF GUILT DEFERRED

DEFENDANT PLACED ON COMMUNITY SUPERVISION FOR: **10 YEARS**

DEFENDANT ASSESSED A FINE IN THE AMOUNT OF $ **3000**

☐ SEE SPECIAL INSTRUCTIONS, incorporated herein by reference.

Time Credited: N/A days toward incarceration   N/A days toward fine and costs   N/A days toward incarceration, fine and costs   COURT COSTS: $ **203.00**

(Mark appropriate selections below, if applicable)

☐ Name changed from N/A.

☐ Judgment Addendum incorporated herein by reference.

☐ It is ORDERED by the Court, that any weapon(s) seized in this case is/are hereby forfeited.

☐ In accordance with Section 12.44(a), Penal Laws of Texas, the Court finds that the ends of justice would best be served by punishment as a Class A misdemeanor. The Defendant is adjudged to be guilty of a state jail felony and is assessed the punishment indicated above.

☐ In accordance with Section 12.44(b), Penal Laws of Texas, the Court authorizes the prosecuting attorney to prosecute this cause as a Class A misdemeanor.

G:\Templates\Judgments\Judgment Type-in Forms\Deferred Adjudication.doc   1 of 2   02/13/06

Deferred adjudication order for Dinny, a slap on the wrist.

Choate Rosemary Hall
333 Christian Street
Wallingford, CT 06492-3800
(203) 697-2325
jdonald@choate.edu

Archives

Robert Blaffer
2933 Del Monte
Houston, TX 77019

October 15, 2002

Dear Mr Blaffer·

John 33

I have enclosed three pages from the 1933 Brief in which your grandfather appears. I'm sorry there's not any more. For the football team photograph, you will have to be the spotter – it's unclear to me which player is your grandfather

I have asked the Alumni Office for the protocol of allowing the public to contact members of any particular class. There may be several ways to do it and I need to hear what they recommend. I will let you know

Enjoy the photographs. I'm very sorry we don't have sufficient inventory of vintage Briefs to offer them for sale.

Sincerely

Judy Donald

Judy Donald (RH'1966)
Choate Rosemary Hall Archives

Send to Arrive   J d   fns
phone 713 942 2322
fax   713 307 8443

Dinny impersonating long dead Robert Blaffer.

COUNTY AUDITOR'S FORM/9999A   OFFICIAL RECEIPT   2 NO 115603
HARRIS COUNTY, TEXAS (V.10/99)

CHARLES BACARISSE DISTRICT CLERK

ACTION: FRAUD   CASE: C-200241613   TRANS NO: 6407529   COURT: 189
STYLE PLT: JOHNSON, WIRT DAVIS
DEF: JOHNSON, JOAN BLAFFER

FEE	DESCRIPTION	QTY	AMOUNT				
100	FILING NEW CASE	1	45.00	PAYMENT 1	CHECK	2514	188.00
121	CITATION WITH 1 COPY	1	8.00	PAYMENT 2			
195	SECURITY SERVICE FEE	1	5.00				------------
199	RECORD PRESERVATION	1	5.00	AMOUNT TENDERED:			188.00
450	JUDICIAL FILING FEE	1	40.00	TOTAL AMOUNT:			188.00
452	LEGAL SRVC FEE-CIVIL	1	10.00	AMOUNT APPLIED:			188.00
475	LAW LIBRARY	1	15.00				
500	JURY FEE (51.604 (GOV	1	20.00	CHANGE:			.00
502	JURY FEE (RULE 216 T	1	10.00	RECEIVED BURNS WOOLEY & MARBROLIA LLP			(LFI09735)
525	STENO FEE	1	15.00	OF 1111 BAGBY #4900			
601	DISPUTE RESOLUTION F	1	10.00	HOUSTON, TX 77002			
775	APPELLANT JUDICIAL F	1	5.00	ONE HUNDRED EIGHTY-EIGHT DOLLARS AND 0/100******************************* DOLLARS			

ISSUED

PAYMENT DATE: 08/15/2002   FILE DATE: 08/15/2002

ASSESSED BY: KUNEE, ELKIN NELSON
VALIDATED 08/16/2002 BY: CARLTON, SHARON JANE

FILE COPY

Certified Document Number: 8658378   Page 9 of 9

Wirt's 2002 suit against his mother for fraudulent depletion of his trust.

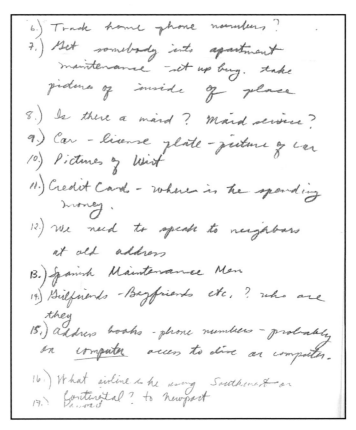

6.) Track home phone numbers?
7.) Get somebody into apartment maintenance - set up bug. take pictures of inside of place
8.) Is there a maid? Maid service?
9.) Car - license plate - picture of car
10.) Pictures of Wirt
11.) Credit Card - where is he spending money.
12.) We need to speak to neighbors at old address
13.) Spanish Maintenance Men
14.) Girlfriends - Boyfriends etc.? who are they
15.) address books - phone numbers - probably on computer access to disc or computer.
16.) What airline is he using Southwest or Continental? to Newport
17.) _____

Dinny's laundry list for surveillance of Wirt.

May 30, 2002

Dear Joan,

I have enjoyed helping you and the children out over the years. I am sure the children will continue to grow and do well in school. I feel as though I have become a godfather to both Seth and Kaleta. I wish you and the children all the best.

Sincerely Yours,

David Collie says "good-bye."

march 2001 - Dinny carpool

SUBJECT Mr. Shaw @ Carpool   DATE 3-26-01

TIME	
3:15	After school In carpool line Mr. Shaw Approached me + Asked
	IF I had talked to Jake Walters. My Reply was yes.
	Mr. Shaw said Seth will have No more Detentions After
	School, Is That understood. I said yes, If Jake said that
	Then That is what will happen. (Then it came up
	What I was Doing) That is when I said Doing my
	Job. He said I have a Nice Family, A Job, + A
	Career To worry About Because I will Sue you.
	I Said I don't want to Be Sued.
Note:	The Conversation Did NOT Bother me, What
	Bothered me was he Brought up my Family out
	of the Blue.
	Told Prince
Note:	His manner Boardel on A Threat (Tone of voice - Firm)
	M. Witter.

PLAINTIFF'S
EXHIBIT
60

Order #

47

Dinny's threat at the car pool line.

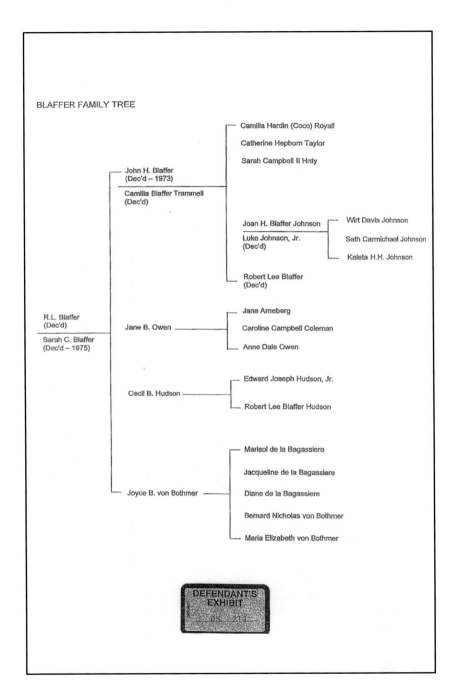

Blaffer family tree.

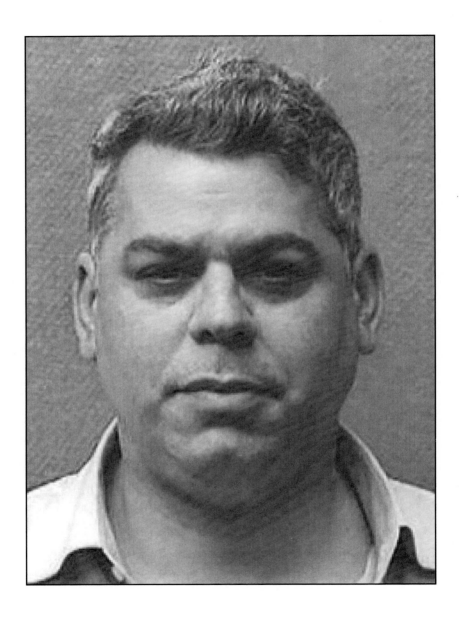

Dinny Shah